D1527678

Beyond Belief
True Stories of Marine Corps That Defy Comprehension

Compiled and Edited By
C. Douglas & Pamla M. Sterner
and Dwight Jon Zimmerman

Respectfully Dedicated to:
LANCE CORPORAL BRITTANY MOUDY
Marine, Mother, Veterans Advocate

Hero Books Publishing

COVER: Birlocho

Table of Contents

Introduction

The ability to tell a good story is an art.

World literature is filled with dramatic, sometimes true, but often fictional stories based on real-life characters whose biographies have evolved and been embellished over the years. Many such stories have been passed down from generation to generation, the tales themselves morphing into legendary status with each re-telling. Such legends have altered the history of their characters, often turning even unscrupulous individuals into heroes. I remember a pair of pajamas I had as a young boy with a badge on it that read: *Billy the Kid—Sheriff.*

The evolution of such stories is perhaps best explained in John Ford's 1962 movie *The Man Who Shot Liberty Valance*, adapted from a 1953 short story written by Dorothy M. Johnson. Towards the end of the movie Ransome Foster, a newspaper editor, utters one of the classic lines in entertainment movie history: *"When the truth becomes legend, print the legend."* It is a mantra that has made storytelling more entertaining.

Our goal in publishing the series, *Beyond Belief—True Stories of American Heroes That Defy Comprehension* of which this book about civilian heroes is the fourth, was to tell stories of real heroes, most of them American, and to do so without literary license or embellishment. This book is a compilation of stories that if you heard someone tell them in a bar you would think: *"There is no way this could have happened."*

But each and every story in this book is TRUE.

During my more than two decades of finding and compiling award citations for the *Military Times "Hall of Valor"* database that I curate, time and time again I have stumbled upon a story that, even I find despite my years of transcribing tens of thousands of award citations, strain my own sense of credibility.

Beyond Belief: True Stories of Marine Corps Heroes

Most of the stories in this book are based on actual award citations, written shortly after the action recounted in them. Such citations were not written by some adept storyteller with a solid grasp of language and drama, but usually by ordinary company/unit clerks and yeomen, based on the signed witness testimony of the men and women who saw the actions. All too often, however, award citations state only a brief synopsis of the actions of a hero in a moment of great danger. When one digs deeper into the witness statements supporting them, fascinating details are discovered.

On Veterans' Day 2020, I published *Beyond Belief—True Stories of American Heroes That Defy Comprehension,* a general military anthology. It was a step I took out of necessity. Over the last decade I have dedicated the vast majority of my working hours to developing the largest and most comprehensive database of military awards ever compiled. In the process I repeatedly read citations that left me shaking my head in wonder and thinking, *"There is a bigger story here that needs to be told."* Reluctant to take needed time away from my database work to write these stories, I thought, *"Why not share these citations with other writers and would-be writers, let them write the stories, and then compile and publish."* It turned out to be both a fun and personally satisfying experience that resulted in one of my favorite books.

After publication of that first book I thought, *"This is great. Let's do it again."* And it was in that vein of thought that I decided to serialize these, leading to: *True Stories of U.S. Navy Heroes That Defy Comprehension, True Stories of Military Chaplains That Defy Comprehension, True Stories of Civilian Heroes That Defy Comprehension* and now this book on Marine Corps heroes. My plan is to release two new books in the series every year, released on Memorial Day and Veterans Day, however this volume is being released a day early, on the Marine Corps Birthday.

-- 0 --

Ten years ago I was living in Alexandria, Virginia, and making regular visits to the Navy Yard to photocopy thousands of Navy Award Cards, 3" x 5" cards containing nearly all citations for awards to members of the Navy, Marine Corps, and Coast Guard. On one visit, when I got home and began to transcribe the Silver Star citation on one card to a U.S. Marine who was serving with the Offices of Strategic Services in World War II, I was not surprised to see it was brief, covering an extended period of time with few details. The award was to Marine Corps Captain John Hamilton. What did catch my attention was a small, hand-written note at the bottom with the words *"Sterling Hayden."* I recognized the name instantly and it piqued my curiosity.

After further research, I learned that famed Hollywood actor Sterling Hayden had enlisted in the Marine Corps under the assumed name of John Hamilton, and been decorated under his assumed name for actions from December 24, 1943, to January 2, 1944. Further research yielded a few more details, which are represented in our series' artist Mario Bircholo on the cover of this volume.

On the night of Christmas Eve, Hayden made a lone voyage in a broken down motorboat, across the Adriatic Sea from an Allied base in southern Italy. Somehow he successfully made the dangerous crossing to the island of Korcula off Yugoslavia, even as the Germans were attacking the island.

His mission was to make contact with future-Yugoslavian President Marshal Josip Broz Tito and his communist rebels, part of the Allied effort against the Axis, to provide supplies and make a reconnaissance of the island to measure the strength of German landing forces.

During his mission far behind friendly lines, his jeep was attacked, his driver killed, and Hayden and his men engaged them only briefly before being forced to flee to avoid capture. They moved to the island of Hvar, which at the time was under attack by German Stuka dive bombers. Despite all this, Hayden successfully completed his mission and secured a boat to return him to Italy with the valuable intelligence information he had obtained.

My good friend Scott Baron, a regular contributor to the "Beyond Belief" series, undertook to write Hayden's biography, and it is the cover story for this book.

Another interesting twist in the evolution of this book occurred in May of this year. With publication of our Memorial Day release, having determined the next book would highlight Marine

Beyond Belief: True Stories of Marine Corps Heroes

Corps heroes and be released on November 10, the Marine Corps birthday, I prepared a list of suggested Marines for my team of writers to select from.

Later that night my wife and I followed our normal pattern, begun during the early days of the COVID pandemic, of watching the nightly news in our living room, and then retiring to our bedroom to watch one or two episodes of whatever old show we are binge-watching before going to sleep. As it happened that night in May, we were nearing the end of the old *"Gomer Pyle, U.S.M.C."* reruns we had been enjoying for more than two months. Half jokingly I turned to Pam and said, *"I should include Gomer Pyle in the Marine Corps book,"* and we both laughed.

While my initial suggestion was not a serious one, the more I thought about it before drifting off to sleep, the more it seemed like a serious idea. While there is no shortage of Marine Corps heroes and icons, known well to every Marine, if one asks the typical American citizen to name a Marine, probably the only one most could name would be the fictional Gomer Pyle. When I brought the subject up with our co-author and editor Dwight Zimmerman, he liked the idea and, based on his reaction, I decided to proceed.

Thankfully, Ronnie Schell, one of the three main cast members of the highly popular sit-com and the lone living member of the regular cast, kindly provided an extensive interview to help me write the story. When I was done with it, while I realized some would question its inclusion, I knew it belonged.

I have chosen to dedicate this book to Marine Lance Corporal Brittney Moudy, my wife's close friend and the woman who for three years was her supervisor at Volunteers of America, where both worked housing homeless veterans. After her own honorary discharge from the Marine Corps in 2007, including two tours of duty in Iraq, Brittney found herself pregnant and homeless. With the determination she had learned through her years in the Corps, she rose above it, found housing, and went to school to get a degree in Social Work.

With her life on track, a loving husband and two children, she never forgot where she came from, or where she had been. She turned her own experiences, and her subsequent education, to help other veterans, specializing in finding and placing homeless veterans, often with spouses and children, in safe and comfortable housing.

Heroes are heroes, not because they did the ordinary or achieved what is expected. Heroes are that because they did something incomprehensible, sometimes seemingly superhuman—an act or lifestyle that defies belief.

To prepare this book we called on some of our friends who have both the ability to tell a good story, and to do it in keeping with the mantra of another fictional entertainment character. Unlike Ransome Foster, *Dragnet* fictional detective Sergeant Joe Friday is remembered for his quote, *"Just the facts, ma'am."* Ironically, in this discussion of fact vs. legend, that well-remembered quote is itself an embellishment. Sergeant Joe Friday never spoke those words in any of the TV shows' eight original seasons from 1951 to 1959. Joe Friday *did* frequently say, while interviewing a woman witness, *"All we want are the facts, ma'am,"* or *"All we know are the facts ma'am."* But the quote as so often remembered reflects another of those alterations in the re-telling of the story of a character, real or fictional.

If you find yourself shaking your head as you read these stories and silently saying to yourself, *"This is unbelievable,"* know that this is the reaction we were seeking to achieve. Each of the authors in this book however, approached their research clinically. Rather than endeavoring to make a good story better through literary license, they have sought to seek and find details behind often abbreviated citations, from credible sources.

Our manta in development is more in keeping with the words that first appeared in Lord Byon's poem *Don Juan* in 1823, *"Tis strange—but true, for truth is always strange,"* or by Margaret Echard in her 1943 novel *Before I Wake*: *"Truth is not only stranger than fiction, but far more interesting."*

C. Douglas & Pamla Sterner

Beyond Belief: True Stories of Marine Corps Heroes

Sterling Hayden (USMC)

The Eternal Sailor

BY SCOTT BARON

Over his lifetime, Sterling Hayden played many roles: Hollywood legend, leading man and later character actor who appeared in over 60 motion pictures He was a novelist and author of **Wanderer** (1963) and **Voyage: A Novel of 1896** (1978). He was a sailor and an adventurer who served as mate on Irving Johnson's schooner *Yankee*. on its noted circumnavigation in 1937. Later he became navigator on the Essex-built schooner *Gertrude L. Thebaud* under Captain Ben Pine in the 1938 Fisherman's Cup races vs the Canadian schooner *Bluenose*. Sterling's photo in the **Boston Post** captioned *"Thebaud Sailor Like Movie Idol"* led to modeling opportunities in New York and a call from Paramount Pictures.

He fought alongside Tito's partisans as part of the Office of Strategic Services (OSS), and appeared in front of the House Un-American Activities Committee in the late 1940's testifying about Communists in Hollywood. But less known is his role as a Marine officer during World War II, a role he would play under the assumed name of John Hamilton.

Hayden was certainly not the only actor in Hollywood to serve in the Marines during the war. Tyrone Power, Louis Hayward, Lee Marvin, Macdonald Carey, Hugh O'Brian, Bill Lundigan, John Russell, George C. Scott, Robert Ryan, Brian Keith, Johnathan

Beyond Belief: True Stories of Marine Corps Heroes

Winters, and Peter Ortiz, all served in the Corps during World War II.

Lieutenant Power flew C-46 Curtiss Commando transport planes assigned to Transport Squadron 353 stationed on Saipan in the Pacific Theater. Captain Hayward was a combat cameraman who filmed the bloody battle of Tarawa assigned to the SECOND Marine Division. Private Marvin was wounded on Saipan while serving with the 3d Battalion, 24th Marines, FOURTH Marine Division. Captain Peter Ortiz served with the OSS in France. Lieutenant Carey was an ordnance officer with Air Warning Squadron Three (AWS-3) at Bougainville. Corporal Lundigan served with Third Battalion, First Marines, FIRST Marine Division and survived the bitter fighting on Peleliu, and Corporal Keith was assigned to Marine Scouting Bombing Squadron Two-Hundred-Forty-Four (VSMB-244) as a rear gunner on Douglas SBD *Dauntless* dive bombers flying missions against Rabaul and other Japanese bases in the Southwest Pacific.

Then there was Sterling Hayden, a restless adventurer who served in the Marines before being seconded to the Office of Strategic Services (OSS), with which he served with distinction in the Balkans, France, Belgium, and Germany.

Hayden did not have an early life that would foreshadow success in his later years, but despite setbacks, he persevered and enjoyed a success that few ever achieve.

Born Sterling Relyea Walter in the quiet neighborhood of Upper Montclair, New Jersey, on March 26, 1916, by all accounts he was wild by nature. One story about him claims that after taking aim at a neighbor's wife with a slingshot, he was beaten with a wet stick by his angry father. When the boy screamed his father collapsed from an apparent stroke and never recovered, dying three months later after a long illness, when Hayden was nine years old.

True or not, he was raised by his mother Frances, who supported them by working for *Good Housekeeping* magazine, commuting to New York while her mother cared for young Sterling. Growing up, he idolized World War I fighter ace Eddie Rickenbacker and played *"Yankees and Huns"* with the neighbor kids while an elderly veteran drilled them with wooden rifles.

Sterling Hayden (USMC)

When his mother married divorcee James Watson Hayden in 1928, Sterling took his stepfather's name, becoming Sterling Walter Hayden. During the Depression the family drifted up and down the East Coast. His stepfather, *"Daddy Jim,"* failed at one endeavor after another, staying in fancy hotels while pursuing big business opportunities that never materialized. Sterling and his mother at times had to skip out on the bill at a boarding house or hotel.

In Maine, young Hayden fell in love with the sea, lighthouses, schooners, fishermen and solitude. He read everything he could about seafaring and sailing. He did not like, nor do well, in school having flunked the third grade. Sent to the Friend's School in Washington D.C., he hated it, as he did all schools, dropping out in the tenth grade with the tuition unpaid.

In November 1932, while enrolled in the Wassookeag School in Dexter Maine, he ran away to Portland, hitchhiking a truck ride to Bangor, then hopping a freight train to Portland where the adventurous 16-year-old made his way to the docks. He spent the night on the schooner *Restless*, and the next morning, the sailors gave him money to return home and finish school. He heeded their advice.

The family moved to a one-room flat in Boston, where Frances sold cosmetics door-to-door. Sterling looked for any work while *"Daddy Jim"* dreamed of the big score. Tiring of the fruitless effort, Sterling eventually made his way to the Boston docks.

Wandering the Boston wharves, he paused to gaze into the window of a nautical instruments store. The shopkeeper advised him that a big schooner, the *Puritan*, was hiring crew for a cruise from New London, Connecticut, to San Pedro, California. He applied for a job, and the captain signed him on as ship's boy at $10 a month, and Hayden went to sea for the first time. A natural sailor, he quickly learned all facets of seamanship.

For the next five years he sailed aboard various vessels from schooners to steamers along the East Coast, first as a seaman, then as a fisherman, fireman, first mate and ultimately navigator, while circling the globe and sailing in the occasional race. He skippered his first ship, the square-rigger *Florence C. Robinson*, at age 22 on a delivery voyage from Gloucester, Massachusetts to Tahiti.

Beyond Belief: True Stories of Marine Corps Heroes

In 1936 as first mate aboard the schooner *Yankee,* Sterling made his first round-the-world voyage. He sailed in schooner races, filled in as a navigator, and showed courage during a competition in October 1938 by crawling along a spar in a howling gale to secure a torn main gaff.

A photograph was taken during the annual Gloucester, Massachusetts, Fishermen's Race which made the cover of a magazine and in newspaper articles about the 6'4", handsome blonde sailor. This led to modeling assignments and, in May 1940, Hayden moved with his mother to Hollywood where he signed a contract with Paramount Pictures, which promoted him as the *"Most Beautiful Man in the Movies."*

"I was completely lost, ignorant, nervous. But the next thing I knew, Paramount made me a seven-year contract beginning at $250 a week, which was astronomical. I got my lovely old mother and bought a car, and we drove to California . . . I was so lost then I didn't think to analyze it. I said, 'This is nuts, but, damned, it's pleasant.' I had only one plan in mind: to get $5,000. I knew where there was a schooner . . .'

Hayden was frequently quoted as saying the only reason he became an actor was so that he could afford to be a sailor. He liked the money, but just like in school, he chafed against the control that movie executives exercised over him.

His first movie, *Virginia* (1941) was directed by Edward H. Griffith and starred Fred MacMurray and Madeleine Carroll. Upon its release, the film was described by the Richmond Times-Dispatch as *"a good picture, with a full load of laughter, action, romance and the touch of pathos that all good pictures should have."* Other critics panned Hayden's performance as *"wooden"* but Hayden developed a romantic relationship with his English-born co-star, ten years his senior, who shared his low opinion of the movie business, considering it shallow and of little importance as much of the world was already at war.

Carroll's sister had been killed in the London Blitz, and she sought a way to contribute, volunteering her time with the Red Cross. Carroll donated a château she owned outside Paris, to house more than one hundred and fifty orphans, arranging for groups of young people in California to knit clothing for them.

They co-starred in a second film, *Bahama Passage* (1941), which again was directed by Griffith and is notable only for being one of the earliest films shot in Technicolor.

Despite some reports stating otherwise, Hayden broke his contract with Paramount, but left on good terms. The studio president, Barney Balaban, understood the young man's desire to *"do something worthwhile."*

In November 1941, Hayden contacted Col. William *"Wild Bill"* Donovan, recipient of the Medal of Honor in World War I and close friend of President Franklin Roosevelt. Donovan was Coordinator of Information (COI) in the Roosevelt Administration. He would go on to become the Director of the Office of Strategic Services (OSS) during World War II, the predecessor of the CIA. Hayden met Donovan through the latter's son, who was also a sailing buff.

Donovan arranged for Hayden to travel to Glasgow, Scotland, for commando and parachute training under the auspices of the British SOE (Special Operations Executive), whose mission was to conduct espionage, sabotage, and reconnaissance in occupied Europe.

After a miserable Atlantic convoy crossing, Hayden arrived at the American Embassy in London to find his arrival was unexpected. He lingered for several days waiting for them to sort things out, and then received orders to report to the Commando Training Center at Archnarry.

Hayden was the only American in the group and the only man with no military experience. The others were all men who had seen combat and knew war. He was taught the latest infiltration and

11

sabotage techniques alongside these hardened combat veterans from France, Poland, Belgium, Norway, and Denmark, whose only desire was to parachute into their home countries to fight the Nazis. Despite his inexperience, Hayden was accepted among them. He worked hard, and at night after training was done, he would join them for the daily whisky ration while they listened to the BBC.

Completing the initial phases of commando training, Hayden was sent to the Parachute School near Manchester. He made ten jumps without incident. On his final jump to become parachute qualified in March 1942, he jumped from a Stirling bomber only to land awkwardly in a quarry, breaking his ankle, tearing up his knee, and displacing his backbone.

Prevented by his injuries from further service, Hayden returned to the United States. While his injuries healed, Donovan urged him to apply for a commission in the Navy. Hayden requested a commission as a lieutenant and an assignment to PT (Patrol Torpedo) boats. Despite the fact that Hayden wasn't a high school graduate, the navy offered to commission him as ensign, but with no guarantee of assignment.

Offended, and feeling that his skills as a sailor merited more than an ensign's slot, instead of enlisting he sailed a schooner to the West Indies where, at the Shell Oil facility on Curaçao, it is alleged that he got drunk with six Marines from the security detachment.

He invited his new drunken buddies up to his room at the Americano Hotel. When the manager informed Hayden that while he could remain, the Marines had to go, the former actor, using his recently acquired commando skills, ejected the manager into the street. Hayden was arrested and thrown in jail.

After his agent put up bail, Hayden sold his boat and flew back to New York. The next day, October 26, 1942, he went to the nearest Marine Corps Recruiting Station. Within hours Hayden was on a train bound for Yamesee, South Carolina, the railhead for the Recruit Depot at Parris Island, South Carolina.

The evening's *New York Daily News* carried a photograph of Hayden as a Private in the United States Marines.

Although Hayden liked the strict discipline and regimentation of the Marines about as little as he liked acting and schools, he was, as his Drill Instructor Private George S. Featherstone described him, *"A Hell of a Good Marine,"* so good that he was one of the two men in his platoon to be selected for Officer Candidate School (OCS). Hayden was assigned as a drill instructor for three weeks while awaiting orders to the Marine Corps School Command at Quantico, Virginia.

Assigned to the 23d OCS Class, Hayden graduated on April 21, 1943, and was commissioned a second lieutenant, U.S. Marine Corps Reserve. Unhappy with his notoriety as a movie star, in late June 1943, he had his name legally changed to John Hamilton. He also contacted Donovan and requested assignment to the Offices of Strategic Services (OSS). When his OCS class graduated, he was one of three posted to the OSS, the remainder shipping out to the Pacific.

Housed in Temporary Building Q in Washington D.C., not far from the Lincoln Memorial, the OSS Headquarters was a hive of activity as the newly operational agency worked to get organized, and it was several weeks before Hayden received orders to report to Cairo, Egypt.

Beyond Belief: True Stories of Marine Corps Heroes

Upon his arrival at Cairo in October 1943, the local commanders had no idea of what to do with the former movie star and put him to work reviewing intelligence reports. But when they realized that Hayden's extensive sailing experience and skill with small boats might prove to be useful in aiding the partisans in Yugoslavia, he was sent to Bari in southern Italy.

From Bari, Hayden was sent south to the port city of Monopoli to set up a base of operations to support Allied efforts in Yugoslavia. Here, Hayden discovered a war-within-a-war as Tito's communist partisans competed for power against the royalist Chetniks led by General Dragoljub *"Draza"* Mihailovic, who had organized the first resistance movement to the invading Axis forces as early as the spring of 1941.

Hayden favored Tito, who confronted the invaders with immediate, determined fighting, as opposed to Mihailovic whose strategy involved stockpiling weapons and supplies, waiting for the moment when his army could help the Allies decisively destroy the enemy without excessive losses and without overturning Yugoslavia's prewar monarchy. This preference for the Communists would have consequences later in his life.

Hayden's command consisted of 400 partisans, 50 of them women, and 14 schooners, six ketches and two brigantines with which to carry weapons and supplies to partisans across the Adriatic Sea to the Balkans.

The small craft would sail under cover of darkness, avoiding the German naval blockade of southern Italy, to unload their cargo on the partisan controlled island of Dalmatia. There, fishing boats would carry the cargo to the mainland to be unloaded on the beach while avoiding German patrols. From there it would be loaded unto mules to be transported up into the mountains.

They made ten trips in all between mid-February and April 1, often unarmed due to a shortage of weapons, and Hamilton later described a routine passage: *"By plunging through the Allied minefield late of an afternoon a schooner always had a fighting chance of reaching Vis at dawn, barely in time to be backed into a precipitous cove where she could be hastily camouflaged with pine boughs festooned in her rigging, unloaded the following night, the camouflage repeated, and then driven toward Italy as soon as the weather served."*

During the summer, Hamilton went on a recon mission, mapping out the best route for the delivery of 40 tons of explosives to the Dalmatian coast in support of a proposed attack on German lines of retreat through northern Yugoslavia. He traveled in partisan launches armed with captured Italian machine guns and anti-tank weapons. The boats' only armor consisted of parallel board walls, the gap between them filled with rocks.

When Hamilton returned to Italy, he learned that, for diplomatic reasons, the entire operation had passed to the British SOE. Disgusted, Hamilton requested a transfer out of the area, but his request was denied.

Hayden came to admire the tough Yugoslav partisans, and considered them more dedicated than anyone he had known. He wrote letters to friends back home extolling their virtues. These experiences influenced his decision later to join the American Communist Party.

Hayden served with the OSS behind enemy lines in Greece and Yugoslavia. In January 1944, Hayden parachuted into Yugoslavia with Marine Gunnery Sergeant John Harnicker and a Navy radio operator. Working with the partisans, they led several downed Allied fliers to safety in Italy.

Hayden also arranged for a rescue of 26 downed American airmen, including 11 nurses who were forced down in German-held Albania by engine trouble. On September 13, 1944, Hayden was promoted to first lieutenant.

In February 1945, Hayden returned to the United States on a 30-day leave, and a promotion to captain on February 14, 1945. Madeleine Carroll remained in Europe, working at Army hospitals in Naples and Foggia, Italy, tending to victims of the Monte Cassino and Anzio campaigns. She also worked aboard hospital trains carrying wounded soldiers to France. In recognition of her wartime service, she was awarded the French Legion of Honor and the American Medal of Freedom.

Beyond Belief: True Stories of Marine Corps Heroes

Hayden returned to Europe, assigned to OSS-Germany, but upon his arrival in Paris, his orders were changed, and he was sent to Belgium assigned to Lieutenant General Courtney H. Hodges' U.S. FIRST Army. These soldiers had just fought in the bitter Ardennes campaign. The FIRST Army would be the first Allied army to cross the border into Germany.

In command of six German-speaking technical sergeants, they followed the advance into Germany from Cologne to Marburg, tasked with locating authentic anti-fascists, but for the most part they were mostly unsuccessful in locating genuine anti-fascists. Following the German surrender in May, Hayden was assigned to visit ports throughout Germany, Norway and Denmark, to assess the damage caused by Allied bombings.

For his actions, Hayden would be recognized with the award of the Silver Star medal in July 1946.

The President of the United States of America, authorized by Act of Congress July 9, 1918, takes pleasure in presenting the Silver Star (Army Award) to Captain John Hamilton (MCSN: 0-22085), United States Marine Corps, for gallantry in action while serving with the Office of Strategic Services in the Mediterranean Theater of Operations from 24 December 1943 to 2 January 1944. Captain Hamilton displayed great courage in making hazardous sea voyage in enemy infested waters and reconnaissance's through enemy held areas. His conduct reflected great credit upon himself and the United States Armed Forces.

Sterling Hayden (USMC)

Besides his Silver Star and two campaign ribbons, Hamilton's (Hayden) decorations included three Bronze Stars, two Bronze Arrowheads, a letter of commendation, and the Yugoslav Order of Merit. He remained in the Marine Corps Reserve until 1948.

Hayden reunited with Carroll in Paris in September 1945, but the couple realized that their marriage was a mistake and they parted as friends, divorcing in Reno at the end of the year. Captain Hamilton was released from active duty on Christmas Eve 1945, and he returned to Hollywood.

Warmly received by Paramount Studios, he returned to making movies. He was still affected by his wartime experiences, and remembering the commitment of the Communist partisans, he, as well as other film actors, joined the American Communist Party in 1946. Hayden only attended a few meetings before he became disenchanted with the rhetoric and dogma, ending his membership after six months. That brief association, however, would come back to haunt him.

Beginning with small parts, his popularity slowly returned to pre-war levels and he would achieve stardom and gain critical acclaim in *The Asphalt Jungle* (1950), John Huston's powerful gangster classic costarring James Whitmore and Marilyn Monroe.

Other notable roles followed; Nicholas Ray's *Johnny Guitar* (1954), and Stanley Kubrick's *The Killing* (1956) and a series of low-budget westerns. He went on to create memorable characters such as General Jack D. Ripper in Kubrick's *Dr. Strangelove* and: *How I Learned to Stop Worrying and Love the Bomb* (1964), the Irish-American policeman Captain McCluskey in Francis Ford Coppola's *The Godfather* (1972), and the alcoholic novelist Roger Wade in Robert Altman's *The Long Goodbye* (1973).

Hayden also portrayed historical figures on the screen. He was frontiersman Jim Bowie in *The Last Command* (1955), an elaborate and sweeping depiction of the last stand at the Alamo. Then, in *The Eternal Sea*, also in 1955, he played carrier pilot John M. Hoskins, who lost a leg in the sinking of the *U.S.S. Princeton* in October 1944, fought to remain in the service, and became a Korean War vice admiral.

Beyond Belief: True Stories of Marine Corps Heroes

Hayden's brief fling with the Communist Party brought him to the attention of the FBI and J. Edgar Hoover during the *Red Scare* and he was called to testify before the House Un-American Activities Committee (HUAC) and allegedly was threatened with losing his children, or even jail time, if he failed to cooperate.

Hayden *"named names"* and later would regret having cooperated. In his autobiography he wrote: *"I don't think you have the foggiest notion of the contempt I have had for myself since the day I did that thing."*

Although he continued to have a successful career as a "B" action movie star, he always maintained that he only acted to finance his maritime adventures, and considered himself more of a sailor or writer rather than an actor.

The actor's private life was less successful. He was not good with money, spending almost everything he earned. His second marriage to Betty Ann De Noon produced four children, but ended eight years later, in May, 1957. A third marriage, to Catherine D. McConnell in 1960, produced two more children.

His last screen appearance was in *Venom* (1982), an British picture that was mediocre at best. He died of prostate cancer at the age of 70 in 1986, and his ashes were scattered over San Francisco Bay by his widow, children, and friends.

One has to wonder what it takes to parachute behind enemy lines or to sail past enemy vessels in the dead of night. Was it patriotism, a desire for adventure, or an effort to find real purpose outside a world of make-believe? Whatever the motivation, it was just another role, uncredited as it might be, that Hayden excelled at, even as he did in his screen portrayals, under an assumed name.

Robert Mullan (USMC)

America's Second Marine Officer

BY SCOTT BARON

By early 1775, relations between the American colonies and the mother country, Great Britain, had deteriorated to the point that the two parties were nearing the point of armed conflict. Earlier, between September 5 and October 26, 1774, the First Continental Congress met in Philadelphia, Pennsylvania, in response to Parliament's attempt to punish Boston and isolate it from the other colonies. But colonial response to the **Intolerable Acts** had the opposite effect of unifying the colonies instead.

On May 10, 1775, the Second Continental Congress convened again at Independence Hall in Philadelphia, to debate the issue of Independence – but by then it was a moot point. On April 19, 1775, the British army met with armed resistance when it marched out to the towns of Lexington and Concord to seize a cache of weapons. The battle between the colonists and the king's troops demonstrated that Americans had ceased to recognize the authority of the royal government in England.

In compliance with the **Continental Marine Act of 1775**, passed by Congress, the **Act** stated that:

"Two battalions of Marines be raised consisting of one Colonel, two lieutenant-colonels, two majors and other officers, as

Beyond Belief: True Stories of Marine Corps Heroes

usual in other regiments; that they consist of an equal number of privates as with other battalions, that particular care be taken that no persons be appointed to offices, or enlisted into said battalions, but such as are good seamen, or so acquainted with maritime affairs as to be able to serve for and during the present war with Great Britain and the Colonies unless dismissed by Congress; that they be distinguished by the names of the First and Second Battalions of Marines"

This resolution, dated

November 10, 1775, established the Continental Marines, and is considered the birth date of the modern United States Marine Corps.

The first attempts at recruiting Marines from Gen. Washington's troops had proved unsuccessful. Washington was reluctant to provide for the Marines, and proposed that they be recruited from civilians in New York or Philadelphia instead.

The Continental Congress commissioned Samuel Nicholas as a captain on November 28, 1775, and directed him to recruit two battalions of men for the new military organization. Upon learning of his commission, Nicholas immediately established a recruiting headquarters at Tun Tavern in Philadelphia. The owner of the tavern, Robert Mullan, became the chief Marine recruiter.

According to tradition, Tun Tavern was where Marines held their first recruitment drive, and it is the officially acknowledged birthplace of the Marines – although the historian Edwin Simmons surmises that it was more likely the Conestoga  Wagon, a tavern owned by the Nicholas family that had this distinction..

In any event, Tun Tavern was rich in history and a significant meeting place for other groups and individuals. It was erected in 1686 at the intersection of King Street and Tun Alley by settler Joshua Carpenter. In 1756, Benjamin Franklin used the inn as a recruitment gathering point for the Pennsylvania Militia in its fight against a Native American uprisings. The tavern also hosted a meeting of George Washington, Thomas Jefferson and the Continental Congress. In October 1775, a seven man Naval Committee including John Adams, met to create articles of war in order to build America's first Navy.

At some point, the tavern was sold to Thomas Mullan, and in the 1740s, a restaurant appellation, "Peggy Mullan's Red Hot Beef Steak Club" was added to the name of the tavern. Thomas had eight children (Harriet, Robert, John, Thomas, Ann, Mary, Elizabeth and Phebe) with two wives, marrying his second wife, Margaret, on October 21, 1758. Thomas was the proprietor of Tun's Tavern and when he died in September 1774, he left a will leaving the tavern to his eldest son Robert.

In November 1775 (some sources say June 1776), Robert Mullan was commissioned a first lieutenant by an act of Congress, to raise the first two battalions of Marines, under the leadership of Captain Samuel Nicholas.

The Continental Marines were to perform a variety of duties, primarily assigned on board armed naval vessels, and were therefore engaged in every important battle afloat. They participated in important landing parties from naval vessels, such as the one at New Providence (Bahamas) in 1776 at Whitehaven, England; at St. Mary's Isle, Kirkcudbright, Scotland; and again at New Providence in 1778.

They served in forts, such as Fort Montgomery in New York and participated in the **Penobscot Expedition** in 1779. They were often detached for service with the Army in such battles as those at Trenton and Princeton. The Continental Marines guarded enemy prisoners, acted as guards at naval stations ashore, and ventured into Indian forest lands to bring out masts for the frigates of the Navy.

Aboard ship, their duties consisted of sentry duty at important posts throughout the ship, and during action, they were often stationed in the tops, where the expert shots were of great assistance and in battle to repel or cover the assaults of boarders.

Beyond Belief: True Stories of Marine Corps Heroes

Captain Robert Mullan helped recruit the first Continental Marine company which was composed of one hundred Rhode Islanders, to be commanded by Captain (later Major) Nicholas.

In March 1776, Nicolas led his men on the first amphibious landing on a hostile shore in Marine Corps history when he commanded approximately 210 Marines on a raid of Nassau, on the Island of New Providence in the Bahamas. Nicholas, the first commissioned officer in the Continental Marines, remained the senior Marine officer throughout the American Revolution.

These first Marines were tasked with supporting a naval expedition to Nova Scotia. However, this mission was subsequently changed to raiding the Bahamas Islands to capture weapons, supplies, and munitions from British garrisons there. The expedition, under the command of Commodore Esek Hopkins consisted of eight hastily armed and equipped ships and approximately 250 Marines, including Nicholas and Mullan.

After departing from Delaware Bay in February 1776, they conducted an amphibious assault on New Providence Island in the British Bahamas on March 3. Under Nicholas' command, 220 Marines and sailors captured Forts Nassau and Montague, Nassau's Government House, and the town of Nassau. They occupied New Providence Island for two weeks and then withdrew, taking with them a great quantity of munitions and guns desperately needed by George Washington's Continental Army. This action also resulted in the death of Lieutenant John Fitzpatrick, the first Marine to be killed in combat.

Sailing back to Rhode Island, the squadron captured four small prize ships, and returned on April 8, 1776, with seven dead Marines and four wounded. Although Hopkins was condemned for failing, Nicholas was promoted to major on June 25 and was tasked with raising four additional companies of Marines for four new frigates, then under construction.

Mullan was commissioned a captain on June 25, 1776, and on December 1, 1776, his command consisted of First Lieutenant, David Love, Second Lieutenant Hugh Montgomery, four sergeants, four corporals, a drummer, a fifer and 73 privates. Captain Mullan's roster lists two Black men among the Marines, Isaac and Orange, the first recorded Black Marines.

Mullan and his Marines fought with the Continental Army in the **Battle of Trenton,** December 26, 1776, where Mullan commanded a company of Nicholas' battalion although they were unable to arrive in time to affect the battle. They fought next at the **Battle of the Assunpink Creek,** also known as the **Second Battle of Trenton** on January 2, 1777. Fighting continued on the following day, January 3, at the **Battle of Princeton,** before entering the winter encampment at Morristown, Pennsylvania.

The January 1922 issue of the *Daughters of the American Revolution Magazine* records that at Morristown, Mullan was detailed for artillery duty. According to a list dated February 27, 1777, Mullan escorted twenty-five British prisoners of war to Philadelphia, and was still serving in Philadelphia on June 1, 1780, and also on April 28, 1783. It appears that Mullan continued his work as Chief Recruiter of the Marines through the end of the war.

At the end of the Revolutionary War, both the Continental Navy and Marines were disbanded in April 1783. In total, 131 Colonial Marine officers and most likely no more than 2,000 enlisted Colonial Marines served during the war.

Mullen died in September 1793 in Philadelphia at the age of 55 and is buried in the Christ Church Burial Ground, Philadelphia. While this might be the end of Robert Mullen's story, it was only the beginning of the Corp's long and noble history.

The establishment of the Continental Navy on October 13, 1775, by a resolution of the Second Continental Congress, predates the founding of the Continental Marines on November 10, 1775, and while the U.S. Navy was disbanded on October 18, 1781, and not re-established until the Naval Act of 1794 when American merchant shipping came under threat while in the Mediterranean by Barbary pirates, the United States Marines Corps wasn't re-established until July 11, 1798.

Both, however, are predated by the U.S. Coast Guard, which was created on August 4, 1790, when President George Washington signed the **Tariff Act** that authorized the construction of ten vessels, referred to as *"cutters,"* to enforce federal tariff and trade laws and to prevent smuggling, making the Coast Guard the longest continuously serving seagoing service. Under Alexander Hamilton, first Secretary of the Treasury, they operated under the U.S. Department of Treasury until 1967.

Marines saw action in the quasi-war with France (1798 - 1801, landed at Santo Domingo, and conducted operations against the Barbary pirates along the *"Shores of Tripoli"* (1805).

"Attack on Derna" Painting by Charles Waterhouse

Naval Agent to the Barbary States William Eaton and Marine First Lieutenant George O'Bannon led six other Marines 600-miles across the Libyan desert to the city of Derna. There, outnumbered ten-to-one despite having hired 500 mercenaries, the Marines led the battle that resulted in taking the city after a bayonet charge. Two Marines were killed, as well as at least nine mercenaries. News of the defeat prompted the leader of Tripoli to quickly settle with the United States.

They participated in several major naval operations during the War of 1812, which was primarily a naval war, and they fought on land in the defense of Washington, D.C. at Bladensburg, Maryland. They also fought General Andrew Jackson in the defeat of the British at the **Battle of New Orleans** (1814).

During the Mexican War (1846-1848), Marines seized enemy seaports on both the Gulf and Pacific coasts and Marines fought with

General Winfield Scott's army at Pueblo and advanced all the way to the *"Halls of Montezuma,"* outside Mexico City.

There were Marines that fought on both sides during the Civil War, with 17 United States Marines earning Medals of Honor during the Civil War. Although most service was with the Navy's blockading squadrons and at Cape Hatteras, New Orleans, Charleston, and Fort Fisher, a battalion of Marines fought at Bull Run and other units saw action in smaller engagements.

The last third of the 19th century saw Marines making numerous landings throughout the world, especially in the Orient and in the Caribbean area, most notably in 1871 during the expedition to Korea, known in Korea as the *Shinmiyangyo* (Korean for *"Western Disturbance in the Shinmi"*) or simply the Korean Expedition. It was the first American military action in Korea, long before the Korean War in 1950. It took place primarily on and around Ganghwa Island and six Marines and nine Navy Bluejackets were awarded the Medal of Honor. They were the first awards of the Medal of Honor for heroism on foreign soil.

Marine Private Hugh Purvis and Marine Corporal Charles Brown were cited for capture of the Corean (as Korea was known at the time) flag after storming the fortress, and posed with that historic flag next to Navy Captain McLain Tilton, who led the combined Navy Bluejacket and Marine force ashore.

Another Marine, Private John Coleman, was cited for: *"Fighting hand-to-hand with the enemy, (he) succeeded in saving the life of Alexander McKenzie."* Boatswain's Mate Alexander McKenzie was a Navy Bluejacket who was one of that action's nine Navy recipients of the Medal of Honor. It was the first, of only three times in history, that a Medal of Honor was awarded to a man for an action that involved saving the life of a Medal of Honor recipient.

Marine Privates John Coleman, James Dougherty, and Michael McNamara were also awarded Medals of Honor for their actions in that battle on June 11, 1871.

Beyond Belief: True Stories of Marine Corps Heroes

Following the **Spanish-American War** in 1898, in which Marines performed with valor in Cuba, Puerto Rico, Guam, and the Philippine Islands, the Marine Corps entered an era of expansion and professional development. They also built a legacy of pride in the Corps and fearlessness in battle.

In remembrance of those Marines who went before, and in respect to the title **United States Marine** that those who have earned the Eagle, Globe, and Anchor, the Marine Corps birthday is a major event for all Marines, active or retired.

Prior to 1921 the Marine Corps birthday was celebrated on July 11, the date when the Marine Corps was re-established in 1798. Then, in 1921, Major Edwin North McClellan of the Marine Corps historical section suggested changing the date to November 10, hearkening back to the Revolutionary War days of the Corp's birth. Major General John A. Lejeune approved and issued Marine Corps Order 47:

MARINE CORPS ORDERS
No. 47 (Series 1921)

HEADQUARTERS U.S. MARINE CORPS

Washington, November 1, 1921

759. The following will be read to the command on the 10th of November, 1921, and hereafter on the 10th of November of every year. Should the order not be received by the 10th of November, 1921, it will be read upon receipt.

1. On November 10, 1775, a Corps of Marines was created by a resolution of Continental Congress. Since that date many thousand men have borne the name Marine. In memory of them it is fitting that we who are Marines should commemorate the birthday of our corps by calling to mind the glories of its long and illustrious history.

2. The record of our corps is one which will bear comparison with that of the most famous military organizations in the world's history. During 90 of the 146 years of its existence the Marine Corps has been in action against the Nation's foes. From the Battle of Trenton to the

---

Argonne, Marines have won foremost honors in war, and in the long eras of tranquility at home, generation after generation of Marines have grown gray in war in both hemispheres and in every corner of the seven seas, that our country and its citizens might enjoy peace and security.

3. In every battle and skirmish since the birth of our corps, Marines have acquitted themselves with the greatest distinction, winning new honors on each occasion until the term "Marine" has come to signify all that is highest in military efficiency and soldierly virtue.

4. This high name of distinction and soldierly repute we who are Marines today have received from those who preceded us in the corps. With it we have also received from them the eternal spirit which has animated our corps from generation to generation and has been the distinguishing mark of the Marines in every age. So long as that spirit continues to flourish Marines will be found equal to every emergency in the future as they have been in the past, and the men of our Nation will regard us as worthy successors to the long line of illustrious men who have served as "Soldiers of the Sea" since the founding of the Corps.

JOHN A. LEJEUNE,
Major General Commandant

The first Marine Corps Birthday Ball was held in 1925, and in 1952, Commandant Lemuel C. Shepherd, Jr. outlined the cake cutting ceremony, which is done with a traditional sense appropriation. The first slice of cake is presented to the oldest Marine present, who in turn hands it to the youngest Marine, a symbol of how the torch not only of freedom, but of Marine Corps tradition, is passed down from generation to generation.

There are no ex-Marines, only Marines.

SEMPER FIDELIS

Beyond Belief: True Stories of Marine Corps Heroes

The Daring Dozen (USMC)

Under Fire in Cuba During the Spanish-American War

By C. Douglas Sterner

May 11, 1898, was an uncommon date in Marine Corps and Naval history. On that date, during the Spanish American War, 52 Navy Bluejackets and Marines from two ships in a joint endeavor, received Medals of Honor. It was the most Medals of Honor awarded for a single action to both members of the Navy, and U.S. Marines – twelve of whom were cited that day. In fact, prior to that battle, only 25 Marines had earned Medals of Honor.

The citations for all 52 heroes are almost identical, and comprise only two sentences. The first sentence gives the place, date, and the ship on which each hero served. The second sentence describes the heroism for which it was awarded. Each citation simply reads:

For extraordinary heroism in action on board the (*U.S.S. Nashville* or *U.S.S. Marblehead*) during the cutting of the cable leading from Cienfuegos, Cuba, 11 May 1898. Facing the heavy fire of the enemy, he set an example of extraordinary bravery and coolness throughout this action

Beyond Belief: True Stories of Marine Corps Heroes

The simplicity of these citations tends to make them pale in comparison to other, contemporary acts of courage, especially in light of the common belief that many early Medals of Honor were given for mundane acts, and handed out liberally. This simply not true.

In 1917, a review of Army awards resulted in 911 Army awards rescinded as having been awarded frivolously. There was no such review of Navy awards, although in the history of the Medal of Honor, 17 Navy awards have been rescinded, most of them for cause (usually desertion).

The simple fact, however, that more Marines earned Medals of Honor on this day than in any other single day of military action in the Corps' history, should give one cause to take a closer look. Upon further research, one quickly finds that like most pre-World War I citations, behind the simple text of one or two sentences, there is a deeper, and much more dramatic story. This certainly proves to be the case with the Daring Dozen Marines who were awarded Medals of Honor, along with 40 of their Naval comrades on May 11, 1898.

THE SPANISH-AMERICAN WAR

In the spring of 1898, the United States went to war with the empire of Spain. It was our Nation's first major conflict since the Civil War, and the first major foreign war in our Country's brief history. It was a war for which the United States was unprepared militarily, but it was a war that had been looking for an excuse to happen for a quarter-century.

The Spanish-American War was a war that lasted less than a year from declaration of war to signing of the Treaty of Paris that ended it. Violent conflict spanned a period of only 115 days with less than 400 American combat deaths. It was an unqualified victory for the United States and a success that propelled our young nation to the forefront as a world power.

It was a foreign war that received popular support on the home front, and is considered by many historians to be our most popular war. It was glamorized in the media and even instigated to some degree by the leading news publishers of the day.

As a direct result of that brief, first major U.S. foreign war, the face of America changed forever. The Spanish-American War led to the liberation of Cuba, a continued American presence in the Philippine Islands, American expansion to Guam and Puerto Rico, and the construction of the Panama Canal. It was a war fought on the ground largely by citizen soldiers from the National Guard, and by Sailors and Marines who mostly fought in what was a largely naval battle against the invincible Spanish Armada. On the fields of combat, lifetime friendships were formed. Upon their triumphal return, American Soldiers, Sailors, and Marines were hailed as heroes in their hometowns.

Indeed, from the perspective of United States history, if ever there was a *"good war,"* it was the **Spanish-American War.** Shortly after hostilities ended in Cuba and the United States entered a period of negotiations for the peace treaty to end the war, John Milton Hay was appointed Secretary of State by President William McKinley. Years later when Theodore Roosevelt occupied the White House, Hay wrote to the President about that war. In that letter he summarized the conflict with a quote that came to be linked with the first war of American expansion beyond her borders. He called it: *"A Splendid Little War."*

THE SPANISH EMPIRE

In the centuries of European exploration and expansion, including Columbus' discover of the West Indies in 1949, two European super powers led the way in discovery and colonization of new territories around the world. Great Britain amassed an empire upon so vast an area, it was said *"The sun never sets on the British Empire."*

Spain, too, which financed Columbus' expedition, colonized areas of North American and South America, as well as islands in the Caribbean, and islands in the Pacific including Guam and the Philippine Islands. Spain maintained is ruling authority with a large, and vaunted armada of war ships, *The Spanish Armada.*

After the American Revolution, the United States began a century of expansion, claiming additional territories throughout North America. In addition to westward expansion into Native-American lands, in 1803 Thomas Jefferson negotiated the Louisiana Purchase, annexing a wide swath of what is now the American mid-

Beyond Belief: True Stories of Marine Corps Heroes

West from the French. The land purchased for fifteen million dollars comprised 828,000 square miles from what is now Montana down to what is now Louisiana.

Sixteen years later President John Quincy Adams negotiated the acquisition of the Florida peninsula from Spain at virtually no cost other than the assumption of $5 million in claims by U.S. citizens against Spain. In the 1820s Mexican holdings gained independence from Spain, and in 1836 the area that is now eastern Texas declared independence from Mexico. That area was annexed by the United States in 1844, and in 1845 Texas was admitted to the Union as our 28th state.

A WAR LOOKING FOR AN EXCUSE TO HAPPEN

Although most of the United States' period of expansion in the 1800s was westward, there was a lustful eye on the Caribbean island of Cuba, 90 miles from the Florida coastline, soon after the acquisition of Florida. In the 1800s, most of Spain's holdings in Latin America declared and ultimately achieved independence; Cuba remained loyal to Spain. However, in 1868 the Cuban people began eyeing independence, and a rebellion began that would drag on in Cuba's **Ten Years War**. Spain resisted, with more than 200,000 troops on the island and the vaunted Spanish Armada quickly available to quell any serious attempt at rebellion. In 1878 the war ended with Spain promising greater autonomy to Cuba, but on the island, resistance continued for another twenty years.

In the United States there was great sympathy for the Cuban rebels who were still fighting for independence. As the fighting became more bitter, in 1896, Spain seated General Valeriano Weyler as military governor of Cuba. Weyler had previously served as Captain-General of the Canary Islands (1878 – 1883), and Governor General of the Philippine Islands (1888 – 1892). While his rule had previously been somewhat admirable, in the Philippine Islands he had taken the unusual step of granting twenty Filipino women the opportunity to receive educations amid the misogynistic resistance of the influential Philippine Islands parish priest of Malolos. For his command of troops fighting an uprising in Tagalogs, he earned the Grand Cross of Maria Christina. However, in Cuba, Weyler was a totally different kind of man.

The Daring Dozen (USMC)

In exercising his assigned duties of pacification of Cuba, on the verge of outright rebellion, General Weyler began by identifying districts that posed the greatest trouble to maintaining control over Cuba. He then herded the civilian populations in those districts to detention camps near military headquarters. It was a policy he called *reconcentrado*. As a result, more than 100,000 Cubans starved or died of disease before General Weyler was recalled in October, 1897.

In the United States there has long been sympathy for the Cuban people in their struggle to be free of Spanish rule. The heavy-handed tactics of General Weyler made for sensational reporting in the media of the United States' *yellow press*. He became known as the *"Butcher,"* and sensational stories of his brutality ran under blazing headlines that read: *"Spanish Cannibalism," "Inhuman Torture,"* and worse. In the traditions of *David and Goliath,* Cuban patriots were portrayed as heroically defending their homeland against a brutal and aggressive enemy with no conscience.

The terms *"yellow press"* and *"yellow journalism"* referred to media practices of the period. In the competitive market to sell more newspapers, publishers of leading newspapers like the *New York Journal* and *New York World*, resorted to publishing the most outlandish stories with unbelievable headlines. They were the "Hillary Clinton Gives Birth to Alien Baby" tabloid journalism of the United States in the late 1800s. The truth of the news didn't matter as much as the ability of a headline to capture attention . . . *"Amazon Warriors Fight for Rebels"* . . . or the potential of a story to incite the emotions of the reader for more; the American people ate it up.

The Spanish recall of General Weyler on October 31, 1897, might have otherwise robbed the media of the prime subject of their inflammatory stories were it not for the continued unrest in Cuba. Building on stories already written and widely known, and with a battery of reporters and artists that included the likes of William Remington, the media survived. Two years earlier a 25-year old author inspired our nation by reliving the sacrifice and glory of Civil War service with the release of his second novel, **The Red Badge of Courage**. Now, Stephen Crane joined the battery of writers chronicling the valiant struggle for freedom in Cuba. Even with the absence of Weyler, tensions mounted and Spain was portrayed as a poor ruler about to leap from the frying pan into the fire in Cuba.

Such news stories pitted the U.S. media against the politicians who were resisting the idea of going to war with Spain in defense of the Cuban rebels. Designed to sway public opinion, they were quite effective. The power of the press to influence public opinion is perhaps best illustrated in a statement by William Randolph Hearst, publish of **The New York World**.

Hearst sent the famous Western artist Frederick Remington to Cuba to sketch Cuban insurgents fighting for their independence from Spain. After several months, Remington had found little to draw, and wired New York, *"Everything quiet, no trouble here. There will be no war. I wish to return."*

Hearst reportedly responded to Remington's appraisal of the situation in Cuba and his request to come home with the statement: *"You furnish the pictures and I'll furnish the war."*

MANIFEST DESTINY

By 1898, little more than 100 years after the birth of the United States of America, the original 13 American colonies had grown into 45 states stretching from sea to shining sea. The successful westward expansion into Indian and Mexican territory was a source of pride. The only war the young nation had ever lost, was the war with itself. Post Civil War there was a strong sense of nationalism and invincibility. This was magnified from the pre-Civil war prevailing doctrine in the 19th century called *"Manifest Destiny."*

Manifest Destiny was an American prevailing doctrine, long before it was given a title when **Democratic Review** editor John L. Sullivan wrote in 1845 that no nation on earth should be allowed to interfere with America's *"Manifest Destiny to overspread the continent allotted by Providence for the free development of our* *yearly multiplying millions.*" Sullivan had published his article in support of annexation of Texas, but the concept that the people of the United States had a sacred obligation to expand its borders to include all of North America (including Canada and Mexico), became the rallying cry . . . and excuse, for all United States incursions into new territory.

Sullivan defined *Manifest Destiny.* in a three-point argument that quickly gained popularity:

1. God Himself was on the side of those eager to expand the U.S. Territories. This line of thinking stemmed from the belief following the American Revolution that the United States was the land of a chosen people, delivered from Great Britain's rule and preserved by Divine providence and in accordance with a Divine plan.

2. *Free Development* meant that the conquest of new regions, placing them under American rule, was the liberation of previously oppressed people. In this regard, the philosophy rendered a concept of the United States as the ultimate savior of the western hemisphere, thereby excusing expansionist activities.

3. Sullivan's third point was the belief that, as the United States population rapidly grew, it was necessary to expand and inhabit new territories to accommodate the needs of the people of this chosen nation.

While the *yellow journalism* fueled the emotions of the American populace in opposition to Spain, the empathy for the plight of the Cuban people and **Manifest Destiny** provided the excuse. It literally created a demand for the United States to go to war with Spain and become the savior of the Cuban people, with an eye to then annexing and making Cuba a part of the United States.

Because of these factors, when war did come, it would become probably the most popular war in our nation's history. Even in the American Revolution and during the two world wars of the 20th century, the American public would have strong anti-war movements. Often unremembered is the fact that in the first year of World War II, after a stunning streak of losses in the Pacific, there was strong sentiment at home for the President to sue for peace with

Beyond Belief: True Stories of Marine Corps Heroes

Japan, and cede to them the territories they had invaded and now ruled. During the **Spanish-American war**, although there was some opposition, it was so small and ineffective as to have little impact. The war with Spain was, perhaps, indeed a splendid little war.

<u>REMEMBER THE MAINE</u>

Amid rising tensions, on January 25, 1898, President William McKinley dispatched the American battleship U.S.S. Maine (BB-2), to Cuba. The *U.S.S. Maine* was an impressive battleship; at 319 feet long. Displacing 6,682 tons, it was the largest ship ever to enter the harbor at Havana. Though only a second class battleship, the nine-year-old vessel was among the most impressive of the U.S. Naval fleet. One of our country's first steel warships, the Maine was unique in the fleet due the fact that it had been totally designed and built by Americans. It was the largest ship ever actually constructed in a U.S. Navy yard. Painted the bright white of a peace-time U.S. Naval vessel, the impressive battleship boasted four huge 10-inch breech-loading rifles in additional to its smaller battery armaments.

Most of Captain Charles D. Sigsbee's 24 Naval officers were graduates of the Academy at Annapolis. At least 20% of the 290 sailors they commanded were foreign born men who sought now to serve their adopted country.

A 40-man Marine guard brought the ship's total strength to 355 American servicemen. The leathernecks, under the leadership of five non-coms, were commanded by First Lieutenant Albertus W. Catlin, who had graduated from the U.S. Naval Academy with the class of 1890. (Sixteen years later as a major, Catlin would earn the Medal of Honor in the engagement at Vera Cruz, Mexico.) Nearly a fourth of the Marines were foreign-born immigrants.

Upon arrival in Havana on Tuesday, January 25, the U.S.S. Maine anchored at Buoy #4, a space reserved for war ships. Despite this, the potential for the unrest in Cuba to turn violent, and the Maine's impressive array of military power, the mission was a peaceful one. Captain Sigsbee informed his crew that there would be no shore liberty while in Cuba. For the most part the men were content to spend a brief time riding peacefully at anchor under the tropical sun of the Caribbean. After this short visit they knew they would return to New Orleans in time for Mardi Gras.

The Spanish welcomed, although somewhat nervously, the arrival of the *Maine*, and sent a case of sherry to the officer's mess along with an invitation to a bull fight at the **plaza de toros**. Captain Sigsbee and a few of his officers dutifully accepted the invite, attending in civilian attire. On his visit ashore the commander of the *Maine* was at one point handed an anti-American propaganda pamphlet by someone in the crowd. Scrawled across it was the message, *"Watch out for your ship."*

Beyond the scrawled message at plaza de toros however, there was little more to indicate that the crew of the *Maine* was facing any undue danger. None-the-less, as a matter of prudence, Sigsbee ordered Lieutenant Catlin to keep his Marines at a careful state of alert.

The *Maine*, by her presence, seemed to have a reassuring effect upon the American Foreign Minister. General Fitzhugh Lee noted this in a communication to President McKinley who requested that when the *Maine's* tenure in Havana expired, another Naval vessel be dispatched to replace her. By Tuesday, February 15, the *Maine* had been at anchor for three weeks without incident. Although Lieutenant Catlin dutifully kept his Marines at a high state of alert, the crew of the *Maine's* biggest problem was boredom.

By the artificial light in his cabin that evening, Captain Sigsbee began writing a letter to his family when Marine fifer C. H. Newton began playing *"Taps"* to signal the end of the day. *"I laid down my pen to listen to the notes of the bugle, which were singularly beautiful in the oppressive stillness of the night,"* Sigsbee wrote. *"The Marine bugler, Newton, who was rather given to fanciful effects, was evidently doing his best. During his pauses the echoes floated back to the ship with singular distinctness, repeating the strains of the bugle fully and exactly."*

It was ten minutes after nine when Newton blew his haunting version of *"Taps."* When the last note had sounded, all became quiet.

Newton returned below deck where most of the enlisted men were billeted. In his cabin, Captain Sigsbee picked up his pen to finish his letter. On deck, Lieutenant John Hood was finishing the day with a fine cigar. As he relished the smoke he noticed someone walking to the starboard side of the ship. Approaching the dark figure, Hood recognized the familiar face of Lieutenant John Blandon as the latter leaned against the railing to peer off at the lights of Havana. It was 9:40 p.m.

> *"You asleep?"* Hood asked with a slight laugh.

> *"No, I'm on watch,"* Blandon answered.

> ### And then . . . the U.S.S. Maine Exploded!

REMEMBER THE MAINE

In the hours after the explosion aboard the *Maine*, the small gigs from the American passenger steamer and the Spanish warship *Alphonso XII* had given good account of themselves in braving the darkness, fires and secondary explosions of the sinking American battleship in search of survivors. Having witnessed this first-hand, Captain Sigsbee was reluctant to immediately blame the Spanish. In his first telegram to Washington he reported details of the event, then closed with the observation that *"Public opinion should be suspended until further report."*

There would indeed be further reports, both officially and unofficially. Two days after the explosion the Navy created the *"Sampson Board,"* an official inquiry into the cause of the disaster. On February 21 the Naval Court of Inquiry began their 4-week investigation in Havana. Simultaneously, the Spanish began their own inquiry into the matter.

The Daring Dozen (USMC)

It would not be an easy process. Captain Sigsbee remembered *"a bursting, rending, and crashing roar of immense volume... followed by heavy, ominous metallic sounds."*

Lieutenant Blandon remembered a single explosion on the port side, followed by *"a perfect rain of missiles of all descriptions."* Lieutenant Hood, who had been next to Blandon to witness the explosion first-hand remembered the explosion as coming on the starboard side.

Marine Lieutenant Catlin reported what he thought to be TWO explosions, the first sounding like the *"crack of a pistol and the second a roar that engulfed the ship's entire forward section."* Some survivors heard one explosion, others a deep rumble followed by one loud explosion, while still others recalled a series of explosions. Reaching any kind of reasonable determination as to what destroyed the *Maine* became a challenge not only to the official Board of Inquiry, but to historians for the following century.

Back in the United States there were few questions about what had caused the *Maine* to suddenly explode in the darkness of night, killing 260 Americas. Two days after the incident, the headline in *The New Your World* read: *"MAINE EXPLOSION CAUSED BY BOMB OR TORPEDO?"*

In the hours after the explosion aboard the *Maine*, the small gigs from the American passenger steamer and the Spanish warship *Alphonso XII* had given good account of themselves in braving the darkness, fires and secondary explosions of the sinking American battleship in search of survivors. Having witnessed this first-hand, Captain Sigsbee was reluctant to immediately blame the Spanish. In his first telegram to Washington he reported details of the event, then closed with the observation that *"Public opinion should be suspended until further report."*

Beyond Belief: True Stories of Marine Corps Heroes

There would indeed be further reports, both officially and unofficially. Two days after the explosion the Navy created the "Sampson Board," an official inquiry into the cause of the disaster. On February 21 the Naval Court of Inquiry began their 4-week investigation in Havana. Simultaneously, the Spanish began their own inquiry into the matter.

It would not be an easy process. Captain Sigsbee remembered "a bursting, rending, and crashing roar of immense volume... followed by heavy, ominous metallic sounds."

Lieutenant Blandon remembered a single explosion on the port side, followed by *"a perfect rain of missiles of all descriptions."* Lieutenant Hood, who had been next to Blandon to witness the explosion first-hand remembered the explosion as coming on the starboard side.

The *New York Journal* was more specific: *"THE DESTRUCTION OF THE WAR SHIP MAINE WAS THE WORK OF AN ENEMY."* Artists created renditions depicting how Spanish saboteurs might have fastened an underwater mine to the hull of the *Maine*, then detonated it from shore. Randolph Hearst offered a $50,000 reward for *"Conviction of the Criminals"* and announced that *"Naval Officers (were) Unanimous That the Ship Was Destroyed on Purpose."*

On March 6, the Spanish government requested the recall of U.S. Cuban Consul Fitzhugh Lee. In the United States, citizens gathered solemnly at Capitol Hill and outside the White House to mourn the loss of 260 Sailors and Marines.

Tensions continued to mount while the Navy conducted its official inquiry. In a Broadway bar in New York City a patron lifted his glass and said, *"Gentlemen, remember the Maine!"* A reporter from the *Journal* happened to be in the bar and wrote about the incident.

When it was published, America had a new war slogan: *"Remember The Main."* It caught on and became a battle-cry. Spaniards were burned in effigy in cities and town across America and soon the slogan became a war cry: *"Remember the Maine, and To Hell with Spain!"*

The Daring Dozen (USMC)

Finally, bowing to the rapidly deteriorating events in Cuba and the overwhelming cries for war at home, President McKinley asked Congress on April 11 to authorize American intervention to end the revolution in Cuba. Five days later the road to war was cleared in Congress when an amendment offered by Colorado Congressman Henry Teller was ratified. Designed to quiet the fears of those who opposed a war based upon an American imperialistic effort to annex Cuba, the Teller Amendment stated that the United States:

> "Hereby disclaims any disposition of intention to exercise sovereignty, jurisdiction, or control over said island (Cuba) except for pacification thereof, and asserts its determination, when that is accomplished, to leave the government and control of the island to its people."

On April 20, while Congress still debated the request for war, President McKinley signed a Joint Resolution for war with Spain, an ultimatum that was promptly forwarded to Madrid with a call for Cuban independence. The Spanish Minister to the United States promptly demanded his passport and, with his Legation, left Washington for Canada.

The following day McKinley received his answer from Madrid. General Steward Woodford, the U.S. Minister to Spain was handed his passport and told to leave the country. The Spanish government considered McKinley's ultimatum to be a declaration of war. With diplomatic relations suspended, President McKinley ordered a blockade of Cuba while the Spanish forces in Santiago began mining Guantanamo. Bay.

The U.S. Naval fleet departed Key West, Florida on April 22 to carry out the President's order for a blockade of Cuba. The American Navy was well prepared for war, especially against the aging Spanish fleet. But the Spanish had at least 80,000 soldiers stationed in Cuba that would require a ground war.

The U.S. Army, with only 25,706 enlisted men and 2,116 officers, was not prepared for war on the ground. On April 23 the U.S. President issued a call for 125,000 volunteers. After months of patriotic fervor generated by tales of Spanish sabotage and atrocity,

41

the recruiting stations were immediately swamped with eager young American would-be soldiers.

On April 25, 1898, the war that had been looking for an excuse to happen, finally became official. The U.S. Congress passed a resolution declaring the United States to be at war with Spain. The Naval blockade of Cuba was already underway, so Congress made the declaration of war effective as of April 21, thereby legitimizing military actions undertaken in the previous four days.

Under Admiral William Sampson, who had earlier headed up the inquiry into the cause of the explosion on the *U.S.S. Maine*, the blockade of Cuba escalated. On the same day that war was declared, American ships bombarded the Spanish at Matanzaras, Cuba.

Cuba, in the Caribbean, was not the only vestige remaining of the old Spanish Empire. Spain also held much of the series of 700 islands in the Pacific known as the Philippine Islands, which had been under the rule of Madrid since Ferdinand Magellan discovered the vast Archipelago in 1521. On the other side of the globe, the U.S. Pacific fleet under Admiral George Dewey was already prepared for war as per the February 25 communiqué from Navy Undersecretary Theodore Roosevelt.

While few Americans gave little notice or concern to events in the Pacific Islands, and even President McKinley confessed that he could not locate the Philippine Islands *"within 2000 miles,"* American Naval planners had long considered the value of the natural port at Manila on Luzon, the largest of the Philippine Islands.

War with Spain was the excuse now, to further expand the influence of the United States, and while Admiral Sampson's ships conducted their blockade in the Caribbean, on April 27 Admiral Dewey sailed his ships out of Mirs Bay, China and set their course for Manila. The **Spanish-American war** would become a battlefield on two, widely separated fronts.

The Daring Dozen (USMC)

THE BATTLE OF MANILA HARBOR

If the prospects for war with Spain had been a foregone conclusion for months, so too was the predicted outcome of such a conflict. The Spanish fleet, while still large, was an aging fleet that no longer reflected the luster and might that had made the terms "Spanish" and "Armada" synonymous. Despite the fact that many ships of the enemy fleet were constructed of steel, as were the newer warships of the U.S. Navy, they were no match for the modern guns of the American sailors. Author Sherwood Anderson had his own unique perspective of America's coming battles with Spain. He said it would be "Like robbing an old gypsy woman in a vacant lot at night after a fair."

Upon receiving orders to proceed, Admiral George Dewey set his own fleet on a course towards Luzon, departing Mirs Bay in China on April 27. His flagship was the first class protected cruiser *U.S.S. Olympia,* followed by three second class cruisers *Baltimore, Raleigh* and *Boston,* the gunboats *Petrel* and *Concord*, the revenue cutter *Hugh McCulloch*, and two transports *Nanshan* and *Zafiro.*

The three-day run across the South China Sea was made, as one Naval lieutenant later reported, *"As directly and with as little attempted concealment as if on a peace mission. Lights were carried at night and electric signals freely exchanged; but gruesome preparations were going on within each ship. Anchor chains were hung about exposed gun positions and wound around ammunition hoists; splinter nets were spread under boats; bulkheads, gratings and wooden chests were thrown overboard; furniture was struck below protective decks; surgical instruments were overhauled and hundreds of yards of bandaging disinfected. The sea was strewn for fifty leagues with jettisoned woodwork unfit to carry into battle."* (Lieutenant John Ellicott)

Beyond Belief: True Stories of Marine Corps Heroes

Once his fleet had put to sea, Admiral Dewey ordered the men to muster on each ship to hear a reading of the proclamation issued five days earlier by General Basilio Augustin Davila, the Spanish governor-general of the Philippine Islands. In that proclamation Davila asserted that, *"The North American people... have exhausted our patience and provoked war . . . with their acts of treachery.*

When morning dawned on April 30, Admiral Dewey's fleet sighted the coastline of the largest of the Philippine islands, Luzon. The United States Navy had finally arrived, prepared for war. First however, they had to locate the enemy fleet. Spanish Admiral Patricio Montojo y Pasaron was no novice at sea, and among the more than 700 islands of the archipelago there were literally thousands of small coves that would hide his vessels.

The logical location for finding the enemy would be somewhere in the vicinity of Manila Bay, a large inlet near the Philippine capital city, midway on the western coast of Luzon. Arriving at Luzon eighty miles north of Manila Bay, Dewey dispatched his warships *Boston* and *Concord* to reconnoiter the smaller bays and inlets while the remaining seven vessels slowly continued southward towards Manila Bay.

The *Boston* and *Concord* found no sign of the enemy fleet, then proceeded to enter Subic Bay at the northwest edge of the Bataan peninsula. Again they found no sign of the enemy vessels, and turned to rejoin the fleet. As they departed the bay they met the *Baltimore*, recently dispatched ahead of the rest of Dewey's warships to meet them.

They did not know that, had their reconnaissance occurred one day earlier, the *Boston* and *Concord* would have steamed directly into the Spanish fleet. Within the previous 24 hours Admiral Montojo had sailed his warships out of Subic Bay after a 4-day stay, opting to enter the shelter of the larger Manila Bay. As the sun began to set on the evening of April 30, Admiral Dewey's full fleet of seven warships and two transports had marshaled outside Subic. He ordered the commanding officers of each ship to join him on the flag ship *Olympia*, where he outlined his plans. For the men of the United States Navy, it would be a long night.

The Daring Dozen (USMC)

Manila Bay is a large inlet on the western coast of Luzon, nearly twenty miles wide and twenty miles long. Entrance to the bay is only achieved through a narrow passageway less than ten miles across, and broken up by the tadpole shaped fortress island of Corregidor, and the smaller islands

of Caballo and El Fraile. At the north end of the entrance is the Bataan Peninsula and the city of Mariveles.

With heavy guns on fortifications at Mariveles and Corregidor, and additional batteries on the two smaller islands and the southern tip of the entrance, an enemy attempting to enter Manila Bay was subject to an intense crossfire from at least five batteries. At the north end of a small peninsula southwest of the capitol city sat Cavite arsenal, as well as additional fortifications on Sangley Point.

Admiral Montojo chose to anchor his ten warships and their transports just outside the city of Manila, knowing that before an enemy could attack him, they would first have to run the gauntlet of shore batteries at the harbor's entrance. Scattered throughout the smaller coves and river inlets to the harbor he had another twenty or more small river boats. It was a perfect place to hide or, should an enemy dare to run the gauntlet, to stand and fight.

Aboard the *Olympia*, Admiral Dewey was planning to do just that. As the ship's band played "There'll be a Hot Time in the Old Town Tonight," the American commander explained his order of battle. The early phase of the moon would provide just enough light for the lead ship to spot the island of Corregidor and the entrance to Manila Bay. By midnight however, the moon would set to provide a darkened passage for his fleet as they ran the enemy gauntlet. If all went well, when morning dawned he would be inside the harbor where he would find and destroy the Spanish fleet.

At 4:00 a.m. on May 1, 1898, coffee was served to the officers and men of Admiral Dewey's fleet. Three vessels of the reserve squadron were sent northward to lay-to, while Dewey's remaining six ships continued their course towards Manila. At 5:05 a.m. the **Stars** and Stripes were unfurled from each of the war ships and Dewey gave the command to *"Prepare for general action."* Ten minutes later the enemy shore batteries at Sangley Point opened fire. The American ships returned fire, and then turned towards the ships of Admiral Montojo.

Within minutes the early morning air was filled with the thunder of heavy guns and geysers of water shooting heavenward as the enemy shells began falling around the American ships. Dressed in his crisp white Naval dress uniform, Admiral George Dewey stood on the bridge of his flagship *Olympia*. In the preceding hours he had done the unthinkable, navigating the Boca Grand to find and meet the enemy. As the smell of smoke filled the air and the shells of the enemy erupted around his fleet, Dewey led the way into battle. At 5:40 a.m. he turned to the Captain Charles V. Gridley of his flagship, and said: *"You may fire when ready."*

When the fighting subsided, with Spanish warships sinking throughout the harbor, at 12:40 Admiral Dewey anchored his valiant fleet abreast of the city of Manila. His untested Sailors and Marines had survived their first engagement and destroyed virtually every ship of Spain's Pacific Fleet; and ten huge warships were now exploding, burning, or sinking. The American forces had also captured an enemy navy yard and more than 400 enemy lay dead or wounded.

For the Americans, not a single ship was disabled, not a life lost. The only casualty of the day was the death of the engineer of the *McCulloch*, a victim of heat stroke.

Spanish ships destroyed were *Reina Christina, Castilla, Velasco, Don Juan de Austria, Don Antonio De Ulloa, Isla de Cuba, Isla de Luzon, Elcano, General Lezo, Marquis del Duero, Argos*

The Daring Dozen (USMC)

As a result of his heroic actions during the decisive battle of Manila Bay, Chief Carpenter's Mate Franz Anton Itrich was awarded the Medal of Honor. It was the first of 110 such awards. As the focus shifted back to the Caribbean, the next Medals of Honor would not be earned until May 11. On that day 52 Americans would be awarded their nation's highest honor, nearly half of the war's total. Twelve would be presented to a **Daring Dozen** United States Marines.

CIENFUEGOS

While Admiral Dewey was busy destroying the Spanish Fleet in Manila, American naval forces in the Caribbean were busy creating a *"sea-wall"* around the island of Cuba to maintain the blockade the President ordered on April 21. Quickly moving out of Key West, the ships assigned to the blockade arrived the following morning, quickly capturing the Spanish merchant steamers *Bonaventure* and *Pedro* While the *New York,* the *Indiana*, and the *Iowa* remained near Havana, other U.S. warships began patrolling the waters elsewhere around the island. On April 24 the Spanish merchant steamers *Catalina* and *Miguel Iover* were taken, and the following day two more Spanish merchant ships were captured.

On April 26 the Spanish made their first successful breach of the American blockade when the Spanish liner *Montserrat* successfully entered the harbor at Cienfuegos to unload a detachment of troops and a cargo of supplies. Ten days later the *Montserrat* again breached the blockade, successfully departing Cienfuegos to return unmolested to Spain.

Beyond Belief: True Stories of Marine Corps Heroes

Cienfuegos was a busy port town on the southern coast of the Island of Cuba, almost directly opposite Havana. The U.S. Naval warships *U.S.S. Marblehead* and *U.S.S. Nashville* carefully patrolled the waters on the southern coastline, hence the two vessels were operating near the site of the only breach in the American blockade. Both ships began taking a closer look at Cienfuegos.

In addition to the Spanish Troops garrisoned at Cienfuegos, the harbor entrance was protected by a large lighthouse. Cienfuegos was a well defended port. It was also a military target. On May 10, Captain B. H. McCalla of the *Marblehead* located the cables that connected the troops at Cienfuegos with the rest of the world. These were large, undersea cables that ran from the Spanish headquarters to transmit communications to and from Havana and Spain. Realizing the value of isolating the Spanish soldiers in Cienfuegos by cutting off their communications, Captain McCalla designed a daring, and almost disastrous, plan of action.

MAY 10, 1898

As evening fell across the Caribbean, Captain McCalla began speaking to his men aboard the *U.S.S. Marblehead.* Nearby, on the *U.S.S. Nashville*, Captain Maynard was giving a similar message to his own sailors and Marines. Briefly, each of the commanders outlined a daring plot to isolate the enemy soldiers stationed at Cienfuegos. *"Tomorrow morning,"* Captain McCalla told his men, *"parties from the Marblehead and the Nashville will enter the bay in small boats, to dredge up and cut the communications cables running out of Cienfuegos."*

The operation would have to be performed close to shore, directly under the guns of the enemy soldiers garrisoned at Cienfuegos. It was not typical Naval duty. In fact, to the Captain's knowledge, such a mission had never been attempted before and may, in fact, not even be successful.

The men of the *Marblehead* listened eagerly to the Captain's plan. When McCalla finished laying it out, he asked for volunteers. Despite the danger, he was met with an eager response from several of his seamen and Marines.

The Daring Dozen (USMC)

Twenty year old Marine Private Herman Kuchmeister was one of those to offer his services. At first, according to later accounts by Kuchmeister, Captain McCalla refused to include the young German immigrant in the group. Because of the great danger the mission posed, McCalla felt Kuchmeister was too young. The Marines of the two ships were to accompany the small boats to draw enemy fire away from, and to provide cover fire for, the sailors who would dredge up and cut the cables. The eager private reminded his captain that he was among the best riflemen aboard ship, *"having won a sharpshooters medal for the best score in target practice."* Captain McCalla took note of Kuchmeister's argument and finally consented to add him to the group of volunteers.

All the men were excited. After weeks at sea with little to do, the prospect of action was well received. At the same time, few if any of the sailors and Marines in the volunteer group had ever heard a shot fired in anger or tasted the fear of confrontation with the enemy. *"That night as I spread my hammock out,"* Private Kuchmeister later said, *"I thought, 'Would I be on board the following night or would I be resting at the bottom of the sea'."*

MAY 11, 1898

The crews of both ships were up before dawn the following day, the men of the cable cutting crews anxiously finishing their breakfast of coffee and hardtack, then quickly assembling their weapons and gear for the unusual mission. *"Cable cutting was something new to all of us and I did not know just how to manage it,"* Navy Blacksmith Austin Durney of the *U.S.S. Nashville* later said. *"To tell the truth, I didn't have the faintest idea of the work. To be prepared for all emergencies we equipped ourselves with every possible tool that suggested itself to us, and thus we took along chisels, hammers, axes, saws, etc."*

49

Beyond Belief: True Stories of Marine Corps Heroes

At 5:00 a.m. the parties launched from both warships. Ensign Magruder of the *Nashville* commanded a steam launch to drop the smaller sailing boats inside the harbor, then pulled his launch back to a position 150 to 200 yards offshore to give covering fire if needed. Overall command of the operation was under the leadership of Lieutenant Camberon Winslow and his second in command, Lieutenant Anderson. The Marine sharpshooters and guards were under the leadership of Sergeant Philip Gaughan of the *Nashville*, and each of the cable cutting boats carried a blacksmith, Durney from the *Nashville* and Joseph Carter from the *Marblehead*. It was these two men who would carry primary responsibility for finding a way to hack or cut through the communications cables.

The waters of the harbor were rough as the small boats began moving towards the shoreline. Near the lighthouse, large rocks could be seen protruding dangerously close to the area where the boats would have to work. To add to the dangerous task, the men could see mines floating in the water beneath them, mines that could be detonated by the enemy on shore from a small switch house. As the cable cutting crews moved closer to the shoreline, the big guns of the *Marblehead and Nashville* began pounding the enemy positions.

At first the Spanish soldiers held their fire, assuming according to Austin Durney's later reports that the Americans were bent on landing on the beach. Then the men of the Spanish garrison noticed the sailors in the cable cutting boats dropping grappling hooks to dredge up the cables, and realized what was happening. From the heights of the cliffs overlooking the harbor the enemy began to fire with great ferocity.

In his boat, Kuchmeister and the other Marines saw a group of nine enemy soldiers sprinting for the switch house. If they reached it, they could begin detonating the mines throughout the harbor. The Marines laid down a deadly fire, dropping all nine of them. Then they turned their two machineguns and their one-pound gun on the small shack itself, leveling it.

Shells from the large guns of the Spanish fortifications began to rain over the harbor, raising geysers of water and adding tumult to the already rough seas. In Durney's boat the men struggled to lift the first cable over the bow, and the blacksmith began trying to cut through it. *"As soon as I got hold of the cable,"* he said, *"I discovered that the only practical tool was a hack-saw."* Durney's small boat was less than 15 yards from shore as he set to his task. Enemy fire rained over his head, some small arms fire striking the boat. Additional and accurate fire began striking the boat from the lighthouse. While the warships and the Marines turned their fire on it, Durney continued his work. Nearby, Seaman Robert Volz was wounded four different times.

Beyond Belief: True Stories of Marine Corps Heroes

For more than an hour the small boats with their crews of brave young sailors and Marines endured the dangerous waters, the ever present mines, the crash of large rounds, and small arms fire, to continue their task. Seaman Harry Hendrickson was shot in the liver and given up for dead. Lieutenant Winslow was wounded in the hand. John Davis took a round to his right leg, and Marine Private Patrick Regan appeared to have been fatally wounded.

In Kuchmeiser's boat, small arms fire began poking holes in the thin wood sides below the waterline. As quickly as a hole sprouted, the Marines would plug it with one of their bullets, then continue to return fire. Kuchmeister noted what appeared to be *"the whole Santa Clara Regiment advanced in company, as on parade."* The enemy force was far too great to continue, but the Marines stayed their position to render cover fire for the sailors cutting through the cables. *"Large shells dropped around us, nearly lifting us out of the water. Shells from our own ship and the Spanish batteries passed over head."* On the *U.S.S. Nashville,* sailors who had not been selected for the mission continued to man the ship's big guns to cover their comrades. Aboard the *Nashville,* Captain Maynard was wounded and First Lieutenant Albert C. Dillingham took command.

Finally, one of the cables was cut through. The shore end was dropped in place and one of the boats from the *Marblehead* towed the other end out to sea where it was dropped after another large section of cable was removed to make it harder to repair. The enemy fire continued to intensify. A flurry of small arms fire began striking Kuchmeiser's boat anew. One round struck the left side of Private Kuchmeiser's face, followed by a second round that shattered his jaw and teeth and cut away a section of his tongue. The second round exited behind his ear, within a sixteenth of an inch of the jugular vein. Kuchmeister was among those given up for dead.

Finally, the second cable was cut. A remaining smaller cable on the shore would have to be ignored. The badly battered sailors and Marines, in small boats barely able to remain afloat, turned to return to their warships. As they fought the seas, the enemy began finding their range. Large shells dropped closer and closer to the small sailing ships. For a few minutes, it looked as if all of the volunteers would be lost.

In the distance Lieutenant Dillingham turned the *Nashville* towards the shore, steaming ahead and then turning again to place his warship between the enemy on the shore and the retreating smaller boats of the cable cutting crews and their Marine guards. It was a bold act that exposed his ship to intense enemy fire, but for the badly battered volunteers, it meant the difference between life and death.

The wounded were quickly taken aboard the warships for medical care. Many of the men had suffered wounds, several of them repeated wounds, and at least three were critical or fatal. Kuchmeister later said, *"The only thing I remembered after being brought aboard ship is that I insisted that I was able to walk to the operating table. As I lain (SIC) in the Captain's cabin, it came to me if I died it was for my country and a glorious cause."* Kuchmeister would survive after two years in Naval hospitals and five operations. He would carry the tell-tale scars to his face and jaw for the rest of his life. He died on February 1, 1923 at the age of 45 – his combat wounds contributing to ill health after the war and his ultimate demise.

All 52 men, 26 from each of the *Marblehead* and the *Nashville*, were subsequently awarded Medals of Honor.

As Naval officers, Ensign Magruder and Lieutenants Winslow and Anderson were not eligible for award of the Medal of Honor. Some Naval records list the name Marine Private Patrick Regan as participating in the cable cutting party and being fatally wounded. The name of Mr. Regan does not appear in the list of 52 Medals of Honor subsequently awarded, however Herman Kuchmeister's account of the actions that day indicate that that one man in his boat was killed.

Amid sometimes conflicting accounts of the casualties, one fact remained from the heroic actions at Cienfuegos on May 11, 1898 – heroism abounded. It so simply related in the few sentences of the Medal of Honor citations as to almost be overlooked. Further, the United States suffered it first major casualties of the **Spanish-American war**, while young sailors and Marines performed their duties with dedication and honor in the face of incredible resistance.

Navy Cable Cutters
Who received Medals Of Honor

U.S.S. Marblehead	U.S.S. Nashville
Bennett, James (US Navy)	Baker, Benjamin (US Navy)
Carter, Joseph (US Navy)	Barrow, David (US Navy)
Chadwick, Leonard (US Navy)	Beyer, Albert (US Navy)
Davis, John (US Navy)	Blume, Robert (US Navy)
Doran, John (US Navy)	Bright, George (US Navy)
Erickson, Nicholas (US Navy)	Durney, Austin (US Navy)
Foss, Herbert (US Navy)	Eglit, John (US Navy)
Gill, Freeman (US Navy)	Gibbons, Michael (US Navy)
Hart, William (US Navy)	Hoban, Thomas (US Navy)
Hendrickson, Henry. (US Navy)	Johansson, Johan (US Navy)
Johanson, John (US Navy)	Krause, Ernest (US Navy)
Kramer, Franz (US Navy)	Meyer, William (US Navy)
Levery, William (US Navy)	Miller, Harry (US Navy)
Mager, George (US Navy)	Miller, Willard (US Navy)
Maxwell, John (US Navy)	Nelson, Lauritz (US Navy)
Oakley, William (US Navy)	Riley, John (US Navy)
Olsen, Anton (US Navy)	Sundquist, Gustav (US Navy)
Russell, Henry (US Navy)	Van Etten, Hudson (US Navy)
Vadas, Albert (US Navy)	Volz , Robert (US Navy)
Wilke, Julius (US Navy)	
Williams, Frank (US Navy)	

The Daring Dozen Marines

Pvt. Daniel J. Campbell	**Pvt. Oscar Wadsworth Field**

U.S.S. Marblehead	*U.S.S. Nashville*
Born: Canada Hometown: Boston, MA Died: April 28, 1944	Born: New Jersey Hometown: New York, NY Died: January 5, 1912
Pvt. Joseph John Franklin	**Sgt. Phillip Gaughan**

U.S.S. Nashville	*U.S.S. Nashville*
Born: New York Hometown: New York, NY Died: April 28, 1940	Born: Ireland Hometown: Yeadon, PA Died: December 31, 1918
Pvt. Frank Hill	**Pvt. Michael Kearny**

U.S.S. Nashville	*U.S.S. Nashville*
Born: Connecticut Hometown: Hartford, CT Died: Unknown	Born: Ireland Hometown: Massachusetts Died: October 31, 1937

Beyond Belief: True Stories of Marine Corps Heroes

Pvt. Hermann Kuchmeister	Pvt. James Meredith
 *U.S.S. Marblehead* Born: Germany Hometown: New York, NY Died: February 1, 1923	 *U.S.S. Marblehead* Born: Nebraska Hometown: Boston, MA Died: January 18, 1915
Pvt. Pomeroy Parker	**Pvt. Joseph Francis Scott**
 *U.S.S. Nashville* Born: North Carolina Hometown: Gates, NC Died: December 20, 1946	 *U.S.S. Nashville* Born: Massachusetts Hometown: Cambridge, MA Died: February 28, 1941
Pvt. Edward Sullivan	**Pvt. Walter Scott West**
 *U.S.S. Marblehead* Born: Ireland Hometown: Uxbridge, MA Died: March 11, 1955	 *U.S.S. Marblehead* Born: New Hampshire Hometown: Bradford, NH Died: September 14, 1943

The Daring Dozen (USMC)

Not until June 10 was any major effort made to land ground forces in Cuba occur. On that date, 58-year old Marine Lieutenant Colonel Robert W. Huntington landed in Guantanamo Bay with 623 Marines, to battle an estimated 5,000 Spanish soldiers in and around the bay. In the earliest ground fighting of the war, two more Marines earned Medals of Honor. Sergeant John Henry Quick was cited for gallantry in action, *"during the battle of Cuzco, Cuba, 14 June 1898. Sergeant Quick . . . signaled the U.S.S. Dolphin on three different occasions while exposed to a heavy fire from the enemy."* The same day, Sergeant John Fitzgerald was cited simply for *"gallantry in action at Cuzco, Cuba."*

By mid-month U.S. Army soldiers began landing in Cuba to engage most of the ground fighting in small skirmishes and major battles such at the **Battle of San Juan (Kettle) Hill**. It culminated with the Naval Battle of Santiago Harbor on July 3 that virtually destroyed what remained of the Spanish War Fleet in the Atlantic and Caribbean. In the decisive battle, aboard the *U.S.S. Brooklyn*, Marine Private Harry Lewis Macneal *"Braved the fire of the enemy . . . displaying gallantry throughout this action,"* earning the final Marine Corps Medal of Honor of **Spanish-American War.**

| Sgt. Quick | Sgt. Fitzgerald | Pvt. Macneal |

With the destruction of the Spanish Fleet at Santiago Harbor, and the surrender of Rear Admiral Pascual Cervera y Topete and his surviving sailors, the war in Cuba wound down to scattered ground actions. On July 17, General Jose Toral's surrender effectively ended the fighting in Cuba, but the war was not yet over. Fighting, now including ground actions.

On July 25, American soldiers began landing in nearby Spanish-held Puerto Rico. In a ground campaign by U.S. Army

Soldiers from August 6 to 13, the Spanish defenders were quickly vanquished.

Meanwhile, across the globe in the Pacific where ground fighting by Army Soldiers has followed the defeat of the Spanish Fleet in Manila Harbor, the war was quickly coming to an end. It culminated with the ground action that came to be called the **Mock Battle of Manila**, a choreographed battle that enabled the Spanish defenders a *face-saving* final dying gasp. By 5:30 in the evening the American flag flew over the Philippine Islands capitol of Manila, and the Spanish-America War was over.

Under the conditions of surrender, the United States barred by the **Teller Amendment** from occupying Cuba, the Island received independence, although the United States maintained, to present, a naval base in Guantanamo Bay.

The Philippines were placed under the occupation and control pending a treaty of peace (Treaty of Paris in 1998). Revolutionary guerrilla and leader Emilio Aguinaldo declared the Islands as Independence on May 1, 1898, although he failed to win international recognition for the island state. Ceded to the United States under the Treaty of Paris, the United States continued its presence, fighting against Aguinaldo and Philippine guerrilla forces for two decades. In 1935, still under U.S. occupation, the Islands became the Commonwealth of the Philippines, with hopes for full independence, delayed only by World War II. Following the war, on July 4, 1946, full independence was granted.

Under the **Treaty of Paris**, Puerto Rico became and remains a United States Territory. So too did the Island of Guam, which was taken by the *U.S.S. Charleston* on June 20, 1898, without a shot fired. Guam was the United States' first possession in the Pacific, providing a much needed Naval base in the far-west Pacific.

More than 300,000 Americans served in the *Spanish-American War*, and 385 of them died in combat, with 1,662 wounded. More than 2,000 died of disease and non-combat conditions. Almost lost to history, due in large part to the simplicity of their citations, are a dozen daring Marines who on May 11, 1898, became a part of Marine Corps history.

Dan Daly (USMC)

The "Fightin'est Marine"

By Dwight Jon Zimmerman

He was short, standing just five feet, six inches tall; the same height as that of Napoleon Bonaparte. And, like the French emperor, during his lifetime he became a larger-than-life legend. Daly was one of only nineteen men to be a double recipient of the Medal of Honor and one of only two Marines to be awarded the decoration for valor above and beyond the call of duty in two separate conflicts (the other Marine being Smedley Butler). But the act that made him legendary was not for something he did, but rather for something that he said: a one sentence challenge, twelve words, so inspirational that they would be immortalized in Marine Corps history: *"Come on, you sons of bitches, do you want to live forever?"*

EARLY YEARS

According to official Marine Corps records, Dan Daly was born in Glen Cove, Long Island, on November 11, 1873, to working class parents John and Ellen Donovan Daly. But there is evidence suggesting that he was actually born three years earlier, on November 23, 1870, in Cork County, Ireland. At one point the Daly family moved to New York City where at age twelve Dan worked as a newsboy in Lower Manhattan selling newspapers.

Beyond Belief: True Stories of Marine Corps Heroes

Back then newsboys literally fought each other for prime locations to hawk their papers. Despite his short stature, or perhaps it helped serve as a goad, it was as a newsboy that young Daly learned how to use his fists. He soon became a skilled boxer and augmented his income by boxing in local clubs. Later, in the 1890s, in order to get a steady income, Daly got a job working at a manufacturing plant that distilled kerosene and made paint, turpentine, varnish, and other resins.

A MARINE IN THE BOXER REBELLION

On January 10, 1899, inspired by the wave of patriotism and national pride that swept the nation as the result of victory in the five-month Spanish-American War, Daniel Daly enlisted in the Marine Corps. At the time the Marine Corps did not have the Parris Island and Camp Pendleton training depots. Daly completed his basic training at the Brooklyn Navy Yard where he underwent two months of physical conditioning and learning the life of a Marine. Though Daly's hardscrabble childhood had inured him to the tough physical demands of the Marine Corps, obeying the service's discipline rules and standards, proved to be another story. For years, his personnel file would reveal a casual, possibly even defiant, attitude, toward regulations, especially returning to base on time from leave.

On March 22, 1899, Daly joined a Marine detachment on the new protected cruiser (a predecessor to armored cruisers) U.S.S. *Newark* eventually arriving at the U.S. Navy base in Cavite, Philippines, on November 25. Six months later, Daly found himself in China, part of a detachment that included Marines, Sailors, and Soldiers sent to protect the American legation in Beijing (then called

American Legation in Beijing

Peking) under threat from an uprising against foreigners and Chinese Christians that came to be called the **Boxer Rebellion.**

Dan Daly (USMC)

Named after the secret society Yihequan *("Righteous and Harmonious Fists")* that practiced martial arts, hence inspiring the name *"Boxers."* It was a people's movement, a culmination of decades of resentment over the military and commercial exploitation of China by European powers. Resentment was further stoked by widespread Christian missionary activity which many

Chinese Christian Refugees

Chinese felt was an insult to the country's own rich religious traditions. Natural disasters in the late nineteenth century that included a severe drought and widespread floods added physical hardship and misery to the emotionally fraught and destitute farmers and laborers. The rebellion began win the hard-hit rural areas with attacks on missionaries and their Chinese converts. The Boxers rapidly gained widespread support to the point where the Empress Dowager Cixi, who initially remained neutral, gave it tacit support that eventually became open.

Daly and the detachment under the overall command of Marine Captain John Twiggs Myers, with Lieutenant Newt H. Hall second in command, arrived at the Legation Quarter on May 31 after a harrowing trip from the port city of Dagu that began with travel upriver on a variety of

Seymour Expedition in China

boats, then on a commandeered train, and finally after a seven-mile double-time march with rifles at the ready and bayonets fixed. Fortunately, the journey was without incident. They were joined by troops sent by other countries for the same purpose as theirs, bringing the total number of reinforcements to 435. Less than a week later The Boxers cut the rail link to the coast. An allied relief force of about 2,000 troops was organized and placed under the command of British Admiral Sir Edward Seymour. Named the Seymour Expedition it embarked by train on June 10. Two days later it was stopped cold by sabotage to the railroad tracks and repeated attacks by The Boxers and eventually forced to retrace its steps.

On June 18, a Chinese government official informed the foreign ministers that a state of war now existed between the Chinese government and theirs and that they had twenty-four hours to leave. The imperial government would provide troop protection from the Boxers until they reached Tinjin. After lengthy discussion, the ministers agreed, but, skeptical of the offer of protection, they requested a meeting with government officials in order to secure guarantees of safe passage. When the German minister was shot and killed while traveling to the Imperial Chinese foreign minister's office to discuss specifics, and after receiving news that The Boxers and Imperial Chinese troops had cut off railroad connections to the coast, Legation leaders prepared for a siege.

Because there were so few troops in the Legation Quarter, one of their first decisions was to shrink its defensive perimeter by half, with each nation's troops assigned a section to defend. Makeshift barricades were constructed with the most distinctive and colorful being the sandbags sewn by the women. Any fabric for the sandbags was fair game, including satin curtains, monogrammed linen sheets, brocades, tapestries, dresses, and more. Daly later recalled, *"[The women] ripped up all their ballroom dresses to sew up sandbags for us, all kinds of colors. I never saw such fancy sandbags. Some of 'em were even trimmed in lace."* A Legation member wrote in his diary, *"There was no doubt that the sky-blue, blood-red, yellow and many other colored sandbags made the most colorful barricades and breastworks in the history of warfare."* Ultimately an estimated 100,000 sandbags were sewn.

Once the Boxers and Imperial Chinese troops surrounded the shrunken Legation Quarter, they began a series of probing attacks. Any time a defense was breached, reinforcements would rush to assist and restore the perimeter. One of the most dangerous attacks occurred on July 13. During the day, about 500 Chinese troops attacked along the German compound, reaching the **Tartar Wall**, the Legation's most important defensive barrier, where they were driven back by Marine sharpshooters. That night, the Chinese staged an attack on the nearby French compound after exploding a mine placed in a tunnel dug beneath two buildings that formed part of the defensive perimeter. This attack, too, was repulsed.

DALY'S FIRST MEDAL OF HONOR ACTION

The following day the Marines began building a makeshift barricade on the sixty-foot-high **Tartar Wall** about 200 yards forward of the existing allied barricade on the top of the wall. On the night of July 14, Hall, recently promoted to captain and now commanding the Marine force due to Myers having been wounded in an earlier attack, took Private Daly with him to reconnoiter the area around the new barricade. They arrived at the barricade, slipped past it and entered a bastion

Boxer Prisoners

about 100 yards further away. After surveying the position, Hall told Daly he needed a volunteer to stay and fight off any Chinese infiltrators while he returned to bring up reinforcements and more sandbags. *"I won't order you to stay out here,"* Hall whispered. *"But if you can hold them back tonight, they'll never drive us back tomorrow."*

Without hesitation Daly replied, *"I'll stay. See you in the morning, Captain."* After handing Daly several bandoliers of ammunition, Hall crept back to the American compound.

Not long after, Daly began to hear voices speaking a Chinese dialect. Suddenly two Chinese men appeared in front of his position. Daly shot each with a single bullet. He expected the Chinese to attack his position en masse. Instead, the Chinese soldiers cautiously approached his position in small groups, apparently unsure of how many troops they faced. As a result, Daly was able to pick them off before they could reach his position. At one point a group of four Chinese soldiers changed tactics and decided to rush his position, Daly managed to shoot three with his bolt-action rifle before they reached him. The fourth he dispatched with his bayonet. The attacks continued throughout the night, with Chinese troops shouting threats in English, and Daly replying with deadly gunfire. When fellow Marines arrived shortly after dawn, they found Daly, still alive, surrounded by dozens of dead Chinese soldiers. Later tellings would inflate the toll to an estimated 200 enemy troops. Marine Corps disciplinary problem child he would continue to be, at least for a while, but now he was also a hero.

The siege of the Legation Quarter eventually lasted fifty-five days, with rescue occurring on August 14, 1900. In 1963, it would be dramatized in the movie *"55 Days at Peking"* starring Charlton Heston, Ava Garner, and David Niven.

Private Daly was one of thirty-three men recommended for the Medal of Honor. In his letter of recommendation, Captain Hall wrote, *"I respectfully invite your attention to the courage and fidelity of Private Dan Daly, U.S. Marine Corps, at all times, and to his conduct on the night of July 15, 1900, when he volunteered to remain alone in the bastion under fire of the enemy while I returned to the barracks for laborers."*

Marines on Parade in China

When it comes to brevity, Daly's Medal of Honor citation is one of the shortest in the history of the decoration.

Dan Daly (USMC)

The President of the United States of America, in the name of Congress, takes pleasure in presenting the Medal of Honor (First Award) to Private Daniel Joseph Daly (MCSN: 73086), United States Marine Corps, for extraordinary heroism while serving with the Captain Newt Hall's Marine Detachment, 1st Regiment (Marines), in action in the presence of the enemy during the battle of Peking, China, 14 August 1900, Daly distinguished himself by meritorious conduct.

With the siege lifted, Daly and the Marines returned to Manila in September. The following month he once again ran afoul of regulations, going on report for being late returning from leave.

A Variety Of Postings, But Little Action

Daly returned to the United States in July 1901. Stationed in the Boston Navy Yard, over the period of several months he repeatedly found himself in the disciplinary doghouse over a variety of offenses ranging from minor (late returning from leave) to major (drunk and disorderly and insubordination on base for which he was court martialed). His chronic misbehavior would continue off and on for more than a decade, only ending in 1913. Yet, for as much as he was a by-the-book headache, the Marine Corps found something in him worth keeping. Every time Daly renewed his enlistment, the Corps not only agreed to keep him in uniform but to promote him as well, first to corporal (1908), then to sergeant (1909). And, in between all that he managed to behave himself for long enough stretches to be twice awarded Good Conduct Medals (1908 and 1912).

In the years following the **Boxer Rebellion** and the outbreak of World War I in 1914, Daly was posted to a variety of ships patrolling the Atlantic Ocean and Caribbean Sea. In 1904 he served aboard the schooner-rigged gunboat U.S.S. *Marietta* that assisted in the U.S.-backed revolt in Panama to achieve independence from Columbia that set the stage for the building of the Panama Canal.

65

Beyond Belief: True Stories of Marine Corps Heroes

In 1912 he was made part of a Marine expeditionary force sent to protect American lives and business interests in eastern Cuba from Cuban rebels protesting a variety of injustices both social and political. The rebellion was put down, but there is no record of Daly having seen action there.

Though Daly widely traveled, with the exception of the **Boxer Rebellion** action at near the start of his military career, he had seen almost no action. That changed in 1914 in Mexico.

MEXICO

In 1910 Mexican dictator Portfiro Diaz was ousted in the Mexican Revolution. The resultant fallout ignited a civil war between three rebel factions led by Pancho Villa, Emiliano Zapata, and Venustiano Carranza, and federal troops under the leadership of self-proclaimed Mexican president General Victoriano Huerta.

Huerta rejected a mediation offer by newly elected President Woodrow Wilson. This was followed by the **Tampico Affair** in which U.S. Navy Sailors attempting to fuel a Navy ship with oil purchased from Mexican officials in the port of Tampico were temporarily arrested. Wilson used the incident, Huerta's rejection of a formal apology, and, more importantly news of a German merchantman attempting to smuggle guns and ammunition into Mexico in defiance of an American embargo of arms shipments to the country, to order the U.S. Navy to *"take [Veracruz] at once,"* the city being the largest and most important Mexican port in the Gulf of Mexico.

A combined U.S. Navy bluejacket and Marine Corps amphibious force landed at Veracruz on April 12, 1914. Ultimately the occupation force would include troops from the U.S. Army. Sergeant Daly was in the first wave of troops to make landfall. The first objectives around the harbor that included port facilities and a rail terminal, were taken without incident.

As a unit of Marines advanced inland to the customs house, it came under rifle and machine gun fire. Marine company commander Captain John Arthur Hughes ordered Daly to take a detachment and establish covering fire and to pick off Mexican snipers while reinforcements got into position to seize the customs house.

Dan Daly (USMC)

Small unit action and house-to-house fighting continued throughout the city as bluejackets and Marines fought to expand the perimeter. Fighting continued into the second day. At one point, Daly and his men were pinned down in a steep gully and taking accurate fire from a nearby house. After ordering his men to provide cover fire, Daly managed to work his way around the back of the house. There he burst through an unguarded door and single-handedly killed the seven Mexican soldiers there. By the third day fighting had all but ceased.

Foreign ministers from Argentina, Brazil, and Chile stepped forward with an offer to mediate. Diplomatic talks stalled and reached an impasse that was only broken when, on July 15, Huerta resigned and went into exile. The last American troops left Veracruz on November 23.

Fifty-six Medals of Honor were awarded for the Veracruz operation. By way of comparison, sixty-four Medals of Honor were awarded for the Battle of Gettysburg, a much larger battle and in World War II, twenty-seven were awarded for the Battle of Iwo Jima. The awarding of so many medals for a relatively small action aroused controversy at the time, the belief that the U.S. Navy was too generous in awarding the decoration.

During the first day's firefight, a U.S. Navy ensign attacked the customs house in an action similar to that of Daly's against a house the following day. The difference was that the ensign led five men in the attack, whereas Daly did so by himself. The ensign was awarded a Medal of Honor, but Daly was not, even though at the time it was possible for military personnel to receive more than one. Instead, Daly would receive his second Medal of Honor for action further east, on the Caribbean island of Haiti.

HAITI AND HIS SECOND MEDAL OF HONOR

Haiti, located on the western half of the Caribbean island of Hispaniola, was the devil's *chew toy* ever since it won its war of independence from France in 1804. Plagued by chronic political and economic unrest and instability, in 1915 the nation erupted into civil war with the bandit/mercenary Cacos taking over most of the countryside and threatening the cities. Newly elected President

67

Beyond Belief: True Stories of Marine Corps Heroes

Woodrow Wilson dispatched a navy squadron and, ultimately, a series of Marine detachments to protect the capital, Port-au-Prince, and Haiti's major port cities, effectively placing the nation under martial law.

On October 22, 1915, Daly was part of a forty-man patrol led by Major Smedley Butler (ultimately a double Medal of Honor recipient as well) tasked with the mission to attack Fort Capois, a Caco stronghold in the mountains of western Haiti.

The patrol was ambushed by about 400 Cacos as it was fording a deep river. Though twelve horses and pack animals were killed by enemy fire, the patrol managed to cross the river without suffering any casualties, taking up a defensive position on high ground several hundred yards from the river.

As his men were establishing their perimeter, Butler discovered that horses were not the only thing lost in the river crossing. Turning to Daly, Butler said, *"Better set up the machine gun, Daly."*

Daly replied, *"It was lost in the river."*

Butler was quiet for a moment as the news sunk in. Then he said, *"Well, we'll have to do the best we can."*

After that conversation, Daly disappeared. About an hour later, he reappeared. He approached Butler and reported that the machine gun was both in position and ready to fire. During the hour that Daly was gone, he had worked his way back to the river, dodging enemy gunfire. Once there, he dived in and swam up and down the river searching for the machine gun strapped to one of the dead horses. He eventually found it. He cut the weapon loose, hauled the heavy weapon ashore and, throwing it onto his back, managed to make his way back to the Marine lines.

It was good that he did. Outnumbered ten to one, thanks to the support of the firepower of the machine gun, the Marines were able to fight off attacks by the Cacos throughout the night. As dawn approached, Butler organized three squads, placing Daly in command of one of them. His purpose was to counterattack. His instructions were *"Just go for those devils as soon as it's light. Move straight forward and shoot everyone you see."* When dawn broke, and supported by the machine gun Daly had rescued, the squads attacked in three different directions, routing them.

For his action retrieving the machine gun, Butler recommended Daly for the Medal of honor. Of that act, Butler later said, *"I wouldn't have had the courage to do that."*

The President of the United States of America, in the name of Congress, takes pleasure in presenting the Medal of Honor (Second Award) to Gunnery Sergeant Daniel Joseph Daly (MCSN: 73086), United States Marine Corps, for extraordinary heroism in action while serving with the 15th Company of Marines (Mounted), 2d Marine Regiment, on 22 October 1915. Gunnery Sergeant Daly was one of the company to leave Fort Liberte, Haiti, for a six-day reconnaissance. After dark on the evening of 24 October, while crossing the river in a deep ravine, the detachment was suddenly fired upon from three sides by about 400 Cacos concealed in bushes about 100 yards from the fort. The Marine detachment fought its way forward to a good position, which it maintained during the night, although subjected to a continuous fire from the Cacos. At daybreak the Marines, in three squads, advanced in three different directions, surprising and scattering the Cacos in all directions. Gunnery Sergeant Daly fought with exceptional gallantry against heavy odds throughout this action.

Daly participated in several more missions against the Cacos and received repeated commendation and praise from superiors including Secretary of the Navy Josephus Daniels. He left Haiti for the United States in January 1916.

Six months later he was back on the troubled island, this time on the eastern half, in the Dominican Republic. Like Haiti, it had been wracked by chronic political and economic crises and Daly was part of a Marine detachment sent to avert civil war. The detachment soon grew into a full-fledged occupation force and a semblance of

Beyond Belief: True Stories of Marine Corps Heroes

order wasn't restored until 1924. But by then Daly had long since departed.

OVER THERE, BUT NOT WANTED OVER THERE

The United States entered World War I on the side of the Allies of France, Great Britain, Belgium, and Italy against the Central Powers of Imperial Germany, Austria-Hungary, and the Ottoman Empire on April 6, 1917.

The large standing army now maintained by the United States only came into being in the 1950s. Prior to that the country had an established military force that could charitably be called *bare bones*. With respect to the Marine Corps, it entered the war with just 419 officers and 13,214 enlisted men. By war's end it had grown five-fold to 2,400 officers and 70,000 enlisted.

Daly was assigned to the 73rd Machine Gun Company, part of the new Sixth Marine Regiment. What set the Sixth Marines apart from other regiments formed in the massive call-up was the fact that sixty percent of its ranks were composed of college educated volunteers. In fact, two-thirds of one company came from one school, the University of Minnesota, where 300 of its male students volunteered en masse.

The regiment was formed on July 11, 1917, and its cadre of officers and sergeants included four Medal of Honor recipients (Daly, Sergeant Major John Quick, Colonel Albert Catlin, and Major John Hughes) and two future Marine Corps Commandants (Major Thomas Holcomb and Second Lieutenant Clifton B. Cates). Training commenced at the new Marine Corps base at Quantico, Virginia. In September the regiment boarded trains to Philadelphia and from there boarded ships for the voyage to France, arriving at the Breton port of St. Nazaire on November 1. There, instead of going to bases for further training, the Marines remained at the port where they were ordered to serve as stevedores and guards.

When the United States entered the war, there was a burst of patriotic enthusiasm and its spirit was captured in a variety of patriotic songs. One of the most famous was *"Over There"* written by George M. Cohan. But while the United States as a whole was united in sending its young men in uniform to France, and the Allies

70

were equally, if not more so, enthusiastic to receive them, there was one organization that was cold to the idea of U.S. Marines in France. That organization was the U.S. Army.

Interservice rivalry has always existed, and not only in the United States military. The combined-arms joint warfare doctrine employed by the U.S. military today only came into effect in 1986 with the **Goldwater-Nichols Act**, later amended to strengthen the doctrine. Though service parochialism can never entirely be eliminated, it is nothing compared to what existed in the early twentieth century.

American Expeditionary Forces commander General John J. Pershing was a U.S. Army general and he was determined to make combat in France an army-only show, thank you very much. But political pressure back in the United States, and the large numbers of Marines in-country forced his hand and the Fifth and Sixth Marine Regiments were organized to form the Fourth Marine Brigade which was finally sent for trench warfare training near Bourmont, about 150 miles northeast of France in late March 1918. They were integrated into the U.S. Army 2nd Infantry Division. After two months of training the brigade was relocated to the front at Verdun for further seasoning.

For more than nine months in 1916, Verdun was the site of one of the bloodiest battles in the war, with more than 750,000 combined French and German casualties. Now that battleground was a relatively quiet zone, it was ideal for rotating in and out green troops in need of learning how to survive and fight in trench warfare conditions.

"Relatively quiet" was the operative term, for German patrols, artillery barrages, and gas attacks gave the Marines a foretaste of what to expect once they were assigned to an active front. In the roughly eight weeks at Verdun the Marines suffered 128 killed and 744 wounded.

THE GERMAN SPRING OFFENSIVE

Also known as the **Ludendorff Offensive** after its creator, General Erich Ludendorff, it was designed to force the Allies to sue

Beyond Belief: True Stories of Marine Corps Heroes

for peace before the full weight of the American Army could be brought to bear on the war in France.

The offensive was a four-stage affair designed to hit the Allied lines at four separate locations. The main attack, codenamed *Michael*, was launched on March 21, with the objective of seizing the Channel ports, dividing the British army from the French and driving it to the sea. This was followed up by attacks further down the front in April and May. The German offensive ripped gigantic holes in the Allied front and Pershing, who heretofore had rejected attempts by Field Marshall Ferdinand Foch, the commander in chief of all the Allied forces in France, to integrate individual American divisions into the British and French armies, gallantly agreed to send American units to wherever they were most needed and under overall French command.

At the end of May, the U.S. 1st Division was sent to the Somme to stop the German advance there at Cantigny, which it did, and the U.S. 2nd and 3rd Divisions were dispatched to Chemin des Dames and thrown into action in what would be called the **Third Battle of the Asine** (after the nearby river). The trip to the battlefield was a bone-jarring thirty-hour truck ride on roads filled with frightened refugees and demoralized French troops heading in the opposite direction.

The Marines arrived just before dawn tired, sore, and hungry. After a brief rest and eating whatever was in their back packs, they began to take up defensive positions, using mess kits and bayonets to dig fox holes and trenches, as the supply convoy that had their food, entrenching tools, and other necessities, would not arrive for another two days.

The improvised American line was intended to be in support of the French Army in position in front of it. But by June 2, what had been a fragmentary retreat by stragglers and individual French units became a general retreat. The American line was now the front and about the receive the full weight of experienced German troops whose morale was sky high.

Marine Colonel Albertus Catlin, commander of the Sixth Marine Regiment of which Daly and his 73rd Machine Gun Company was a part, issued an order stating, *"The Germans are advancing and as far as I know we are the only troops between them and an open gate. We will occupy this line and hold at all cost."*

At 3:00 p.m. Marines saw the lead elements of the German Army appear at the edge of the wheat field in front of their line. Buoyed by the routing of the experienced, though demoralized, French Army, the German troops confidently expected to do the same to the, for all practical purposes, raw American troops.

Instead, they were brought short by a devastating hail of gunfire that stopped them in their tracks. The Marine Corps takes pride in the slogan *"every Marine a rifleman"* and almost every Marine unit there had earned a marksmanship badge of either sharpshooter or expert. Wave after wave of advancing German troops were cut down by accurate rifle and machine gun fire.

The German advance was stopped. But the issue remained in doubt. During the initial after-battle lull the Americans consolidated their position, expecting at any moment a renewed German assault. But, for two days that did not happen. The overall German success in its offensive had, ironically, contained within it the seeds of its failure. By the time the Germans had reached the American lines, they were at the end of their tether. Equally important, they had outrun their supply lines. So the combination of rest and re-supply caused what amounted to a fatal two-day delay in the renewal of the German attack. And that set the stage for the **Battle of Belleau Wood.**

On June 5, a German artillery barrage hit a Marine ammunition dump, setting fire to it. Ignoring exploding ammunition and continuing enemy artillery, Daly led a group that managed to put out the fire before the whole building exploded.

THE BATTLE OF BELLEAU WOOD

John Toland, in *No Man's Land*, his history of World War I, described Belleau Wood as follows: *"It was not a large wood. The trees were about six inches thick and so densely planted that one could scarcely see twenty feet ahead except where ax or shell had cut a swath. Unlike American forests, it had been constantly under care of a forester who cleared out the underbrush and those trees ready for timbering. Despite the lack of undergrowth there was ample shelter in the high, rocky ground which was scarred with gullies and crags. It was an irregular area not much more than a square mile that from the air reminded some of a sea horse, some of a twisted kidney."*

Forcing the Germans out of the forest would be a daunting task. The craggy terrain made it a natural fortress that the Germans took full advantage of. Brigade Commander Army Brigadier General James Harbord ordered that both Belleau Wood and the town of Bouresches on its southeast corner be taken on June 6, 1918.

The destroyed town of Bouresches, France, on the edge of the Belleau Wood

The attack began with an assault on German-occupied Hill 142, which overlooked the wood from the west. Two companies of Marines took the hill at heavy cost, with one company suffering more than fifty percent casualties. Reinforcements were rushed to assist the Marines and a total of four German counterattacks were repulsed. By midafternoon the hill was securely in Marine hands. The stage was now set for an attack on the wood itself. But the Marines would do so blind, as no reconnaissance had been made of the German defenses there.

The attack was scheduled for 5:00 p.m. To reach the German lines the Marines had to first cross 400 yards of open ground. The first wave of Marines had not even covered a hundred yards when it came under intense rifle and machine gun fire that threatened to stop the attack before it could reach the wood.

Daly and the 73rd Machine Gun Company were attached to the assault force and were stationed at its southern end at the town of Lucy-le-Bocage (pronounced **"Lucy Birdcage"** by the Marines), and was delivering suppressing fire on the German positions. Despite their help, the heavy German gunfire continued, with Marines diving to the ground in order to avoid the deadly streams of bullets.

Dan Daly (USMC)

The City of Lucy-le-Bocage showing in center over housetops the Belleau Wood captured by the Americans in 1918.

Floyd Gibbons, a war correspondent from the *Chicago Tribune*, was attached to one of the Marine units and was thrice wounded in the battle. In the after-battle dispatch for the newspaper he wrote what happened next:

"The enemy gun fire was terrific. The oats and the wheat in the open field were waving, and snapping off, not from the wind but from rifle and machine gun fire of German veterans in their well-concealed positions. A runner came scrambling through the brush, and handed the old Gunnery Sergeant a sheet of paper. He read it quickly, then glanced along the line of his dug-in platoon. He stood up and made a forward motion to his men. There was [a] slight hesitation. Who the hell could blame them? Machine gun and rifle bullets were kicking up dirt, closer and closer. The sergeant ran out to the center of his platoon—he swung his bayonet-rifle over his head with a forward sweep. He yelled to his men: 'Come on, you sons-of-bitches. Do you want to live forever?'" So inspired (or shamed), the Marines got up, charged, and routed the enemy.

As with many defining moments in combat, much debate has been made over what exactly was said that day by the *"old Gunnery Sergeant"* who, of course, was Daly.

Daly himself later claimed he said, *"For Christ's sake, men, come on! Do you want to live forever?"* Daly's account has the better ring of truth, but given the religious mores of the time, either

Gibbons or his editors in Chicago, decided that taking Christ's name in vain would offend their readers, thus toned it to the milder curse of *"sons-of-bitches."* And, because the original newspaper article and subsequent book on World War I written by Gibbons that included the incident were the most widely read, that version has become the one best known to history.

The Battle of Belleau Wood would continue for another twenty days. On June 10, Daly single-handedly attacked a German machine gun emplacement with grenades and pistol, taking fourteen prisoners and later that day rescuing twelve wounded Marines.

On June 26, Harbord received the message: *"WOODS NOW U.S. MARINE CORPS ENTIRELY."* Historian Dick Camp, a retired Marine colonel who fought in Vietnam, wrote that Belleau Wood *"became more than a bloody battleground for the men of the Marine Brigade. It became hallowed ground, synonymous with valor and self-sacrifice, and a reference point by which to judge all other events in their lives."* In honor of their victory, French 6th Army commander Jean Degoutte, under whose command the Marines were serving, issued an order on June 30 changing the name of Belleau Wood to that of "Bois de la Brigade de Marine." General Pershing sent his praise, calling the Marine victory the "Gettysburg of the War."*

Even the Germans praised them, bestowing on the Marines the cognomen *"Teufelhunde"—"Devil Dogs."*

Belleau Wood after the battle.

A THIRD MEDAL? – DENIED.

Nineteen men have the distinction of receiving two Medals of Honor. Daly's superior, Marine Lieutenant Colonel Harry Lee was so impressed with Daly's actions at Belleau Wood that he took the unprecedented move of recommending First Sergeant Dan Daly for a third Medal of Honor. He cited four specific actions:

- Extinguishing a fire in an ammunition dump at Lucy-le-Bocage (June 5, 1918)
- Visiting all the gun crews under his command, ignoring incoming enemy fire to inspire his men (June 7).
- Singlehandedly attacking an enemy machine gun emplacement with hand grenades and pistol and capturing fourteen enemy troops (June 10).
- Repeatedly rescued wounded while under fire (June 10).

General Bundy, the division commander and an Army general, agreed, endorsing the recommendation on July 12. On Sunday, August 25, 1918, before some 5,000 troops, First Sergeant Dan Daly was one of thirty-eight officers and men of the 4th Marine Brigade to receive the U.S. Army Distinguished Service Cross.

What happened?

Two things. Actually, perhaps even three. All serving to downgrade the recommendation. First some background is necessary.

The Medal of Honor has a rocky history. Both versions of the Medal of Honor were authorized during the American Civil War. Even though it was an Army officer who initially suggested the decoration, the Navy Medal of Honor was the first to become official (1861), with the army version authorized the following year. But up until World War I it was the nation's only decoration for military valor. And therein lay the rub. Not only that, but its criteria as originally written was so vaguely worded that, even after several revisions, awarding it was vulnerable to abuse. For example, for decades an individual could make the recommendation for himself, something that Theodore Roosevelt did for his action at San Juan Hill in the Spanish American War. His recommendation was rejected. He received it posthumously in 2001.

Though there was some abuse of awarding it in the U.S. Navy, the biggest problem was with the army's Medal of Honor, the most egregious example being the awarding of its Medal of Honor to the Twenty-Seventh Maine Volunteer Infantry Regiment where all 864

Beyond Belief: True Stories of Marine Corps Heroes

men received the decoration. The battle? Gettysburg. The action? Re-enlistment and garrison duty at Washington, D.C. for four days. It gets worse. Only half the regiment re-enlisted and served garrison duty, the rest returned home to Maine because their enlistment had expired just before the Gettysburg battle. Yet, *all* of the men received the medal. As you might expect, those men who received theirs for bravery in combat were more than a little miffed over this.

Over the years, attempts were made to correct the problem. Finally, in 1916 the War Department established a strict criteria that identified and closed all the loopholes and convened a commission composed of retired generals, some Medal of Honor recipients, to review all 2,625 citations to date and make a list of those whose medal awards should be culled. On February 5, 1917, the board presented its finding. Called the **Purge of 1917**, a total of 911 names on the list were eliminated, including all of those from the 27th Maine. That took care of one problem. But, thanks to World War I, another problem arose.

When America entered the war, Pershing found himself in an embarrassing situation. As the American Expeditionary Forces (AEF) Commander later observed in his memoir: *"The problem of decorations in our army had long been a knotty one, and except for the Medal of Honor and Certificate of Merit we had only campaign badges and those given for marksmanship. The Allies desired to confer their decorations on our men who served with distinction under them, but we were not permitted to accept foreign decorations without permission from Congress. . . . As it was a matter of importance to our officers and men, the whole question of decorations was taken up by the War Department on my suggestion with the result that Congressional action established certain medals of our own and authorized our soldiers to receive those of foreign governments."*

Thus was created the Army Distinguished Service Cross, Distinguished Service Medal, and Citation Star (later the Silver Star), Navy Distinguished Service Medal, and Navy Cross, with other medals authorized later. In a footnote, the U.S. Navy convened its own Medal of Honor review board after the war and struck seventeen from its list.

Dan Daly (USMC)

Okay, you say, *"That's the* Army *Medal of Honor. What's that to do with Sergeant Daly? He's a Marine. Shouldn't he have been subject to the U. S. Navy's criteria and receive its Medal of Honor?"*

Nope. And you can thank General John J. Pershing for that. In an order issued by him, he stated that all AEF units under his command, regardless of branch of service, had to submit such recommendations through U.S. Army channels. And, in fact, five Marines did receive the Army Medal of Honor.

So it seems petty, meanspirited even, that Daly would be denied a third Medal of Honor, especially since it would have been the Army version. But because it would have been the Army version and, thanks to war correspondent Floyd Gibbons, such a suggestion cannot be dismissed out of hand.

For reasons of military security, Pershing had imposed a ban on identifying any AEF military unit in war correspondent dispatches – an understandable precaution as Pershing did not want the enemy to know the location of any of his units through intelligence gathered from published newspaper articles. And therein was the rub.

On June 6, prior to him accompanying the Marines into battle, Gibbons wrote what's called a *skeleton dispatch*, which basically is an outline in which details would be filled in later. In it he included the line, *"I am up front and entering Belleau Wood with the U.S. Marines."* As there was only one Marine brigade in France, this vague phrase was actually quite specific and should have been caught and excised by censors in Paris. Normally it would have been.

One of the censors in Paris was an ex-newspaperman and friend of Gibbons. When he heard that Gibbons had been severely wounded, with rumors that he had been killed at Belleau Wood and believing that he was dead and that this dispatch was the last thing he had written, his censor friend said, *"This is the last thing I can ever do for poor old Floyd."* The dispatch was released without change.

When the *Chicago Tribune* published the dispatch under the headline *"U.S. MARINES SMASH HUN, GAIN GLORY IN BRISK FIGHT ON THE MARNE"* and followed it up the next day with another article headlined, *"MARINES WIN HOT BATTLE, SWEEP*

Beyond Belief: True Stories of Marine Corps Heroes

ENEMY FROM HEIGHTS NEAR THIERRY," it was as if the green-eyed monster of jealous interservice rivalry had been prodded with a white-hot poker. There was hell to pay in the headquarters of the AEF at Chaumont and the commands of every Army unit in France. Though the breach in secrecy was bad enough, it was the way the articles were written that set off a furor in the army.

The articles gave the appearance that the Marines were winning the war on their own. Which was untrue, of course, and unfair. But the damage had been done. To underscore how deeply and long-lasting the contretemps affected the U.S. Army, one example: General Douglas MacArthur was an army brigade commander in World War I. In World War II he was the Southwest Pacific Theater Commander. When he received a recommendation that the Fourth Marine Regiment receive the Presidential Unit Citation for its heroic stand in the Philippines, he rejected it, stating, *"The Marines received enough credit during the last war."*

After the war the Navy Department awarded its Medal of Honor to the five Marines who had received the army version, thus making them the last double recipients. This seemed like the perfect opportunity for the U.S. Navy to right a U.S. Army wrong. But again Daly was denied a third Medal of Honor, the Navy probably thinking it best not to pour salt on a still-raw public relations wound. Instead, he was awarded the Navy Cross, equivalent to the Distinguished Service Cross. Daly also received the Citation Star.

The President of the United States of America, authorized by Act of Congress, July 9, 1918, takes pleasure in presenting the Distinguished Service Cross to First Sergeant Daniel Joseph Daly (MCSN: 73086), United States Marine Corps, for repeated deeds of heroism and great service while serving with the Seventy-Third Company, Sixth Regiment (Marines), 2d Division, A.E.F., on 5 June and 7, 1918 at Lucy-le-Bocage, and on 10 June 1918 in the attack on Bouresches, France. On June 5th, at the risk of his life, First Sergeant Daly extinguished a fire in an ammunition dump at Lucy-le-Bocage. On 7 June 1918, while his position was under violent bombardment, he visited all the gun crews of his company, then posted over a wide portion of the front, to cheer his men. On 10 June 1918, he attacked an enemy machine-gun emplacement unassisted and captured it by use of hand grenades and his automatic pistol. On the same day, during the German attack on Bouresches, he brought in wounded under fire.

The President of the United States of America takes pleasure in presenting the Navy Cross to First Sergeant Daniel Joseph Daly (MCSN: 73086), United States Marine Corps, for repeated deeds of heroism and great service while serving with the 73d Company, 6th Regiment (Marines), 2d Division, A.E.F., on June 5 and 7, 1918 at Lucy-le-Bocage, and on 10 June 1918 in the attack on Bouresches, France. On June 5th, at the risk of his life, First Sergeant Daly extinguished a fire in an ammunition dump at Lucy-le-Bocage. On 7 June 1918, while his position was under violent bombardment, he visited all the gun crews of his company, then posted over a wide portion of the front, to cheer his men. On 10 June 1918, he attacked an enemy machine-gun emplacement unassisted and captured it by use of hand grenades and his automatic pistol. On the same day, during the German attack on Bouresches, he brought in wounded under fire.

It's worth noting that Daly was not the first person to be considered for a third Medal of Honor. In the aftermath of the **Battle of Little Big Horn**, there was discussion of awarding the Medal of Honor to Lieutenant Colonel George Armstrong Custer and the men in his command who died with him in that battle. Captain Tom Custer, younger brother to George, was a double recipient, having received both of his decorations in the American Civil War. At the time the decoration was not awarded posthumously. Had it been so, Tom Custer would have been the first triple recipient.

Beyond Belief: True Stories of Marine Corps Heroes

Wounded at Belleau Wood, Daly returned to action in August and participated in the **Battle of St. Mihiel** where he repeatedly distinguished himself in the thick of battle and, as a result, was wounded twice. World War I ended with him in the hospital recovering from those wounds. Upon his recovery in December 1918 he was posted to occupation duty in Germany. In April 1919 he boarded a ship for return to the United States and it arrived in New York Harbor on May 7.

Upon completing twenty years of service in the Marine Corps, on September 11, 1919, he requested transfer to inactive service. In December he was temporarily recalled to duty and promoted to sergeant major, returning to inactive duty a month later.

Upon retirement Daly lived with his sister and her family, which included their mother, in the Canarsie neighborhood of Brooklyn. They later moved to Glendale, Queens. He took a job as a bank guard for the Wall Street investment bank of Brown Brothers. Daly also became a favorite of the neighborhood kids, playing catch with his nephew and doing a variety of activities with the neighborhood kids.

For the most part Daly declined invitations to public events involving veterans. In 1937 he made a rare exception and accepted an invitation to march in the inaugural parade for President Franklin Roosevelt, to be held for the first time on the new date of January 20, the original inaugural date being March 4. The day was cold and wet. Daly spent several hours outside in the inclement weather and wound up catching a severe cold that turned into pneumonia. He died on April 27, 1937, at age sixty-three.

He was buried with full military honors at Cypress Hills National Cemetery located on the border between Brooklyn and Queens. Cypress Hills is the final resting place for twenty-four Medal of Honor recipients, three of them double recipients: Daly, Seaman Louis Williams, and Coxswain John Cooper. According to Major General Smedley Butler, another double recipient of the Medal of Honor, Dan Daly was America's *"fightin'est Marine."*

Clifton Bledsoe Cates (USMC)

"I Will Hold!"

By Scott Baron

On July 19, 1918, as the Battle of Soissons raged in France, most the 2d Battalion, Sixth Marine Regiment had been annihilated by enemy artillery so intense that Captain Clifton Cates, one of the few surviving Marine officers, had lost most of his britches in an explosion that nearly cost him his life. After capturing an old abandoned French trench, he sent a runner back to his battalion headquarters with a situation report for Lt. Colonel Lee:

"I am in an old abandoned French trench bordering on the road leading out of your P.C. and 350 yards from an old mill I have only two men out of my company and 20 out of some other

company. We need support, but it is almost suicide to try to get it here as we are swept by machine gun fire and a constant barrage is on us. I have no one on my left and only a few on my right. I will hold."

"I will hold" would become the phrase most identified with Cates as he advanced through the ranks to become a Marine legend, and is today recognized throughout the Marine Corps as a battle cry or slogan intended to improve morale and inspire confidence.

In thirty-seven years of active duty, Cates saw action on the Yangtze River in China, in five major engagements in the First World War, and another five in the Second World War. He is one of very few officers who commanded a platoon, a company, a battalion, a regiment, and a division, each in combat, and as the 19th Commandant of the Marine Corps, he commanded the entire Corps during the Korean War.

His thirty combat awards include the Navy Cross, two Distinguished Service Crosses (Army), two Distinguished Service Medals, four Silver Star Medals (Army Awards), the Legion of Merit with Combat "V," two Purple Hearts, Croix de Guerre w/Gilt Star & 2 palms, the Legion of Honor, Knight grade (France), and the Order of Orange-Nassau, rank of Grand Officer w/crossed swords (Netherlands).

Clifton Bledsoe Cates was born August 31, 1893, in Tiptonville, Tennessee, the older of two children born to Willis Jones Cates, a planter, and Martha Darnall (Bledsoe) Cates. He and his younger sister, Katherine Nell Cates Prothro (1896), grew up on the family plantation and attended public schools in Tiptonville.

After elementary education in country schools, Cates attended the Missouri Military Academy, where he became an honor student and a four-letter man in sports. He earned a Bachelor of Laws degree from the University of Tennessee in 1916, where he played on both the baseball and football teams, and was admitted to the Tennessee Bar. Cates was a member of the Kappa Tau Chapter of Phi Gamma Delta.

Following America's entry into World War I on April 6, 1917, Cates was commissioned as second lieutenant in the Marine Corps

Clifton Bledsoe Cates (USMC)

Reserves, and reported for active duty at the Marine Barracks, Port Royal, South Carolina, on June 13, 1917.

On August 28, 1917, Second Lieutenant Cates was assigned as a platoon leader in the 96th Company (H&SC), 2nd Battalion, Sixth Marine Regiment. He was promoted to first lieutenant on July 1, 1918, and received a temporary promotion to captain on March 5 through September 25, 1919. The Sixth Marines sailed for France in January 1918, where Cates would join them in fighting in France.

During World War I, the Fifth and Sixth Regiments of Marines were attached to the U.S. Army's 2d Division, American Expeditionary Forces. As such, Marines were often decorated with the Army Medal of Honor, the Army's Distinguished Service Cross, and the Army's Silver Star. After the war, some of these Marines were subsequently awarded the Navy Medal of Honor in addition to the previously awarded Army Medal of Honor, as well as the Navy's only other combat decoration, the Navy Cross, often for the same action that merited the Army awards.

At Belleau Wood, on June 6, 1918, Cates' company was ordered to attack the village of Bouresches. The company commander was mortally wounded early in the battle, leaving Cates in charge despite his not knowing the attack's intent or objective. He organized the available men of his company as well as some other Marines in the vicinity and carried out a successful attack, and subsequent defense of the village. The Germans responded with mustard gas nearly wiping out the entire company

For his heroism in the Aisne defensive at Bouresches, near Chateau Thierry on June 6, 1918, he was awarded both the Distinguished Service Cross and the Navy Cross.

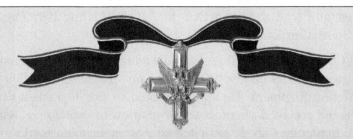

The President of the United States of America, authorized by Act of Congress, July 9, 1918, takes pleasure in presenting the Distinguished Service Cross to Captain Clifton Bledsoe Cates (MCSN: 0-155), United States Marine Corps, for extraordinary heroism while serving with the Ninety-Sixth Company, Sixth Regiment (Marines), 2d Division, A.E.F., in action near Chateau-Thierry, France, 6 June 1918. While advancing with his company on the town of Bouresches their progress was greatly hindered by withering machine-gun and artillery fire of the enemy which caused many casualties, one of whom was his commanding officer. Taking command, Captain Cates led them on to the objective despite the fact that he was rendered temporarily unconscious by a bullet striking his helmet and that this was his first engagement. Exposing himself to the extreme hazard, he reorganized his position with but a handful of men.

The President of the United States of America takes pleasure in presenting the Navy Cross to First Lieutenant Clifton Bledsoe Cates (MCSN: 0-155), United States Marine Corps, for extraordinary heroism while serving with the 96th Company, 6th Regiment (Marines), 2d Division, A.E.F. in action near Chateau-Thierry, France, 6 June 1918. While advancing with his company on the town of Bouresches their progress was greatly hindered by withering machine-gun and artillery fire of the enemy which caused many casualties, one of whom was his commanding officer. Taking command, Captain Cates led them on to the objective despite the fact that he was rendered temporarily unconscious by a bullet striking his helmet and that this was his first engagement. Exposing himself to the extreme hazard, he reorganized his position with but a handful of men.

During the continued fighting in Belleau Wood from June 13 - 14, 1918, he received an Oak Leaf Cluster in lieu of a second Distinguished Service Cross. He was one of only nine Marines to receive two Distinguished Service Crosses in World War I.

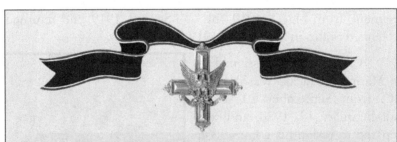

The President of the United States of America, authorized by Act of Congress, July 9, 1918, takes pleasure in presenting a Bronze Oak Leaf Cluster in lieu of a Second Award of the Distinguished Service Cross to Captain Clifton Bledsoe Cates (MCSN: 0-155), United States Marine Corps, for extraordinary heroism while serving with the Ninety-Sixth Company, Sixth Regiment (Marines), 2d Division, A.E.F., in action near Bois-de-Belleau, France, June 13 - 14, 1918. During the night, a severe gas attack made it necessary to evacuate practically the entire personnel of two companies, including officers. Captain Cates, suffering painfully from wounds, refused evacuation remaining and rendering valuable assistance to another company.

The Army also awarded Cates the Citation Star (subsequently converted to the Silver Star Medal) at Chateau Thierry, France, for his actions from June 6 to July 10 1918, and an Oak Leaf Cluster in lieu of a second Silver Star for actions at Somme-Py, France, October

2 - 1918, and a third Silver Star in the Battle of Blanc Mont Ridge (October 1 -10, 1918). By the end of the war he received his fourth Silver Star.

Apart from these decorations and a two Purple Hearts which he received for wounds, the French Government recognized his heroism with the Legion of Honor and the Croix de Guerre with Gilt Star and two palms. He was also cited twice by the Commanding General of 2d Division, AEF, and once by the Commanding General, AEF, and was entitled to wear the Fourragere awarded the Sixth Marines.

Following the Armistice, Cates served with the Army of Occupation in Germany and was assigned to Company E, Composite Regiment, from May 1, 1919, through Sep 19, 1919, and returned to the United States in September 1919.

Cates was next assigned to the Marine Barracks, Washington, D.C. from September 20, 1919, until February 14, 1920, and was prepared to resign his commission until he was dissuaded by Major General George Barnett, Commandant of the Marine Corps, who took Cates on as his aide-de-camp. Cates also served as an aide in President Woodrow Wilson's White House in Washington DC.

On November 15, 1920, continuing as Barnett's aide, Cates followed him to San Francisco, California, where Barnett served as Commanding General of Department of the Pacific, San Francisco. It was there that Cate's promotion to captain was made permanent on April 2, 1921, with a date of rank of June 4, 1920. He remained in that post until June 10, 1923, when he was assigned as Commander of the Marine detachment aboard the battleship U.S.S. *California* (BB-44).

Assigned to the Battle Fleet in the Pacific, *California* served as its flagship and was occupied with routine training exercises,

Clifton Bledsoe Cates (USMC)

including joint Army-Navy maneuvers and the annual fleet problems. On the night of November 11, 1924, Navy Lieutenant Dixie Kiefer took off from the ship, the first night aircraft launch in history. Further experimentation with aircraft continued into early 1925, when the ships of the Battle Fleet received a squadron of Curtiss TS-1 floatplanes on March 31, 1925.

On April 29, 1925, Cates left the *California* and on May 9 reported to the Fourth Marine Regiment at San Diego, California. There he commanded a company until he was reassigned to recruiting duty on May 26, 1926, first at Spokane, Washington, then on May 6, 1927, at Omaha, Nebraska until February 23, 1928. Following a tour of duty with the American Battle Monuments Commission in Washington, D.C. (March 6, 1928 – May 3, 1929), Cates returned to duty commanding the 2d Battalion, Fourth Marines at Shanghai, China from August 5, 1929 until June 1932, serving as regimental athletic officer, with a promotion to major on October 1, 1931.

From January 28 through March 3, 1932, his battalion participated in defense of International Settlement during the emergency of the Chinese-Japanese Operations, where he was awarded the Yangtze Service Medal and the Marine Corps Expeditionary Medal for his China service.

From August 17, 1932, through June 23, 1933, Cates attended the Army Industrial (War) College, then took command of 2d Battalion, Seventh Marines, Fleet Marine Force (FMF) serving off Cuba and the Caribbean (1933-1934). He later attended the Senior Course at the Marine Corps Schools, Quantico, Virginia, from September 10, 1934, until July 26, 1935.

On July 26, 1935, as tensions mounted in the Pacific from Japanese expansionism, and with the rise of Fascism in Europe, Cates was promoted to lieutenant colonel and was assigned to the War Plans Section, Operations and Training, Headquarters, Marine Corps at Quantico.

On June 30, 1937, Cates was assigned as the Executive Officer of the 2d Battalion, Fifth Marines, 2nd Brigade, FMF, at Shanghai, China, assuming command in September 1937. On February 1, 1938, he took command of 2d Battalion, Fourth Marines.

Beyond Belief: True Stories of Marine Corps Heroes

While attending the U.S. Army War College (September 1, 1939 – June 22, 1940), Cates was promoted to Colonel on April 1, 1940, and later reported as the Director of The Officers Basic School at Philadelphia Navy Yard, Philadelphia, Pennsylvania (July 6, 1940 – April 23, 1942). In the interim, the Japanese attacked the U.S. Fleet at Pearl Harbor, Territory of Hawaii, on December 7, 1941, initiating America's entry into WW II.

Transitioning from training Marines to fighting as one, Cates took command of the First Marine Regiment, FIRST Marine Division at New River, North Carolina on May 3, 1942.

The First Marines were at a low state of readiness when Cates took command, having just been reconstituted from cadre status; however, the regiment possessed strong leadership and in June 1942, the FIRST Marines set sail from San Francisco on board a mix of eight ships headed for the South Pacific. They landed on the island of Guadalcanal, part of the Solomon Islands, on August 7, 1942, initiating the first major land offensive by Allied forces against the Empire of Japan.

Cates led the First Marines at Guadalcanal, codenamed *Operation Watchtower* as Allied forces, predominantly U.S. Marines, landed on Guadalcanal, Tulagi, and Florida Island in the southern Solomon Islands, with the objective of using Guadalcanal and Tulagi as bases in supporting a campaign to eventually capture or neutralize the major Japanese base at Rabaul on New Britain.

Some of the heaviest action the regiment saw on Guadalcanal took place on August 21, 1942, during the Battle of the Tenaru, which was the first Japanese counterattack of the campaign. The First Marines fought in the Guadalcanal Campaign until relieved on December 22, 1942.

Following their first campaign, the regiment was sent to Melbourne, Australia, to rest and refit. During their stay, there they were billeted in the Melbourne Cricket Grounds. On February 11,

Clifton Bledsoe Cates (USMC)

1943, Cates turned the regiment over to Colonel William John *"Wild Bill"* Whaling. For his command of the First Marine Regiment in the Guadalcanal-Tulagi landings and the capture and defense of Guadalcanal, Cates was awarded the Legion of Merit with Combat *"V"* *"for exceptionally meritorious conduct in the performance of outstanding services to the Government of the United States in the Pacific Theater of Operations during the period from 7 August to 15 December 1942."*

With the experience gained at Guadalcanal, Cates was returned to the United States in March for his first tour of duty as Commandant of the Marine Corps Schools at Quantico, Virginia, with a temporary promotion to Brigadier General on September 16, 1942, which was made permanent on April 3, 1943, and subsequent promotion to Major General on February 1, 1944. He remained at Quantico until June 20, 1944.

On July 12, 1944, Cates relieved Major General Harry Schmidt and assumed command of the FOURTH Marine Division in the Marianas operation, the Tinian campaign, and the seizure of Iwo Jima. The planning for Tinian included the first complete aerial reconnaissance of an enemy base by the key commanders, including Cates. For his services at Tinian, Cates received the Navy Distinguished Service Medal, the citation reading:

"For exceptionally meritorious service to the Government of the United States in a duty of great responsibility as Commanding General, FOURTH Marine Division, prior to and during the conquest of enemy Japanese-held Tinian Island in the Marianas Group, from 12 July 1944 to 1 August 1944. Assuming command of a division depleted in physical strength by twenty-five days of continuous combat on Saipan, Major General Cates brought his officers and men to the peak of battle-readiness and, organizing his attack plans with decisive clarity, landed the division as the leading assault group or the beaches of Tinian on

Beyond Belief: True Stories of Marine Corps Heroes

24 July. Expeditiously establishing a beachhead and deploying his units, he stormed the island's strong defenses, annihilating a powerful enemy counterattack before dawn of the next day, and, continuing his relentless aggression for two days as he advanced beyond the assigned objective to seize Mt. Lasso, thereafter moved forward within the assigned zone without interruption until the island fell to our forces nine days later. His forceful leadership, indomitable courage and tenacious determination in reducing his objective in a minimum of time contributed materially to the conquest of this important stronghold."

Cates again led the Division during the Battle of Iwo Jima and near the end of the fighting, he attempted to persuade the remaining Japanese brigade to surrender honorably rather than fight to the death. Cates was awarded a Gold Star in lieu of a second award of the Distinguished Service Medal, the citation reading *"For exceptionally meritorious service to the Government of the United States in a duty of great responsibility as Commanding General of the FOURTH Marine Division, prior to and during the seizure of enemy Japanese-held Iwo Jima, in the Volcano Islands, from 19 February 1945 to 20 March 1945. Inculcating in the officer sand men of his regiments his own indomitable spirit of aggressiveness, Major General Cates organized, trained and welded his depleted division into a formidable fighting command in a relatively brief period between critical operations. A bold tactician, he landed his force on the southeast shore of the island against heavy infantry resistance and, defying the continuous, terrific bombardment laid down by enemy guns located strategically on high ground which afforded direct observation and complete coverage of his entire zone of action, pushed his relentless advance inch by inch through the shifting volcanic sands. Fighting furiously without respite for twenty-four successive days despite heavy casualties, his Division progressed slowly but steadily toward the objective, driving the Japanese garrison from its intricate system of defenses with inexorable determination until the fanatic opposition of a desperate and ruthless enemy was crushed. Repeatedly disregarding his own personal safety, Major General Cates traversed his front lines daily to rally his tired, depleted units and by his undaunted valor, tenacious perseverance and staunch*

Clifton Bledsoe Cates (USMC)

leadership in the face of overwhelming odds, constantly inspired his stout-hearted Marines to heroic effort during critical phases of the fierce campaign

In the photo above, Marine Division Commanders observe the official flag raising ceremonies on Iwo Jima, on March 14, 1945. Present, from left to right, Major General Keller E. Rockey, FIFTH Marine Division, Major General Graves B. Erskine, THIRD Marine Division, and Major General Clifton B. Cates FOURTH Marine Division.

Cates continued to lead the Division in the Pacific theater through the end of the war, and the FOURTH Marine Division was awarded two Presidential Unit Citations and a Navy Unit Commendation. Following the Japanese surrender on September 2, 1945, the FOURTH Marine Division was inactivated on November 28,1945.

Ordered back to the United States in December of 1945, Cates was appointed President of the Marine Corps Equipment Board at Quantico on January 14, 1946, holding that position for six months before he was named Commanding General of the Marine Barracks, Quantico, on June 1, 1946. He held that command until January 1, 1948, when he was advanced to the rank of 4-Star General and was nominated, confirmed, and sworn in as the 19th Commandant of the Marine Corps.

Beyond Belief: True Stories of Marine Corps Heroes

At the outbreak of the Korean War in June 1950, despite the Marine Corps being down in strength to 75,000 officers and men, the 1st Provisional Marine Brigade was sent to South Korea within nine days. As Commandant, General Cates contributed to the passage of Public Law 416, which set the Corps' active strength at three divisions and three aircraft wings. Also during his tenure, he directed the Marine Corps in the development of a doctrine for the employment of helicopters in vertical envelopment and a practical test of their use in the Korean War.

When General Cates completed his four-year term as Commandant, he reverted to the rank of lieutenant general on January 1, 1952, and began a second tour as Commandant of the Marine Corps Schools, Quantico. He retired on June 30, 1954, after two and a half years with the schools and was again promoted to General on the retired list.

In 1920, Cates married Jane Virginia McIlhenny and they had two children, Clifton Bledsoe Cates Jr. (1921) and Ann Willis Cates Hilbish (1931). His son attended the U.S. Naval Academy, graduating with the class of 1943 on June 19, 1942, and served throughout the remainder of World War II in the Gunnery Department of the *U.S.S. Pennsylvania*. He retired from the Navy as a captain.

General Cates died June 4,1970, at the U.S. Naval Hospital, Annapolis, Maryland, after a long illness. He was buried with full military honors on June 8 at Arlington National Cemetery.

Cates' high school alma mater, the Missouri Military Academy in Mexico, Missouri, honored his memory with the creation of the *"General Clifton B. Cates 'I Will Hold' Award for Leadership"* during the academy's 125th anniversary celebration in 2014. The award specifically recognizes the leadership traits of perseverance and determination.

Charles Ream Jackson (USMC)

West Point Marine

By Scott Baron & C. Douglas Sterner

There are so many parts of Charles Jackson's story that are beyond belief, that it is truly beyond belief. Because of the First World War, he graduated the U.S. Military Academy at West Point, New York, twice, only to resign and later enlist in the Marines as a private. After the war, he survived the Spanish Flu. Trapped on Corregidor at the start of World War II, he was taken as a POW, survived the Bataan Death March, and endured brutal conditions at the Cabanatuan Prison Camp as well as wet and dry beriberi, malaria, dysentery, chronic diarrhea, internal bleeding, and malnutrition as a prisoner of the Japanese, dropping in weight to 98 pounds.

He escaped and operated in the Philippine Islands as a guerrilla, only to be taken prisoner a second time. He survived three years of brutal captivity and testified regarding his treatment at a Court of Inquiry in August 1947. His memoirs, written in 1948, would remain unpublished until 2012, 41 years after his death.

Charles Ream Jackson was born on July 14, 1898, in Petersburg, Virginia, to Army Captain Montgomery Chamberlayne Jackson and his wife, the former Isabel Biscoe Ream. His younger brother, Montgomery Chamberlayne, Jr. was born on August 30,

Beyond Belief: True Stories of Marine Corps Heroes

1900. Montgomery, Sr. was President of the Jackson Coal and Coke Company, and the children had a comfortable upbringing.

Both boys attended Petersburg High School, where Charles studied Plane Geometry, Algebra, Civil Engineering, French, and Drawing. They both attended Virginia Military Institute (VMI) where Montgomery graduated in 1920. Charles pursued a civil engineering degree for two years, then left VMI and was given an appointment to West Point by the Honorable Walter Allen Watson of the 4th Congressional District of Virginia, and was admitted on June 14, 1917.

At the academy, he was known as *"Charlie"* or *"Jack"* and was assistant manager of the baseball team and served on the Crest Committee. but America's entry into World War I created a vital shortage of officers for the rapidly expanding army and this need directly affected West Point. As Lieutenant General Sidney B. Berry, the 50th Superintendent of West Point later observed: *"World War I almost destroyed the Military Academy. Emphasis on quickly producing large numbers of officers for the war led to early graduation of five classes, disrupted the staff and faculty, and virtually turned West Point into simply another training camp for officers."*

Jackson's class graduated early, on November 1, 1918. He was commissioned a second lieutenant (unassigned). When the Armistice was signed on November 11, 1918, the two classes that had graduated on November 1 had only been in the active Army for ten days. The newly minted second lieutenants were ordered back to West Point on December 1, 1918 as the **Student Officer Battalion**. During this time, Douglas MacArthur became the 31st Superintendent of the U.S. Military Academy (1919-1922).

At a West Point formation, one would see a battalion of these **student officers** in olive drab, another battalion of plebes in gray, and yet another battalion of new cadets in *oriole* hats. Designated the Class of June 1919, its ranks included General Nathan F. Twining, Chief of Staff of the Air Force, General Albert C. Wedemeyer, who replaced Joe Stilwell (Class of 1904) in the China-Burma-India Theater, General Alfred M. Gruenther, Eisenhower's protege at NATO and later president of the American Red Cross, and General

Charles Ream Jackson (USMC)

Anthony C. McAuliffe, best known for his *"Nuts!"* response to the German surrender offer at the Battle of the Bulge, and who went on to command U.S. Army Europe. In total, the class of 1919 had a total of six full generals, believed to be an academy record.

Jackson graduated the academy a second time on June 24, 1919, and went overseas during the summer of 1919, departing for France in July where he visited Belgian French, and Italian battle fronts and observed the Army of Occupation in Germany, remaining until September 17. He returned to U.S. on September 26, assigned as a student officer at the Camp Benning, Georgia, Infantry School on October 1, 1919.

Jackson served on active duty in the Army until he resigned his commission on January 19, 1920. He then accepted a commission as a First Lieutenant in the Virginia National Guard on February 20, 1920, and held it until June 17, 1920, when he again resigned. After leaving the National Guard, Jackson accepted a commission in the Regular Army Infantry on November 30, 1920.

What followed was a series of brief assignments as the Army downsized following the end of the war. Jackson was assigned to the 22d Infantry Regiment at Fort Porter, Buffalo, New York, from November 30, 1920, through September 16, 1921, then returned to Fort Benning on September 17 until June 1, 1922. After briefly serving at Fort Sam Houston, Texas, assigned to the 23d Infantry Regiment, Jackson transferred to the Coast Artillery on June 8, 1923, assigned to the 16th Coast Artillery at Fort Ruger, Hawaii, where he was promoted to First Lieutenant on July 25, 1924.

On September 16, 1924, Jackson was assigned at Fort Shafter, Hawaii, but for an unknown reason, he resigned from active duty on July 27, 1925. Jackson held a Reserve Officer's commission as First Lieutenant, Infantry, from October 23, 1925, through April 11,1927, but saw no active duty.

During this period, he worked as an engineer for the Dupont Chemical Company, but civilian life appears not to have agreed with him and on September 3, 1927, he returned to the military, enlisting at Detroit, Michigan, as a private in the United States Marine Corps.

Beyond Belief: True Stories of Marine Corps Heroes

In his memoir "I Am Alive" Jackson recalled of his service in the Marines *"While in the Marine Corps, I served in China several times, in the Philippines, Japan, Guam, Hawaii, [on] most of the West Coast and at a few of the East Coast naval stations in our own country, as well as in Nicaragua, Panama, Haiti, Cuba, Puerto Rico, and the Virgin Islands. I have also been seagoing and have had at least a year's service on transports."*

Rising to the rank of First Sergeant, he was promoted temporary Sergeant Major on August 14, 1940. Jackson was sent to Pearl Harbor, Hawaii, on July 2, 1940, then to Shanghai, China, on November 14, 1940, assigned as the battalion Sergeant Major of the 2d Battalion, Fourth Marines. The Fourth Marines had garrisoned Shanghai since 1927, an origin of the term *"China Marine."*

Sometime during his time in China, Jackson met Margaret Duncan MacRae, the only daughter of the Rev. Cameron Farquhar MacRae, a Christian missionary, and his wife, Sarah Nicoll Woodward. Born in Shanghai, Margaret was sixteen years younger than Jackson. The two were subsequently married

Late in 1941, as war loomed in the Far East, the regiment sailed for the Philippine aboard the SS *President Madison* and the era of the China Marines ended as the last of the regiment departed on November 28, 1941.

The Fourth Marines arrived in the Philippine Islands on December 1 and were assigned to protect the naval station at Olongapo and nearby Mariveles. Seven days later, Japanese troops landed in Luzon, and the Fourth Marines were placed under U.S. Army control and subsequently assigned to defend the island fortress of Corregidor, which guards the entrance to Manila Bay.

Jackson later recalled *"We evacuated Shanghai on November 28, 1941 and went to the Philippines and landed at the Olongapo Naval Base. On Christmas Eve, after the war had started, we were bombed by the Japanese. The naval base was hit pretty hard, as was the little barrio outside the base. The word came down that the Japanese were driving down our way, and we had to leave Olongapo for fear of being cut off from the rest of the Regiment."*

Charles Ream Jackson (USMC)

The fighting on Bataan was intense, with an outcome pre-ordained by forces beyond the control of the Army, Navy, and Marine Corps defenders. The Japanese threat to the Philippines had been recognized twenty years earlier, and a war plan for the defense of the Philippines was written in 1928. Known as "Orange No. 3" or "WPO-3," the defense of the islands called for a tactical delay of the invading enemy. Rather than battling the enemy throughout the island, if they could not defeat the invaders at their point of landing, the army would pull back to the peninsula of Bataan at the opening of Manila Bay. There they would delay the enemy for up to six months until reinforcements could be brought in to end the siege.

Unknown to the valiant defenders, those reinforcements would never come.

Ten months before the attack at Pearl Harbor, British and American military tacticians had established a war plan known as *"ABC-1."* The agreement between the two nations specified that, in the event that there would be hostilities on two fronts involving both the Germans and the Japanese, both Allied powers would concentrate most of their military resources on defending Europe. Of course, the brave men fighting hunger, disease and starvation in the dense jungles of the Philippines were not aware of ABC-1. For this reason they believed President Roosevelt when he gave his year-end speech promising "the entire resources of the United States" would be committed to defending the Philippine Islands.

Two days later the Japanese took control of Manila. Meanwhile, more than 80,000 American and Filipino soldiers had withdrawn to the 500 square mile Bataan peninsula to maintain the delaying defense called for in Orange No. 3. Across the island the Philippine Scouts, many of whom were not aware of Orange No. 1, continued to battle the enemy. It was a brave effort, many of them fighting with outdated World War I British Enfield rifles. Ammunition began to run out, food was in short supply, and disease depleted their ranks. But they, along with their brothers at Bataan stubbornly held out, anxiously awaiting the resources of the United States that had been promised by the President. Amazingly the soldiers stopped the Japanese advance at the Abucay line, and held it for 12 days. Then, on February 8, General Homma received an infusion of fresh troops from Tokyo. For the Americans and

99

Beyond Belief: True Stories of Marine Corps Heroes

Filipinos there were no fresh troops, no resupply. When Singapore fell on February 15, 1942, it was becoming apparent to the Philippine defenders that the United States would be sending no reinforcements. They were expendable.

Their anthem was echoed in the words of American War Correspondent Frank Hewlett who wrote:

> *We're the battling bastards of Bataan.*
> *No Mama, no Papa, no Uncle Sam.*
> *No aunts, no uncles,*
> *no nephews, no nieces.*
> *No rifles, no planes,*
> *or artillery pieces.*
> *And nobody gives a damn.*

Jackson recalled: *"The bombing began on Christmas Eve, and by morning everyone had begun the evacuation. Being assigned to the Battalion's Intelligence Section, along with a Lieutenant Sidney F. Jenkins and five other Marines, we were the last ones to leave Olongapo with Lieutenant Colonel Anderson.*

We were all riding in a truck driving down the Bataan Peninsula toward Mariveles where we would bivouac before going over to the Island of Corregidor."

During the fighting on Corregidor, Jackson was awarded the Purple Heart on May 2, 1942, and a Gold Star in lieu of a second Purple Heart on May 6, 1942. He was also awarded the Silver Star on April 13, 1942. As positions fell and units disintegrated, stragglers from the U.S. Army and Navy, as well as Filipino units were assigned to the Marines.

Jackson modestly refrained from writing about his actions in combat, so we have only the citation for his Silver Star Medal to inform us of his first heroic actions. His Silver Star was awarded by the Army; as the Navy didn't have the Silver Star Medal as an authorized award until August 1942.

Charles Ream Jackson (USMC)

The President of the United States of America, authorized by Act of Congress July 9, 1918, takes pleasure in presenting the Silver Star (Army Award) to Chief Warrant Officer [then Sergeant Major] Charles Ream Jackson (MCSN: 212786), United States Marine Corps, for gallantry in action as a member of Headquarters and Headquarters Company, Fourth Marine Regiment, on 13 April 1942 following a heavy Japanese artillery barrage upon Battery James, Fort Mills, Corregidor, Philippine Islands. When personnel of the battery were trapped as they sought shelter in nearby tunnels, he readily volunteered, although the position was under close enemy observation and steady fire, to rescue his comrades. Disregarding the imminent danger of collapsing walls and roofs, Warrant Officer Jackson heroically entered the tunnels, assisted in extricating trapped soldiers, and gave first aid to the wounded. The gallant actions and dedicated devotion to duty demonstrated by Chief Warrant Officer Jackson, without regard for his own life, were in keeping with the highest traditions of military service and reflect great credit upon himself and the United States Marine Corps

On April 9, 1942, the Japanese landed 50,000 fresh combat troops on the Island. Army General Jonathan Wainwright issued orders to General Edward King to resist by all means. General Edward King responded that he and his staff had determined his force was reduced to 30% of their efficiency. General Wainwright continued to order not only resistance, but ordered a counterattack to repel the new Japanese offensive. It was not to be. With less than two days rations remaining, his troops paralyzed by exhaustion and disease, further resistance to the fresh Japanese offensive would have resulted in the slaughter of his beleaguered command. On April 9 General King surrendered, and Bataan fell to the Japanese. The only

Beyond Belief: True Stories of Marine Corps Heroes

active American presence in the Philippine Islands was now on the small, tadpole-shaped island of Corregidor and three smaller nearby fortified islands where what remained of the Fourth Marines continued to resist, despite being isolated, surrounded, and hopelessly abandoned.

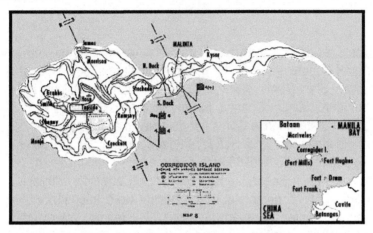

Jackson was one of more than 11,000 defenders including mostly Army soldiers, as wells as the small contingent of Marines, 500 stranded Naval sailors, and 500 Filipino soldiers, abandoned to struggle to survive on the small island for nearly 28 days after the fall of Bataan. Rations quickly were depleted, and without any hope for reinforcement or re-supply, it was a meager, miserable existence.

"The Japanese were the unwitting cause of adding to the scant rations of our beleaguered garrison," Jackson recalled. *"They can by no means be considered among the world's best bombers. The little island was a hard place to hit, at best, and, in addition, the antiaircraft guns of the 60th Coast Artillery unnerved the Japanese pilots to the extent of causing bombers to deflect from their courses. Many bombs were dropped in attempts to hit The Rock, but exploded harmlessly in the waters offshore. Consequently, large numbers of fish were stunned and floated to the surface.*

"Filipinos are generally good swimmers and absolutely fearless in the water when they are hungry. So after each bombing, the water was black with the heads of swimmers, and they bagged

large quantities of fish. Frequently the white soldiers, sailors, and Marines would join in the foraging."

Although rations were sparce, ammunition was plentiful to man the island's 45 coastal guns and mortars, and seventy-two anti-aircraft guns split between thirteen batteries. So resist, they did.

One unknown Marine who was later captured and never seen again, wrote the Fourth Marine Regiment's valiant defenders, who became known as Corregidor Marines, their own anthem to the tune of the "Marine Corps Hymn":

"First to jump for holes and tunnels and to keep our skivvies clean, We are proud to claim the title of Corregidor's Marines.

"Our drawers unfurled to every breeze from dawn to setting sun, we have jumped into every hole and ditch, and for us the fightin' was fun.

"We have plenty of guns and ammunition But not cigars and cigarettes, At the last we may be smoking leaves wrapped in Nipponese propaganda leaflets.

"When the Army and the Navy looked out Corregidor's Tunnel Queen, They saw the beaches guarded by more than one Marine!"

Corregidor was literally the World War II *Battle of the Alamo.* The Japanese pounded the defenders relentlessly from April 10 to May 6. Japanese pilots flew 614 missions, dropping more than 1,700 bombs, before finally launching their land invasion on May 6, 1942. The end was foreordained, and with total annihilation of his forces the only other option, on May 5, 1942, General Jonathan Wainwright surrendered the fortress, the last American stronghold in the southwest Pacific.

Lieutenant Colonel Donald Curtis, Executive Officer of the Fourth Marines, ordered Captain Robert B. Moore to burn the Fourth Marines Regimental colors. Captain Moore took the colors in hand and left the headquarters. On return, with tears in his eyes, he reported that the burning had been carried out. Colonel Samuel l. Howard, the Regimental commander, placed his face into his hands and wept, saying, *"My God, and I had to be the first Marine officer ever to surrender a regiment."*

Beyond Belief: True Stories of Marine Corps Heroes

For his own heroic actions in the period, Howard was awarded the Navy Cross. The text of his citation gives a glimpse into the important role his Fourth Marines played in the defense.

The President of the United States of America takes pleasure in presenting the Navy Cross to Colonel Samuel Lutz Howard (MCSN: 0-452), United States Marine Corps, for distinguished service in the line of his profession as Commanding Officer of the FOURTH Marines, U.S. Marine Corps, in the Philippines from 7 December 1941 to 6 May 1942. Although this regiment reached the Philippines just prior to the outbreak of war, and was without its complete equipment, Colonel Howard successfully and efficiently employed his force in the defense of Olongapo until ordered to withdraw on 24 December 1941. The regiment was then shifted to Corregidor where it rendered outstandingly courageous service in the defense of the beaches of that Island Fortress. During the prolonged siege of Corregidor, Colonel Howard commanded all beach defenses with a mixed force of approximately 3,000, which included some Army light artillery units, coast defense weapons, Filipino Army Air Corps personnel as infantry, remnants of other Army units from Bataan and 700 Bluejackets. Although exposed to many and repeated bombing and strafing attacks, and terrific artillery bombardments, Colonel Howard displayed outstanding qualities of courage, leadership and efficiency, by maintaining his force at the peak of battle efficiency under most difficult and hazardous conditions. His service at all times was in keeping with the highest traditions of the United States Naval Service.

Marine casualties in the defense of the Philippine Islands totaled 72 killed in action, 17 dead of wounds, and 167 wounded in action. Worse than the casualty levels caused by combat in the Philippines was the brutal treatment of Marines in Japanese hands.

Charles Ream Jackson (USMC)

Of the 1,487 members of the Fourth Marines captured on Corregidor, 474 died in captivity.

Following the surrender of Corregidor, Jackson and the others were marched north to Cabanatuan. He would later write of the horrific conditions of the march *"Don't stop for water, they just stuck a fellow" was the word passed. We looked at the moving column up ahead, and there as that column divided itself like a*  *swift, rushing stream around a rock in its bed, we saw a pitiful, crumpled figure lying in the road, his bright blood reflected against the shining sun. "Let the chow alone, they just got another!" was barked at me as I was stuffing my shirt with C rations from a roadside dump. I looked up, and there was a man in the ranks passing by, supported by a comrade and trailing a few drops of red in the gray dust...."*

At Cabanatuan, the prisoners daily faced brutal conditions including disease, malnourishment and torture. The prisoners feared they would be executed by their captors. Many died of untreated wounds, starvation, and even summary execution by their Japanese captors.

Jackson's wife would only learn of her husband's fate later that year upon receiving a postcard from the Imperial Japanese Army, forwarded by the War Department, upon which Jackson had written three words; *"I AM ALIVE."* He would later use those words as the title of his memoirs I am Alive.

"While a prisoner, I suffered partial blindness, the result of prolonged starvation," Jackson later wrote. *An Army Medical Corps doctor, Lieutenant Colonel Warren A. Wilson, procured for me, after some ten months of helplessness, a pair of eyeglasses from one of our dead. With these glasses I was able to sew my clothes, do my work, and read such books as our meager stock provided. Had it not been fore these blessed volumes, I doubt my capacity to have pulled through, mentally."*

Beyond Belief: True Stories of Marine Corps Heroes

Little more, however, is known about Jackson's own actions. When writing his memoirs that were published decades after his death, he focused on telling the stories of others, his comrades in confinement and suffering.

What is known is that Jackson managed to escape in the middle of August 1944. In the jungles he then helped a small group of Americans to organize a Filipino guerrilla unit to harass the Japanese. When the Japanese organized a major retaliation against the guerrillas, Jackson headed south, hoping to work his way to Borneo or to Australia. While traveling south he contracted a severe case of malaria and lost consciousness. Having planned to escape himself, he had given away most of his supply of quinine to others.

When the Japanese found him, they gave him quinine and recaptured him. He was sent to the Bilbad Prison Camp in Manila, a staging area for prisoners who were slated for transport by ship to working prison camps in Japan.

Escape was no longer an option. In the Bilibid Prison the captives were shown an order signed by General Masahru Homma who had commanded the Japanese 14th Army in its invasion of the Philippine Islands, and who was the architect of the Bataan Death March. The order read: *"For every man who escapes, ten men will be shot to death."* Further, he could not erase from his memory, witnessing the horrific fate that had befallen four Army Ani-Aircraft Artillery soldiers who had once escaped, recounted in his memoirs. (General Homma was charged with war crimes after the end of the war and was executed by an American firing squad on April 3, 1946.)

> *"At nine o'clock that evening they were brought in after a six hour absence. Major Mori's myrmidons trussed them up in a most effective fashion. They were tied to wooden posts, the supports of a shed in the motor pool area, on the south side of the building. Bareheaded they were, and between the calf of their legs and the back of their thigh was lashed a piece of timer two inches by four inches in size. Their hands and ankles touched, drawn tightly together by a piece of line. Here, they knelt on the ground covered with jagged gravel.*

Of their anguish and pain, their knees in the sharp stones probably hurt them the least, for that cruel timber was a diabolical torture. And some men told me afterward of how the sentries would now and then, throw a handful of dirt in their mouths when the men begged for water.

Until three o'clock in the afternoon of the next day these four men writhed in the pitiless sun with, I repeat, and handful of dirt thrown in their mouths from time to time when they begged for water. We all saw them that terrible day, and we all wondered who would be the forty to die with them. But a grave for only the four was dug, just outside the gate on the way to the swift flowing Cabanatuan River. At three o'clock they were untied and dragged, for they could not walk for some little time, before a drumhead court-martial.

We watched the proceedings from a short distance away. A Japanese officer or two, a handful of noncommissioned officers, were the tribunal of death. It may have lasted an hour. We saw them start down the path to the open grave, awaiting its prey, the sentries guarding those doomed young men. Behind them followed the firing squad. Some of us turned away for we could look on no longer, but though we ceased to look, it seemed to us that these four young boys walked with the eager steps of bridegrooms on their way to the nuptial alter. For after such torture, death was a welcome release.

Sitting in the nipa-thatched barracks, I could hear the comments of those who watched their deaths. 'They are tying their hands! They are blindfolding them. No, they refused it! They are standing them up in the Grave! They are putting lighted cigarettes in their mouths, but the big fellow, Private Gordon, spit his out! Right in their faces, too! Their heads are high. They have lots of guts!'

I heard the scattered rifle volley ragged and torn. Then came more cries of wonderment. 'The big fellow got up again!' A few more scattered shots came, to be followed with a 'He's down at last!' Then there was the sound of four mercy shots, one after the other. Outside the barracks were comments. 'The big guy cursed them to their faces to do their damnedest!' It was over.

Beyond Belief: True Stories of Marine Corps Heroes

Jackson recounted that for days, he and his comrades worried for the fate of the other forty that would be executed. For whatever reason, it never happened.

Late in 1944, Jackson boarded a Japanese *Hell Ship* for transport to Japan. Unlike many of his comrades who made that deadly voyage, he survived and was sent to the Hanowa Prisoner Of War Camp #6 at Honshu, Japan. There he worked in the Mitsubishi copper mine and in the scrap metal department of a Japanese steel mill. There were 500 prisoners and four officers, two of whom were doctors.

The camp was commanded by First Lieutenant Asaka, Infantry, Imperial Japanese Army: Jackson would write of him *"His stern and rigid treatment was tempered by a real regard for our welfare while I was imprisoned in Japan; an enigmatic figure, we think he saved many lives entrusted to his care."*

He would also recall their little Marine mongrel mascot Soochow. The mongrel dog was adopted by the Fourth Marines in Shanghai, China in 1937. Soochow was a steak-eating, beer-drinking Marine that became legendary in Shanghai, before the Marines took him with them to the Philippine Islands in 1941. Soochow survived the bombardment of Corregidor, and then spent three years with his loving comrades during their imprisonment. He was liberated at Bilibid Prison in February 1945, and flown to the United States, where he lived out his life at the Marine Corps base.

Technical Sergeant Paul J. *"Pappy"* Wells and Private First Class Soochow shortly after being liberated.

Jackson wrote of Soochow's time as a Japanese prisoner of war noting, *"His keen ears often detected bombing and strafing planes ahead of the air raid warning. Unlike most other dogs, who gave warning by scurrying for shelter with their tails tucked between their legs, this little fellow stood his ground, barking furiously at the sky raiders before he would take cover. By doing so, he saved the lives of many of his Marines."*

Upon being liberated at the end of the war, Jackson was returned to the United States where he was appointed a Commissioned Warrant Officer, United States Marine Corps on November 13, 1947. Assigned to the Marine Corps Recruit Depot, San Diego, California, he was reunited with Soochow, mascot of the Fourth Marine Regiment.

On April 7, 1949, Jackson married Margaret MacRae in Alexandria, Virginia. His serious eye trouble, a result of vitamin deficiency when a prisoner of war, forced his retirement on November 1, 1951, when he moved to San Diego and lived there until his death. After retirement, his diminishing eyesight became worse, and by 1970 he was practically blind. This, plus the fact that he was developing Parkinson's Disease, so depressed him that on May 4, 1971, he took his own life. Cremated, his ashes were scattered off the coast of San Diego, California.

Perhaps most unbelievably, Jackson would write of his time as a POW *"Strange as it must seem to some of you, I bear no hatred toward the Japanese, except for a few individuals with whom I came into close contact and earned their disfavor. Judged by our own standards, there were even some "good men" among our enemies."*

Evans Fordyce Carlson (USMC)

Gung Ho - Marine Corps Raiders

By Jim Furlong

As I write my sixth chapter for the *Beyond Belief* series it is becoming obvious to me that many of the people we write about are *mavericks* — especially those who were officers. In this book we have Greg *"Pappy"* Boyington and in the most recent book on *Civilian Heroes* we had John Paul Vance. The term *"maverick"* can have both negative and positive connotations. Negatively, you might also describe a maverick as someone who is a *"loose cannon,"* going off in all directions at once. But on the positive side, you might use it to describe someone who is firm in their convictions, willing to go against the grain, and one who leads by example.

Evans Carlson certainly fits both descriptions. Certainly, the man who *"invented"* Special Operations in the U.S. Military, and his ideas regarding guerilla warfare were not universally received by his Marine Corps superiors. But in true *maverick* style, Carlson ignored his chain of command and went directly to the top — President Franklin D. Roosevelt. His friendship with the President and his eldest son, James Roosevelt, developed when Carlson was assigned to security at the President's Warm Springs, Georgia, Summer White House, allowed him to do it.

EARLY YEARS

Evans Fordyce Carlson was born on February 26, 1896, in Sidney, New York. His father, Thomas, was a Congregationalist Minister, and his pastorates would result in several moves in Carlson's childhood which would see him in New York, Massachusetts, Vermont, and New Hampshire. He idolized his father but didn't care for his mother, Joetta, who, he seemed to imply, was from a family dating back to the American Revolution but had no money. She was always imploring her son to act in a proper manner. Despite the rules of his father's strict home, Carlson always felt he should live up to the high standards that his father not only set for his children, but the same way he lived his own life. Carlson would continue to correspond with his father throughout his life.

At age eleven, with $2.34 in his pocket, he left home by train to Boston, and then by boat to Portland, Maine. There he found a job in a match factory, running blocks of wood through the saws to make match heads. He worked long, hard days for only three weeks when, weak and sick, he decided it best to return home, aborting his attempt to prove to his father that he could live on his own.

Carlson remained restless. When he was fourteen he left home for good after being suspended from school for a year. The rope to the school bell had been cut and Carlson emerged as the leading suspect. Whether he did it or not, or was just looking for a way to get out of school, Carlson confessed to the act and was given the suspension as punishment.[1] This time, however, Carlson kept in touch with his family, writing to them that they should not worry — but he wouldn't see them for seven years. Moving to Vermont, he was a laborer on the railroad, and also learned Morse Code — a valuable skill in those days. He later moved to New Jersey, staying with friends of his mother and going to night school. He dropped out after only a month, ending his formal education. Nonetheless, he was a voracious reader and was self-taught in many subjects.

JOINING THE ARMY

At sixteen, Carlson explored his life's options. In New Jersey he decided he would visit the Navy Recruiting Office near the Hoboken Ferry. However, en route he passed the Army recruiting office and was intrigued with the posters of China and the Philippines he saw there. So, he decided to go inside. There he found out that the minimum age to enlist was twenty-one. Standing at slightly over 6 feet, and weighing 150 pounds, he probably looked older then his

---

[1] Blankfort, Michael. *The Big Yankee: The Life of Carlson of the Raiders.* Boston: Little, Brown, 1947.

sixteen years. He indicated he was 22 on his enlistment papers and was inducted into the Army. When his mother's friend found out, she wired the Carlson's and indicated they could cancel the enlistment and asked for advice. Carlson's parents agonized over their son's actions, but ultimately concluded that he needed to learn from his mistakes and advised their friend not to do anything.

During his first enlistment in the Army he served in the Philippine Islands and at Schofield Barracks in Hawaii. He was promoted rapidly, and when his enlistment expired before his twenty-first birthday he was discharged as a first sergeant. He reenlisted shortly thereafter. Poncho Villa had invaded the United States and raided the town of Columbus, New Mexico, and nearby Camp Furlong. Carlson participated in the **Mexican Punitive Expedition** conducted by General John J. Pershing. A minor skirmish, it is it is interesting to note that it was the first-time motorized vehicles and airplanes were used by the armed forces in the U.S.. It was also the last time horses were used in military operations by the calvary.

During World War I he saw action in France and earned a **Wound Chevron**. On August 7, 1932, General Douglas MacArthur reinstituted General George Washington's Purple Heart Award for wounds in combat, and. also made the award available to those wounded during World War I. Carlson exchanged his Wound Chevron for the Purple Heart. It was during this period that Carlson met his future wife Dorothy (Etelle) who, in 1917, bore him a son, Evans Charles Carlson.

During the war he was commissioned a second lieutenant in May 1917, and was made a captain of field artillery in December 1917. After the Armistice, he served in Germany with the Army of Occupation. Eventually, he was discharged from the army in 1921, as America reduced its Armed Forces in peacetime.

JOINING THE U.S. MARINE CORPS

The call to military life, with its excitement and structure, impressed Carlson. In 1922 when he enlisted in the Marine Corps as a private. His leadership skills continued to impress and, in 1923 he was once again commissioned as a second lieutenant. He was assigned duty at the Marine Corps Barracks (MCB) Quantico, Virginia, and in 1924 sailed for Culebra, Puerto Rico, and then was ordered to the west coast for duty with the **Pacific Fleet**. He applied for aviation training in 1925, and was sent to the Naval Aeronautical Station, Pensacola, Florida, for instruction.

For reasons that aren't clear, he subsequently left and returned to duty with ground infantry Marines. He served another foreign tour from 1927 to 1929 at Shanghai, China, with the Fourth Marine Regiment. It would be the first of many trips to China for him.

At first, Carlson languished in the hot, sultry, Shanghai summer. He became bored with the routine of garrison duty and lost considerable weight. But as summer cooled to fall, his fortunes changed. He was promoted to first lieutenant and became the Fourth Regiment's intelligence officer. Carlson's life took on new meaning in this role which required him to develop expertise in Chinese history, culture, and politics. He immersed himself in this endeavor and read everything he could that was written in English. Not satisfied, he began studying the many Chinese dialects. He is quoted by his biographer, Helen Snow, as saying: *"I didn't know anything about intelligence work but I went ahead just the same. I now became interested in politics in China for the first time."*[2]

Although he didn't realize it at the time, his assignment in military intelligence would be a very transformative moment in his life, and even likely, in the outcome of the Marine Corps' war in the Pacific during World War II.

NICARAGUA

The Panama Canal was completed in 1914 and the Marines, who had been occupying Nicaragua to prevent other countries from building a canal, remained to provide security and oversee the formation of the Nicaraguan National Guard (Guardia Nacional). It was their mission to deal with roving bands of guerilla fighters that were attempting to overthrow dictators in Nicaragua who were perceived to be friendly to the United States. The Marines were still at war with the guerillas in May 1930, when first lieutenant Carlson reported for duty and was made a Captain in the Guardia Nacional.

---

[2] Snow, Helen, *"Autobiography of Evans Carlson: Reminiscences Told to Helen Snow in China, 1940,"* L. Tom Perry Special Collections, Harold B. Lee Library, Brigham Young University.

Evans Fordyce Carlson (USMC)

He was sent to a remote village to command a group of thirty-five Guardia Nacional troops. Carlson knew some Spanish, but was not yet fluent – but he was able to communicate effectively with them. Again he demonstrated his ability to relate to his men, even when they were from a different culture. *"I met the Nicaraguans as equals and developed the principles of fair play and justice. The men were shooting their officers. I went to one place where they had just killed two. I had no trouble as I treated the men as I would have liked to be treated myself and won their confidence." [3]*

Soon after arriving inland, about 100 insurgents raided a village near his encampment. Carlson took a band of sixteen men, and when they caught up with them, they engaged them and in just ten minutes of fighting killed five insurgents. Carlson lost none of his own men.

Eventually, Carlson contracted Malaria and when he was cured, he was transferred to a desk job in Managua. On Christmas Day, Managua suffered a major earthquake that killed over 1,000, injured many more, and caused over $15 million in damages. First Lieutenant Carlson immediately organized recovery efforts and received high praise for his actions. Several high-ranking Nicaraguan officials sent letters to Washington praising his actions, not only in the earthquake recovery, but for his earlier raid of the insurgents with Guardia Nacional. He was awarded his first Navy Cross for those efforts.

The President of the United States of America takes pleasure in presenting the Navy Cross to First Lieutenant Evans Fordyce Carlson (MCSN: 0-3613), United States Marine Corps Reserve, for extraordinary heroism while attached to the Guardia Nacional from 16 May 1930 to 1 May 1931. Upon joining the Guardia Nacional, First Lieutenant Carlson was assigned at Jalapa in the bandit area of Nueva Segovia. On 8 July 1930, he received a report that a group of one hundred bandits were

[3] Ibid.

looting the town of Portillo. He immediately left with a detachment of sixteen men to gain contact. Four the men deserted en route but with the remaining twelve men he pushed on and overtook and gained contact with a group of forty bandits, completely routing them, killing two and wounding seven, without any casualties to his detachment. Arms, ammunition, equipment and clothing looted from the town of Portillo were recaptured. Lieutenant Carlson maintained his district in a most excellent manner and by his activities and well-directed operations kept it singularly free from banditry.

Carlson returned to the United States when malignant malaria made it impossible for him to continue his duties, but not before absorbing lessons from guerilla warfare in Nicaragua that he would later utilize in forming the Second Marine Raider Battalion. Carlson focused on five points. The first concerned the proper use of small unit tactics. Like other Marine officers with service in-country, Carlson recognized the futility of large-unit maneuvers in the wilds of Nicaragua. To fight bands of guerrillas, who favored speedy strikes before disappearing into the countryside, smaller groups of men worked better in jungles and streams. *"The only successful offensive operations,"* stated a Guardia officer, *"have been by small, very mobile patrols capable of living off the country and of following bandit wherever they have been able to go."*[4]

Combined with the second tactic – *concentrate as much firepower on the enemy as quickly as possible* –Carlson had the foundations for much of what he later advocated with his Marine Raiders. A third tactic was *hit and run*. Hit them fast and do not get tied up with long, protracted battles. The fourth tactic was to be able to *live off the land* which closely dovetails with the fifth tactic, to *blend in with the local populace and gain their confidence.*

SECOND CHINA ASSIGNMENT

In 1933 Carlson received orders to return to China. Anxious to see the *"real"* China he had previously studied in his assignment as intelligence officer, he appealed to his superiors to be assigned

---

[4] Blankfort, Michael. *"The Big Yankee: The Life of Carlson of the Raiders,"* Boston: Little, Brown, 1947.

somewhere other than the **Westernized International Settlement** in Shanghai. His superiors acquiesced and he was given an assignment in Peiping (today, Beijing). With Dorothy and Evans Jr., he rented and lived in a home just inside the **Forbidden City**.

He was assigned as the adjutant to the **American Legation,** and his duties allowed him to further immerse himself in the Chinese culture, of which he was becoming particularly fond. He and Dorothy entertained often, and met many notable political and cultural figures. He also taught classes in Chinese history and culture to many of those military assigned to him in the **Legation Guard.** Previous to Carlson's assignment, the **Legation** had been plagued with morale and disciple problems, and Carlson noted that when the Marines were exposed to Chinese culture, and educated as to the reason for their assignment, discipline problems all but disappeared.

Carlson noted that *"when soldiers are given information about the situation in which they act and live, they derive from it a sense of responsibility . . . He would never forget this lesson."*[5] That lesson would be reinforced on his third trip to China, and his sharing a sense of purpose with the troops would become another cornerstone in the philosophy which eventually became part of the Second Marine Raider Battalion model.

Carlson's second Chinese tour ended in 1935. He was promoted to Captain and returned to the United States and stationed at the Marine Corps Barracks in Quantico, Virginia. He was soon to have another transformative experience where he would meet the most powerful man in the United States of America.

SERVICE TO THE PRESIDENT

In 1935, Captain Carlson was posted as second-in-command of a Marine Unit to augment the President's Secret Service detail when he travelled to Warms Springs, Georgia, where the water eased the pain in his legs.

"Captain and Mrs. Evans Carlson stood up when the tall, rather ungainly woman entered the room followed by Jack and Jill, two Irish Setters. The others who had been waiting for lunch also

---

[5] Ibid

rose. They included Marine Lieutenant Colonel and Mrs. Lemuel Shepard, Assistant Secretary of State Francis B. Sayre Sr., and Episcopal Bishop Julius Atwood.

"'Shall we go into the dining room?' the woman said. 'Franklin is already at the table.'

"Franklin was Franklin Delano Roosevelt, and the woman who showed them to the table was his wife, Eleanor. The luncheon was only an hour on that cold day in February 1936, but the bond forged between the U.S. President and the Marine captain lasted years."[6]

The two particularly bonded over a mutual admiration for Chinese culture. Roosevelt fondly recalled the exploits of his maternal grandfather, Warren Delano, who made his wealth, according to Roosevelt, importing teas and silks. (*Author's note: In fact, the bulk of Warren Delano's wealth came from the illegal import of Turkish opium into China. Though opium was illegal in China, China's social caste system had merchants near the bottom of the social stratum which made merchants susceptible to corruption. Thus, many of the monied East Coast families such as the Russells, Delanos, Peabodys, Cabots, Forbes, and Lodges made their "fortunes" importing opium to China." For more on this I suggest you read* The China Mirage" by James Brady.

While the bond between the President and the young Marine deepened, the President's oldest son James, also came into the circle.

As the President gained more confidence in Carlson, Carlson continued to express a desire to help the President any way he could. Carlson was corresponding frequently with Roosevelt through the intermediary of Roosevelt's private secretary, Missy LeHand. He expressed that not only would he help Roosevelt and his family, but that he would keep that assistance in strictest confidence.

Eventually Roosevelt did see a way to have Carlson help him, and in a much needed confidential way. On the eve of Carlson's third assignment in China, Roosevelt summoned him to a meeting in the White House on July 15, 1937.

---

[6] Ibid.

Evans Fordyce Carlson (USMC)

"'I want you to drop me a line now and then – direct to the White House,' Roosevelt told Carlson. 'Let me know how you're doing. Tell me what's going on. I suspect there's going to be a great deal going on this summer in China. I'd like to hear what you have to say about it.' When Carlson readily agreed, Roosevelt added, 'Shall we keep these letters a secret? Just between the two of us? Shall we?'"[7]

Roosevelt was signaling that he would like the letters to be routed through his intermediary, his personal secretary Missy LeHand. Roosevelt. He no doubt sensed future problems with an aggressive Japan who was embroiled in the Second Sino-Japanese War. Fighting with an isolationist Congress, Roosevelt thought that Carlson could give him information he might not otherwise receive through normal diplomatic channels.

Clearly. Carlson's agreement with Roosevelt to send reports directly to the President was contradictory to normal chain-of-command protocol. If he was found out (and eventually he was), he would be viewed un favorably by those superiors left out of the loop.

Over the next two years Carlson sent seventeen reports on his observations to Missy LeHand, for confidential distribution to President Roosevelt.

THIRD CHINA TOUR AND THE ORIGINATION OF *"GUNG HO"*

If politics makes strange bedfellows, then wars make even stranger bedfellows – or to use another cliché, *"The enemy of my enemy, is my friend."* For instance, the World War II Allies including the Soviet Union, who would become adversaries after the War. Also, during the Second Sino-Japanese War the adversaries for control of China, the Chinese Nationalists led by Chiang Kai-shek, and the Chinese Communists led by Mao Zedong, buried the hatchet, so to speak, to fight to repel the Japanese invaders.

When Carlson reported for duty in China in 1937, the Second Sino-Japanese War was raging. The Japanese already controlled, or at least they thought they did, the Northern Provinces of China and

---

[7]Ibid.

119

the major cities of Peiping (Beijing) and Shanghai. Carlson, initially assigned to the **American Legation** in the **International Community**, often observed fighting in the streets between the Japanese and the **Chinese Nationalist Army**, literally right under his nose.

Carlson was assigned to U.S. Naval Intelligence as an observer under the command of Admiral Harry Yarnell, commander of the Asiatic Fleet. Yarnell implored Carlson to not only observe and report how the Chinese fought, but more importantly, how the Japanese fought.

Word got out on Carlson's letter writing activities to the Commander-in-Chief. Not only was this frowned upon, but it caused unknown higher ups to begin tracking Carlson's activities. It was not uncommon, given Carlson's charge from Roosevelt, to observe all goings on in China and for Carlson to meet with some people whose loyalties to the United States might be questioned.

One of those was purported communist sympathizer Edgar Snow, a journalist from Kansas City who had just finished the manuscript for **Red Star Over China**. Snow gave Carlson a copy of the manuscript and, when returning it after he read it, Carlson inquired of Snow if Mao Zedong and Chou Enlai were real people. Snow challenged him to find out for himself. Shortly after Christmas 1937, Carlson set out on a 51-day journey behind enemy lines. En route, he encountered another Communist sympathizer, 45 year old writer Agnes Smedley. The attraction between the two was one of two human beings who loved each other as true equal human beings, or comrades.

Evans Fordyce Carlson in China

Evans Fordyce Carlson (USMC)

Carlson's own marriage was troubled at the time, but there is no evidence whatsoever that he and Smedley had anything more than an abiding deep respect for each other. Carlson's friendships with Snow and Smedley would last the rest of his life.

There were two highlights of this trip for Carlson.

The first was a night visit with Mao. It would establish a lifetime impression on Carlson who wrote about it in detail. Under the light of a single candle in the room, the two talked about politics throughout the ages, current politics in American and Europe, the influence of religion on society, and what a potential world organization would look like.

The second highlight was his participation in an operation with the **Eighth Route Army** (the name for a unit in the Chinese Communist Army or Red Army). He marched on foot with a subunit of 600 Chinese soldiers over eight mountains, covering a distance of 58 miles in under 32 hours. Though they were poorly equipped, he was amazed at the comradery, discipline, and morale of these soldiers. He described it as an experience he would never forget.

It was during this march that Carlson observed that *"every man would have input into the plans and officers had no distinct privileges until everyone thought they were earned."* Marine Raider Major Jon T. Hoffman described "gung ho" as an unconventional military philosophy that was an admixture of Chinese culture, Communist egalitarianism, and New England town hall democracy.

Carlson told *Life* magazine, *"I was trying to build up the same sort of working spirit I had seen in China where all the soldiers dedicated themselves to one idea and worked together to put that idea over. I told the boys about it again and again, I told them of the motto of the Chinese Cooperatives, Gung Ho. It means Work Together—Work in Harmony."*[8]

But *Gung Ho* doesn't mean that. Its meaning has evolved over time but in Chinese the literal translation means *"industrial cooperative."*

---

[8] Jess Kung, *The Long, Strange Journey of "Gung Ho,"* National Public Radio, Code Switch Word Watch, October 18, 2019.

Beyond Belief: True Stories of Marine Corps Heroes

The phrase *"Gung-ho"* describes enthusiasm — often to the point of naivete. But it didn't always. The original Chinese is 工業合作社, which means *"industrial cooperative"* – 工業, *(gōng yè)* meaning *"industry,"* and 合作社 *(hé zuò shè)* meaning "cooperative." It refers to organizations democratically run by workers producing industrial goods like blankets and military uniforms.

工業合作社 was abbreviated, as many long Chinese proper nouns are, to the first character of each part, 工合. Today, we would Romanize it to gōng hé, but in the 1930s, the same sounds turned into *kung ho*, or *gung-ho*.[9]

Gung Ho, as Carlson envisioned it, was a true coming together of fighters who were deemed to be equals with their officers, and who understood exactly why they were there fighting, and who would participate as equals in the strategies and planning of military operations.

Carlson pledged from the first moment he observed the fighting spirit of the **Eighth Route Army** that if he ever commanded Marines in war their motto would be ***Gung Ho.***

And that is how the term was incorporated in the Marine lexicon, and subsequently that of other branches of military service.

CENSURE AND RETIREMENT FROM THE CORPS

While on patrol with the Red Army, Carlson was continuously reminded by the Chinese that much of the Japanese aggression was made possible by United States companies selling vital war materials, including oil, to the Japanese. Carlson was deeply troubled by this, and also clearly saw the writing on the wall that before too long these same war supplies would be used by Japan against the United States.

The highly principled Carlson felt he had to speak out and tell the American people of the impending danger. He knew he would be jeopardizing his career and, his many friends and peers warned him of the danger. Agnes Smedley called him *"crazy"* and *"innocent."* But when he arrived back in Hankow on August 7, 1938, he sought

---

[9] Ibid

Evans Fordyce Carlson (USMC)

out three American reporters and warned them not only of the dangers to China, but what he saw as the impending danger to the United States. Two days later the *Chicago Daily News* mentioned Carlson by name in an article critical of U.S. companies profiting from the sale of war materials to Japan.

On September 17 Carlson received a censure from the Marine Corps and was warned of harsh repercussions if he continued to speak openly to the press. Once again he was at a crossroads of his career. He felt obligated to continue to speak out on a subject he was certain was of critical importance to his country. His friends rallied and tried to dissuade him.

There was also a financial consideration as Carlson was a mere two years away from retirement. He told a few friends he was considering retiring from the Marines. Marine Commandant Thomas Holcomb, both a friend to Carlson and a confidant of the President, tried to talk him out of it. His Asiatic Commander Admiral Harry Yarnell sent a complete report to Washington, D.C., praising Carlson for his service and even held up his retirement papers hoping Carlson would change his mind. But Carlson wrote the President, through Missy LeHand in March 1939, telling him he felt he could be more useful as a civilian because he felt he had to say what was on his mind, and as a military man that would embarrass the Corps.

Roosevelt expressed his sorrow over Carlson's decision but wished him well.

Carlson's resignation from the Marine Corps was effective March 17, 1939. He would devote the next two years to making speeches and granting media interviews, in an effort to halt Japanese war material sales by American companies. During this period he wrote several magazine articles and penned two books: *The Chinese Army,* published in the fall of 1939, and *Twin Stars of China*, published in 1940. These books were met with positive critical reviews and argued against American policy that allowed war material sales to Japan by American companies.

They also promoted the guerilla style of warfare being used by the Chinese Communists against the Japanese invaders. All that these books seemed to do, however, was give the impression Carlson was, at the least, a *"Red sympathizer."*

Beyond Belief: True Stories of Marine Corps Heroes

Carlson was continually frustrated in that he felt he *"was preaching to the choir."* The attendees already seemed to be in agreement with his stance, and he wasn't reaching those he needed to reach. Frustrated, in the fall of 1940, Carlson returned to China for the fourth time to observe the Japanese invasion there. His visit only reinforced the value of guerilla units, as used by Mao's Communist forces, in fighting Japanese aggression. He eventually returned to the United States in the Spring of 1941, convinced more than ever that the Japanese would attack the United States in the next few months.

Another one of those transformative moments for Carlson occurred after he gave a speech to the **Army and Navy Club** in early April 1941. A former colleague, a Marine colonel, approached him and engaged him about the possibility of returning to the Marines. Carlson was convinced, and with the help of Marine Commandant Thomas Holcomb, was returned to active duty on April 28, 1941. Despite Holcomb's and President Roosevelt's support, there were numerous objections to Carlson's return by many senior Marine Corps officers. He was perceived by them as being too *"left leaning"* (i.e. a Communist sympathizer), and a maverick (willing to go outside the book.) Back in uniform, Carlson was subsequently assigned to Camp Elliott in San Diego, California.

Then came the fateful *"day that will live in infamy."* On Sunday, December 7, 1941, Carlson was stopped at the gate while attempting to go on leave from Camp Elliott. He was informed that the Japanese had bombed Pearl Harbor.

JAMES ROOSEVELT AND CARLSON'S RAIDERS.

James Roosevelt, the eldest son of the President of the United States, joined the Marines Corps in 1936 at the rank of Lieutenant Colonel. Bespeckled, balding, and somewhat sickly, Roosevelt hardly fit the poster image of a Marine recruit or officer. Coming into the Corps as a Lieutenant Colonel afforded him the luxury of avoiding the rigorous training and testing that all other Marines had to endure. The derision he felt, and that was heaped on him, caused him in 1939 to subsequently resign his honorary commission and join the Marine Corps Reserves, at the more appropriate rank of Captain. He was still looked upon with skepticism by his peers and superiors, who viewed him as a Marine who was benefiting from being the son of the President of the United States.

After Pearl Harbor, on the evening of December 8, Roosevelt had helped his father into bed. Jimmy, as he was known, asked his father to assign him to a combat billet. Like any father, the President offered some half-hearted objections but saw the legitimacy of James' argument. How could the President order the sons of his citizens into harm's way, and hold back his own son from combat. The President relented and granted James' wish.

Almost simultaneously, the President met with his cabinet and confided in his old friend William J. *"Wild Bill"* Donovan that British Prime Minister Winston Churchill was hailing the effectiveness of his small elite unit, the **British Commandos** who were striking at the Germans in hit and run type raids. Donovan had recently been appointed by the President as an Army colonel charged with gathering intelligence on our enemies. Donovan was now urging the President to take a more active combat role in the war and the President seemed to agree. Donovan would eventually be made Director of the **Office of Strategic Services** when it was created in June 1942.

James Roosevelt, meanwhile, had his desires granted and was activated from the Reserves and assigned to Camp Elliott where, probably not coincidentally, he was assigned to work with his old friend from Warm Springs, Georgia, days – Evans Carlson.

With the two friends reunited and seemingly on the same page regarding Carlson's advocacy for a guerilla unit, Roosevelt penned a January 1942 memo to the Marine Corps Commandant and others in the Chain of Command. The memo was titled *"Development Within the Marine Corps of a Unit for Purposes Similar to the British Commandos and the Chinese Guerillas."* In it he proposed *"an outfit based on Carlson's observations of the Communist Eighth Route Army's notion of ethical indoctrination, which called for a policy of close relationships between officers and men, elimination of class distinctions, and full sharing of information in all ranks."*[10]

Beyond Belief: True Stories of Marine Corps Heroes

Unquestionably the ideas conveyed in the memo were Carlson's, but Roosevelt's enthusiasm of Carlson's methods and influences enabled him to persuade the reluctant Marine Corps leadership to authorize the controversial plan. To be sure, it helped his and Carlson's efforts that the proposal was written by the President's son, but absent such a cogent synthesis of Carlson's experiences with the **Chinese Communist Army** and **British Special Forces**, the inception of the Marine Raiders might have been thwarted by the conservative Marine Corps Command.[11]

But now the Marine Corps Commandant, General Thomas Holcomb, had a quandary. He was being leaned on by the President of the United States to form a commando style force. On the one hand, the President was advocating for his confidant Colonel. Donovan of the Army to be assigned to the Marine Corps and promoted to Brigadier General. Holcomb knew an Army man would not be welcomed into the Marine Corps hierarchy. He was reluctant to make that move.

Now the President had a proposal from his own son on his desk, and he seemed to be pushing that. But James' proposal would involve making radical structural changes from the Marines usual way of doing things. The *"everybody's equal,"* and changes to squad size and equipment, would not be received well by the Corps. To further the quandary, Merritt Edson, like Carlson, was a hero of the Marine Corps operation in Nicaragua. Additionally, he had a Medal of Honor he had earned, and he was pushing to command any new commando-style group in a more traditional Marine Corps organization.

Commandant Holcomb's solution was elegant and simple. He urged his Navy superiors and the President to let Donovan operate in Europe while still in the Army. He also proposed two new battalion's for the Marine Corps. It included a more traditional TO&E: **First Marine Raider Battalion** commanded by Edson for the East, and

---

[10] Duane Schultz, *Evans Carlson, Marine Raider,* Westholme Publishing, Yardley, Pennsylvania, 2014.

[11] LCpl Evan F. Weiss, USMC, *The Forgotten Marine, The Legacy of James Roosevelt, Marine Corps Innovator and Navy Cross Recipient,* Leatherneck Magazine, June 2017.

Carlson would command the **Second Marine Raider Battalion** in the West (the Pacific). That unit would follow the concepts and organization advocated by Carlson and Roosevelt.

"As a testament to James Roosevelt's growing importance as a military leader, Carlson trusted him with more than just the 'politics' of their mission. In fact, Roosevelt was involved in selecting the 1,000 Marines who would compromise Carlson's Raiders."[12]

Moreover, the physically unimposing Roosevelt surprisingly kept up the pace with the other Raiders during their grueling training activities. These included a 35-mile hike two times per week, and a 70-mile nighttime trek once a week, all on a near starvation diet of raisins and rice. Among those who knew him best, Roosevelt dispelled the perception that he was a Marine *"in name only"* having earned the respect of the Corps' most elite warriors. The only accommodation the President's son received was a medical waiver – James Roosevelt had flat feet, and during training as well as subsequent combat in the Pacific, he was authorized to wear tennis shoes in lieu of combat boots.

When **Carlson's Raiders** were recruited, trained, and had become a viable fighting force, they were ready for their first mission.

In the first nine months of World War II, the United States and its allies in the Pacific lost battle after battle, and island after island. The United States' war planners were about to embark on a bold endeavor – the first major American offensive of the war to capture not only Guadalcanal in the Solomon Islands, but also take control of a strategic landing field there that endangered both New Zealand and Australia.

Navy and Marine Corps strategists felt it would be helpful to have a diversionary raid elsewhere in the Pacific that might preclude the Japanese from reinforcing their troops on Guadalcanal. The Guadalcanal amphibious assault was planned for August 1942.

Carlson's Raiders were selected to provide not only the needed diversionary attack, but were also tasked with gathering intelligence

---

[12] Ibid.

on the Japanese, and to hopefully strike fear in the Japanese troops by assaulting a well-fortified outpost in the Pacific surrounded by other Japanese-held territory. That strike would be on the Makin Atoll.

As the planning began, it was obvious that James Roosevelt, Executive Officer of the **Second Marine Raider Battalion,** would be part of the attack. That gave military brass in the Pacific fits. What if James Roosevelt was killed in action? Worse, what if James was captured? The brass, not Carlson, made the decision to exclude the President's son from the Makin Raid.

"Surely . . James Roosevelt was justified in his outrage when he learned that military brass planned to exclude him from the Raiders' first combat mission for fear of a propaganda nightmare if he were to be killed or captured. Upon receiving this news, Roosevelt again petitioned the help of his father, who agreed that his son deserved to fight with Carlson and the newly formed Raider Battalion, no matter the risk. (O)ne very stern call by President Roosevelt to Admiral Chester W. Nimitz, the Commander in Chief of the U. S. Pacific Fleet, was enough to ensure that Roosevelt would be included in the now-legendary raid of the strategically significant Makin Atoll."[13]

On August 17, 1942, ten days after the landings at Guadalcanal, two companies of Carlson's raiders arrived in the submarines *Nautilus* and *Argonaut,* and were launched in motorized rubber rafts for an amphibious landing on Makin Atoll. The sea was heavy and the rains were heavier − and the weather battered the invaders. The rafts flooded and most of the motors failed under the deluge. But even so, the invaders somehow reached shore intact.

Carlson and his men set up a command post manned by Roosevelt, and the rest of the group set out to engage the garrison stationed on the volcanic island. They were met with heavy resistance and the Japanese mounted two banzai attacks. The Japanese also quickly attempted to reinforce the island, but the same rough weather and attacks from the Raiders prevented that from happening. The

[13] Duane Schultz, *Evans Carlson, Marine Raider,* Westholme Publishing, Yardley, Pennsylvania, 2014.

Evans Fordyce Carlson (USMC)

Raiders did suffer casualties and, unknown to Carlson and his men, they had destroyed and killed most of the Japanese defenders.

The raid had always been envisioned to reflect Carlson's tactics of a hit-and-run style attack. But the Raiders found exfiltrating the island to be even more hazardous and dangerous. Many motors on the boats were still inoperative, and the pounding surf pushed the rafts back

Elements of Carlson's Raiders on Makin Atoll

to shore. Some rafts capsized and the radios used to communicate with the submarines were lost. Some rafts might have made it, but it was impossible to tell with so many capsizing.

During the chaos that was occurring, James Roosevelt noticed three Raiders floundering after their raft had capsized, and rushed out to rescue them. He would receive a Navy Cross for his heroic actions. Back on the Island, Carlson, true to his tactics, held a war council in which the troops made the agonizing decision to surrender, and sent a Raider messenger to convey the message.

The messenger was killed before he could deliver the offer. Eventually, however, Carlson was able to communicate by flashlight with the submarines and he successfully messaged them to come into the calmer waters of the lagoon to rescue the remaining Raiders. The *Nautilus* and *Argonaut* did maneuver into the lagoon, and the makeshift rafts successfully rendezvoused with their rescuers.

The two submarines returned to Pearl Harbor where upon disembarking, the Raiders were finally able to make sense of the final toll. Two-hundred eleven Raiders participated in the raid – 19 were killed and 17 wounded. Nine Raiders were captured and later reported to have been decapitated by the enemy while in captivity.

The President of the United States of America takes pleasure in presenting the Navy Cross to Major James R. Roosevelt (MCSN: 0-5477), United States Marine Corps Reserve, for extraordinary heroism and distinguished service as Executive Officer, and second in command of the SECOND Marine Raider Battalion, during the Marine Raider Expedition against the Japanese-held island of Makin in the Gilbert Islands on 17 and 18 August 1942. Risking his own life over and beyond the ordinary call of duty, Major Roosevelt continually exposed himself to intense machine-gun and sniper fire to ensure effective control of operations from the command post. As a result of his successful maintenance of communications with his supporting vessels, two enemy surface ships, whose presence was reported, were destroyed by gun fire. Later during evacuation, he displayed exemplary courage in personally rescuing three men from drowning in the heavy surf. His gallant conduct and his inspiring devotion to duty were in keeping with the highest traditions of the United States Naval Service.

Evans Carlson also performed heroically and earned his second Navy Cross.

The President of the United States of America takes pleasure in presenting a Gold Star in lieu of a Second Award of the Navy Cross to Lieutenant Colonel Evans Fordyce Carlson (MCSN: 0-3613), United States Marine Corps Reserve, for extraordinary heroism and distinguished service as Commanding Officer of the SECOND Marine Raider Battalion, during the Marine Raider Expedition against the Japanese-held island of Makin in the Gilbert Islands on 17 and 18 August

Evans Fordyce Carlson (USMC)

> 1942. In the first operation of this type ever conducted by United States Forces, Lieutenant Colonel Carlson personally directed his forces in the face of intense fire of enemy ground troops and aerial bombing barrage, inflicting great personnel and material damage on the enemy. In the withdrawal of his forces under adverse sea conditions, he displayed outstanding resourcefulness, initiative and resolute purpose in evacuating all wounded and disabled men. His high courage and excellent leadership throughout the engagement were in keeping with the finest traditions of the United States Naval Service.

Was the Makin Atoll Raid a success? It did not meet all its objectives. It did not return with any sizeable hard intelligence; and it didn't capture any of the Japanese Garrison. But it did accomplish two psychological objectives. First, it was a tremendous morale boost for Americans back home — we were finally giving it to the enemy. At least 46 Japanese were killed in the raid, and they suffered losses of two airplanes and two small ships in their reinforcement effort. Secondly, it put the Japanese on notice that the United States, by this action and the invasion of Guadalcanal, was now on the offensive in the war. It served notice that we intended to win this war, and this action proved we could strike anywhere in their Empire at any time.

In November the U.S. Army's 27th Infantry Division returned to Makin Atoll to again invade it, but this time to also occupy it. With them was James Roosevelt, who was attached as an observer. In the fighting that followed he earned a Silver Star.

The President of the United States of America, authorized by Act of Congress July 9, 1918, takes pleasure in presenting the Silver Star (Army Award) to Lieutenant Colonel James R. Roosevelt (MCSN: 0-5477), United States Marine Corps, for gallantry in action at Makin Atoll, Gilbert Islands, 20 to 23 November 1943. Attached as an observer to the units of the 27th Infantry Division which effected the landing on Makin Atoll, Lieutenant Colonel Roosevelt voluntarily sought out the scenes of the heaviest fighting. Throughout the three-day period, he continually accompanied the leading elements of the assault, exposing himself to constant danger. His calmness under fore and presence among the foremost elements of the attacking force was a source of inspiration to all ranks.

CARLSON'S LONG PATROL

After the near disaster at Makin Atoll, the Raiders wanted badly to have another shot at the enemy. Carlson wanted an engagement to prove his controversial concept of guerilla fighting would work. They would be given that opportunity in early November 1942, in an operation that would become known as **Carlson's Long Patrol**.

Marine General Alexander Vandegrift was desperately trying to expand the perimeter around the captured Japanese airfield his Marines had captured and renamed **Henderson Field**. There were still sizeable Japanese pockets of resistance both north and south of **Henderson Field**. However, the American perimeter effectively blocked large Japanese troop movements, which prohibited the two forces from joining up and becoming a more formidable force.

Vandegrift decided that in order to free the island of all Japanese resistance, he would have to attack in force against the Japanese emplacements north of the airfield. Before long, reports, began filtering back to Vandergrift that some Japanese were escaping to the south, too small in number to be detected but still the general feared if they met up with the Japanese forces in the south, they could wreak havoc.

Vandegrift decided he needed someone to operate behind enemy lines and this appeared to be a job designed for the **Second Marine Raider Battalion**.

Carlson and his troops, initially consisting of Companies C and E, were dispatched on the transport ship *U.S.S. Manley* and landed in Aola Bay on Guadalcanal, on November 6. Aola Bay is about 30 miles south of **Henderson Field**. The Raiders came ashore in Higgins Boats and secured a perimeter just inland, while they awaited orders which were air-dropped to Carlson that evening. The next morning they began their sweep, looking for piecemeal instances of Japanese troops moving South along the Coast. The patrol would last about four weeks until December 4, 1942.

During that time, the Raiders engaged in several small unit skirmishes that resulted in about 500 Japanese killed, and numerous others injured. Carlson's Raiders suffered only 16 killed and 17 wounded. However, jungle diseases took a far greater toll on the Raiders, including their commander. Carlson would earn his third Navy Cross on the Long Patrol.

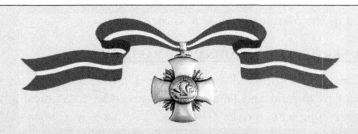

The President of the United States of America takes pleasure in presenting a Second Gold Star in lieu of a Third Award of the Navy Cross to Lieutenant Colonel Evans Fordyce Carlson (MCSN: 0-3613), United States Marine Corps Reserve, for extraordinary heroism and distinguished service as Commanding Officer of the SECOND Marine Raider Battalion in action against enemy Japanese forces at Guadalcanal, in the British Solomon Islands, during the period from 4 November 1942 to 4 December 1942. In the face of most difficult conditions of tropical weather and heavy growth, Lieutenant Colonel Carlson led his men in a determined and aggressive search for threatening hostile forces, overcoming all opposition and completing their mission with small losses to our men while taking heavy toll of the enemy. His personal valor and inspiring fortitude reflect great credit upon Lieutenant Colonel Carlson, his command and the United States Naval Service.

Carlson's Raiders, the Marines of the Second Marine Raider Battalion, were hailed as heroes from a country desperate for heroes in World War II. They had secured their place in Marine Corps lore for eternity with their Long Patrol.

On March 15, 1943, the now four Marine Raider battalions were placed under the control of the newly created First Raider Regiment, commanded by the former commander of the Third Raider

Beyond Belief: True Stories of Marine Corps Heroes

Battalion, Colonel Harry B. Liversedge. A week later Carlson was relieved as commander of the Second Raider Battalion by Lieutenant Colonel Alan Shapley, an officer of much more orthodox thinking, and Carlson was made Executive Officer of the **First Raider Regiment.** Within a month, Shapley had reorganized the **Second Raider Battalion** into a traditional organization, and Liversedge then standardized the organization of the four raider battalions along the lines of the **First Raider Battalion,** although all of them adopted the three fire-team squad organization pioneered by Carlson. It was soon adopted by the Marine Corps as a whole.[14]

<u>LATER SERVICE, RETIREMENT AND EARLY DEATH</u>

Carlson was ordered back to the United States for medical treatment of malaria and jaundice, and served as a technical advisor to Walter Wagner's movie *Gung Ho!: The Story of Carlson's Makin Island Raiders* that was released in December 1943.

He subsequently returned to the Pacific campaign and participated in the **Battle of Tarawa** in November 1943, as an observer, and was cited for volunteering to carry vital information through enemy fire from an advanced post to division headquarters. During the **Battle of Saipan** in 1944, he was wounded while attempting to rescue a wounded enlisted radioman from a front-line observation post, and was awarded his second Purple Heart.

It seemed Carlson's gunshot wound to his shoulder was a lot worse then first thought. He had several surgeries to try and ease the constant pain he felt. Several bone grafts wee unsuccessful, and he was put on sick leave back in the United States.

Physical disability resulting from wounds received on Saipan caused Carlson's retirement on July 1, 1946. He was advanced to the rank of Brigadier General on the retired list at that time for having been specially commended for the performance of duty in actual combat.

Despite the pain in his arm, Carlson continued an aggressive speaking tour. Around Christmas 1945, he began to feel pain in his

---

[14] Hoffman, Maj. Jon T., (USMC). *Creating the Raiders: From Makin to Bougainville. Marine Raiders in the Pacific War,* October 2013.

arm and chest. He told no one, not even his second wife Peggy. He wrote the pain in his chest off as simply a chest cold and the pain in his arm as being from his many surgeries. Finally, a mere few days after Christmas 1945, he was admitted to the hospital having suffered a heart attack. It would not be his last.

Carlson did not have time left . . . .he was wearing out and wearing down from all his years of hard service, the lingering pain in his arm, and now a damaged heart. He was too weak to continue giving more impassioned speeches around the country, or to even meet with reporters and supporters at his home for very long. He moved to a nursing home outside of Portland, Oregon, in the town of Brightwood. He died on May 27, 1947, at age 51.

In death, as in life, the Marine Corps brass seemed determined to heap one more humiliation on the Marine who had given so much of his life to the Corps, but had essentially been a burr in the saddle of the Marine Corps hierarchy. Evans Fordyce Carlson had been a hero to the American people in the early days of the war, when the American public so desperately needed a bright, shining light in those dark early days. His daring raids captured the American spirit and showed the country that, indeed, there was light at the end of the tunnel. It reassured them that brave Americans existed who could defeat the Japanese, given time.

On June 4, 1947, Carlson was buried in Section 1, Lot 653, at Arlington National Cemetery. But even in death, Evans Carlson would continue to be humiliated by the Corps. Most military headstones carry recognition of Military Awards – especially valor awards. Carlson's headstone gives no hint of the fact that that he received three Navy Crosses and two Purple Hearts.

There were no tributes to Carlson from either peer Marine Corps officers or top brass. The newspapers, however, provided lavish coverage. Marine Corps Commandant General Alexander Vandergrift paid his respects, but was one of the few Marines participating in the ceremony officially. There was a very sparse crowd at the interment and most were there were there at the behest of Carlson's family. The *Washington Post* wrote about it in an editorial entitled *"Honor Slighted,"* and referred to the lack of official Washington's participation as *"shabby treatment"* for one of its war heroes.

Why was this so? Well, there was much jealousy over Carlson's relationship with President Roosevelt and his son, James. Carlson's letters directly to the President outside of the chain-of-command wasn't a simple matter of jealousy – his peers harbored an animosity over this slight. Nowhere is this more evident then when he was essentially stripped of his command mere months after the very successful **Long Patrol**. Yes, Carlson was sick with malaria at the time, but even after he recovered from malaria, he was still only allowed to be an observer for the rest of the war. He was never given a command again. That speaks loudly as to how he was viewed by Marine hierarchy.

CARLSON'S LEGACY

So, what was Evans Carlson's legacy, not only to the Marine Corps but to the country as a whole?

In the early planning for this volume of Marine Heroes, I asked the editor for this assignment. You see, I was fortunate enough to have been taught in high school by a man who was a **Carlson Raider**. His name was James Arneberg.

As we get older, we tend to think of those teachers who had a great influence on us. Mr. Arneberg was one of those for me. You see, he wasn't really Mr. Arneberg – he was Arne. And as I wrote this story, I could see those traits of Evans Carlson in my teacher Arne. He was tough, but fair. He was principled – no cheating would ever be allowed. If you won, you had to do it fair and square. There were no favorites – everyone was equal. As I look at myself today, I see myself as having *some Arne* in me who, of course, had a lot of Evans Carlson in himself. I am so thankful for that.

James Roosevelt went on to have a storied career as a soldier and a citizen, being a six term Congressman from California.

"None of the successes matched his time with Carlson."
According to his widow, Mary Roosevelt, up to his August 13,

Evans Fordyce Carlson (USMC)

1991, death in Newport Beach, California, Roosevelt claimed that his service with the Raiders was absolutely "'the love of his life'. He liked the fact that everybody was in this together with no favorites. To some extent I think he enjoyed the anonymity. Not that he was completely anonymous, but he liked that there were no favorites." She repeated James's assertion that if he were to be remembered for one achievement, he would want it to be his work for and with the Raiders."[15]

In his book, **American Commando**, John Wukovits detailed the many recollections that the Raiders had of their leader, Evans Fordyce Carlson, from their reunions. The comments below, from Mr. Wukovits book, detail Evans Carlson's legacy.

Captain Washburn of Company E of the **Second Raider Battalion**, who went on to embark on a profitable business career attributed his successful trademarks to lessons learned in commanding the men of Company E. Those admiral attributes are decency, trust, hard work, and equity. In a 1980 interview he credited Carlson for showing him how to handle his employees.

A tapestry of individual gallantry weaves the story of the **Second Raider Battalion**. The Raiders could not have fashioned their legacy without Carlson and Roosevelt's calm guidance at the helm. These leaders, likewise, could not have registered their lofty deeds without the contributions of men like Captain Washburn, Lieutenant Miller, and Transport Madhakian.

"Once I walked with Giants," proclaimed Private John Cotter of Company D. *"Nowhere have I known men like the Raiders."*[16]

Evans Carlson was both a warrior and a man of peace, I leave you with a quote from Douglas MacArthur.

"The soldier above all others prays for peace, for it is the Soldier who must suffer and bear the deepest wounds and scars of the war."

---

[15] John Wukovits, *American Commando: Evans Carlson, His WWII Marine Raiders, and America's First Special Forces Mission*, NAL Caliber, A division of Penguin Group, USA, New York.

[16] Ibid.

Beyond Belief: True Stories of Marine Corps Heroes

Evans Carlson was really a man of peace. His early passing at 51 years of age, shows that he wore the deepest wounds and scars of war.

John Basilone (USMC)

Machine Gun Hero

BY JIM FAUSONE

The service of John Basilone, a Medal of Honor and Navy Cross recipient, is unbelievable and made more remarkable in that the only U.S. Coast Guardsman to ever receive the Medal of Honor, Douglas Munro, saved Basilone's life. Only with the backdrop of the World War II Pacific Theater could this be possible. Not even Hollywood could dream up this story. John Basilone served both in the Army and in the Marines, so both services can claim his heroics. He has been called one of the most badass Marines in history. Even

today, Marines visit and pay honor to a statue of *"Manila John"* in Washington, DC.

EARLY LIFE

Giovanni (John) was born to a large and loud Italian-American family with roots in Buffalo, New York. and Raritan, New Jersey. The ten children in this Catholic family would not have been unusual in the early 1900s. John was the sixth child born to Salvatore, who emigrated from Italy, and Theadora, who grew up in New Jersey. Theadora's parents had also emigrated from Italy. In classic fashion, Sal and Theadora met at a church gathering and they married three years later. John was born on November 4, 1916, at home in Buffalo.

Beyond Belief: True Stories of Marine Corps Heroes

The family returned to Raritan in 1918, as Buffalo averages 89 inches of snow each year as compared to New Jersey's 25 inches and 50 more days of sunshine. The Basilones were back home near the big extended Italian family. Basilone grew up in the nearby Raritan Town (now Borough of Raritan) where he attended St. Bernard Parochial School. After completing middle school at age 15, he dropped out prior to attending high school.

Raritan was a small town in 1920 with 4,500 people, and today its size has not doubled. The area is between New York City to the northeast and Allentown, Pennsylvania, to the west. The Delaware and Raritan Canal (D&R Canal) was built in the 1830s to connect the Delaware River to the Raritan River. It was an important feature of the agricultural area. This was a time of peace and expected prosperity. A strong hard-working young man could make his way in the world, even if he did not have clear direction. In 1931, after dropping out of school, Basilone worked as a golf caddy for the local country club before joining the military. But the world was about to change.

Two events occurred that would have been in the news in 1932, but would not have been of interest to young John who was free from the constraints of education. First, World War I veterans were making their way to Washington, D.C., to demand the bonus payments they had been promised. This should have foretold  John that not all promises to military recruits are kept. As reported by the National Park Service:

"In the years after World War I, a long battle over providing a bonus payment to WWI veterans raged between Congress and the White House. Presidents Harding and Coolidge both vetoed early attempts to provide a bonus to WWI veterans. Congress overrode Coolidge's veto in 1926, passing the World War Adjusted Compensation Act, otherwise known as the Bonus Act.

"The act promised WWI veterans a bonus based on length of service between April 5, 1917 and July 1, 1919; $1 per day stateside and $1.25 per day overseas, with the payout capped at

John Basilone (USMC)

$500 for stateside veterans and $625 for overseas veterans. The catch was this bonus would not pay out until each veteran's birthday in 1945, paying out to his estate if he should die before then...

In May 1932, jobless WWI veterans organized a group called the "Bonus Expeditionary Forces" (BEF) to march on Washington, DC. Suffering and desperate, the BEF's goal was to get the bonus payment now, when they really needed the money..."

"By summer, at least 20,000 people had joined the camps, with some estimates putting the total number above 40,000. Many were joined by their families."[17]

President Hoover called out the Army to push the Bonus Army out of the nation's capital. That action impacted Presidential politics and ultimately Congress. With Democrats holding majorities in both houses, they passed the Adjusted Compensation Payment Act in 1936, authorizing the immediate payment of the $2 billion in World War I bonuses, overriding President Roosevelt's veto of the measure.

Second, young John should also have noted in the news that the NSDAP (Nazi Party) won more than 38% of the vote in German federal election in July 1932. The seeds of the next World War had been planted. Little did the Raritan caddy know how the world winds were blowing, and if he could rely on the nation's promises to its servicemen.

THE FIRST STINT

Storm clouds were brewing in Europe and in the Pacific. The Nazis were causing rumbling in Europe; and the Japanese were causing rumbling in China and the Pacific. After World War I there was a natural drawdown of the U.S. armed services. A modest rebuilding of the force strength began during the 1930s under the War Department Chief of Staff, General Douglas MacArthur from 1930 to 1935.

During the same period, the economic crash had many young men looking for gainful employment to support their families. In 1933, Congress passed an act that put large numbers of jobless young

---

[17] https://www.nps.gov/articles/bonus-expeditionary-forces-march-on-washington.htm

141

men into reforestation and other reclamation work. President Roosevelt directed the Army to mobilize these men and thereafter to run their camps making the Civilian Conservation Corps (CCC) program. This was not a job the Army wanted; but options were limited.

One additional option for a hungry and unemployed young man was to join the regular Army. After John Basilone turned 18 years old, he enlisted in the Army in July 1934. As an infantry grunt, Basilone completed basic training and after stateside training, had his first overseas assignment to the Philippines.

The American military had been in the Philippines since the end of the **Spanish-American War** under terms of the Treaty of Paris, when the United States took possession of the Philippines from Spain. This arrangement had to be implemented by force in 1898 and American troops were still on the Island in the mid-1930s. Philippine Independence would not be achieved until July 4, 1946, when the United States declared the Philippines an independent nation.

Basilone's tour in the islands would have been exotic for a New Jersey boy with little risk of engagement. He enjoyed the food, temperature, women, and comradery of his Army buddies. When he left the Army and returned stateside, he often thought about how to get back to Manila. He drove a truck for three years in Raritan, but the tropical breezes of Manila were always on his mind. The coldest month on average in Manila measured 78 degrees and no snow. John had to feel it was much better than Buffalo, New York or New Jersey. Good duty if you could get it.

John thought about getting back to that good duty and felt his best opportunity to get back to Manila was with the Marines.

THE SECOND STINT

When asked about re-enlisting or multiple tours, a common refrain from veterans is, *"It was a blast....but I would never do it again."* Maybe for most men it is the pull of a normal life, or family, or age, or wisdom, but at 24 years old, John had no such pull to stay in New Jersey. Also, a more experienced John would at this time have been aware of the world events with the Axis war in Europe and Japanese aggression in China.

John Basilone (USMC)

The United States was getting prepared for a war that seemed inevitable. Congress passed several laws related to national defense, including the **Selective Training and Service Act of 1940**, which provided for drafting and training men for the Army, Navy, Marines, and National Guard. More than 16 million men registered for the draft. Congress authorized money to build planes and ships, housing for soldiers, and established new military bases across the country. In this backdrop, Basilone joined the Marines in June 1940.

He did his initial training like all Marines, although he was older and more experienced based on the Army stint. He was sent to Guantanamo Cuba as his first overseas assignment with the Marines. His next assignment would not be as idyllic.

GUADALCANAL

The name *"Guadalcanal"* is said with reverence in the Marine Corps. Even today, finding it on a map in the Pacific would be a challenge for most Americans. There have been dozens of movies made about the Guadalcanal campaign depicting heroes on air, sea and land. That tradition continued in 2005 with the film, *"I'm Staying with My Boys: The Heroic Life of Sgt. John Basilone, USMC."*

As part of the Solomon Island chain, Guadalcanal was the first land campaign against the Japanese in World War II. The Battle of Guadalcanal, code named *Operation Watchtower* by American forces, was fought between August 7, 1942, and February 9, 1943. Since Pearl Harbor on December 7, 1941, the Pacific war had been primarily a sea campaign and Japan moved swiftly throughout the Pacific taking islands at will. Nine months after that fateful day, amid a string of stunning American defeats, it was time for the United

Beyond Belief: True Stories of Marine Corps Heroes

States to show it could fight the mighty Japanese Army, and beat it. In *Operation Watchtower* the reputation and honor of the U.S. Marine Corps hung in the balance.

On August 7, 1942, America mounted its first major amphibious landing of World War II at Guadalcanal, using innovative landing craft built by **Higgins Industries** in New Orleans. The goal was to capture a strategic airfield site on the island (later named **Henderson Field** for a U.S. pilot lost in the Battle of Midway). This island was the furthest south that the **Rising Sun Empire** had captured, and to halt Japanese efforts to disrupt supply routes to Australia and New Zealand, victory was paramount but uncertain. The invasion ignited a ferocious struggle marked by seven major naval battles, numerous clashes ashore, and almost continuous air combat over eight months.

The Solomon Islands remain strategically important almost 100 years later. In 2022, China, having learned from World War II, signed a new security pact with the island-nation for ship visits, logistical replacement, protection of the safety of Chinese personnel, and major projects. In the future, American blood may again have to be shed on Guadalcanal.

The men who landed ashore at Guadalcanal in 1942 upheld the lore of the Marine Corps tradition in blood, sweat, and fear. Getting ashore turned out to be easier than predicted by the war planners, but holding the island airfield was harder than anticipated.

The Navy, with the assistance of Coast Guardsman, gave the Marines a ride to share. The boat of choice was the **Higgins Landing Craft.** They would be famous for the D-Day landing at Normandy, France, nearly two years later. Their wooden construction and flat bottom drew  almost no draft. Its innovation was the front-lowering ramp that enabled the men to disembark quickly. (With previous boats, men had to jump over the sides, exposing them to enemy fire.) The ramp allowed for a more orderly landing − although it was certainly still risky. Dissatisfied with the landing boats designed by the Navy, the

John Basilone (USMC)

United States Marine Corps tested several commercial designs in the late 1930s, eventually settling on the former bootlegger boat designed by the Higgins Boatbuilding Company.

SEMPER PARATUS AIDS SEMPER FIDELIS

After ferrying Marines to Guadalcanal, the U.S. Coast Guardsmen (Coasties) under the command of the Navy, stayed on the island through August 1942. Coasties also served as signalmen from the shore to the ships off the coast. Signalman First Class Douglas A. Munro set up blinkers to signal the ship at night until he returned to his ship.

However, in September a plan by the commander of the Fifth Marines did not proceed as envisioned. As the Higgins boats approached the shore on September 27, they were forced to re-direct due to coral reefs. After they successfully landed the men further down the cove, the boats returned to their operating base. The Marines were quickly trapped between a larger enemy force and the sea. Having lost the radio which was their only means of communication to call in supporting aerial bombardment, the men used their white shirts to spell *"HELP"* on the sand. This attracted the attention of a Marine Corps dive bomber who communicated the situation to the command post. Relief was immediately organized and Coast Guard Signalman Doug Munro volunteered to lead the rescue effort.

"Munro led a group of 10 Higgins boats toward the island under continuous strafing fire by the enemy. With four other boats, he approached the shore and attracted the enemy fire while the other 20 landed to evacuate the Marines. As the rescue craft left the island, one fully loaded boat was stranded on the coral reef. Munro pulled his own boat between the shore and the trapped boat in order to divert the enemy fire. On the disabled boat, the abled-bodied Marines climbed into the water to

lighten the load and release it from the coral. Once free, it turned toward the sea and departed, Munro's boat behind it. In the next few seconds, Doug Munro was shot in the back of the head and as he lay dying in Ray Evans' arms, his final words were 'Did they get off?' "[18] (Dexter, 1942).

Amongst the Marines rescued that day was future Medal of Honor recipient Sergeant John Basilone. For his sacrificial courage, the Canadian-born United States Coast Guardsman from Cle Elum, Washington, was awarded the Medal of Honor. Although the Coast Guard has served in every war in our nation's history, and its sailors have earned many combat decorations including the Navy Cross and Silver Star, Douglas Munro is the only Coast Guardsman to be awarded the Medal of Honor.

The President of the United States of America, in the name of Congress, takes pride in presenting the Medal of Honor (Posthumously) to Signalman First Class Douglas Albert Munro, United States Coast Guard, for extraordinary heroism and conspicuous gallantry in action above and beyond the call of duty as Petty Officer in Charge of a group of 24 Higgins boats, engaged in the evacuation of a battalion of Marines trapped by enemy Japanese forces at Point Cruz Guadalcanal, on 27 September 1942. After making preliminary plans for the evacuation of nearly 500 beleaguered Marines, Munro, under constant strafing by enemy machineguns on the island, and at great risk of his life, daringly led five of his small craft toward the shore. As he closed the beach, he signaled the others to land, and then in order to draw the enemy's fire and protect the heavily loaded boats, he valiantly placed his craft with its two small

---

[18] www.cmohs.org/news-events/blog/douglas-a-munro-the-coast-guards-only-medal-of-honor-recipient/

guns as a shield between the beachhead and the Japanese. When the perilous task of evacuation was nearly completed, Munro was instantly killed by enemy fire, but his crew, two of whom were wounded, carried on until the last boat had loaded and cleared the beach. By his outstanding leadership, expert planning, and dauntless devotion to duty, he and his courageous comrades undoubtedly saved the lives of many who otherwise would have perished. He gallantly gave his life for his country.

BACK ON THE ISLAND

The first few months on Guadalcanal were brutal. The Imperial Japanese Army fought bravely but the Marines had a similar resolve. Japanese soldiers clearly would rather die than dishonor the Emperor or disobey an order. Strategic moves were made by each side, sometimes costing hundreds of lives. It is reported that up to 30,000 Japanese and 7,000 Americans died in the battle for this rock in the Pacific. The Marines ran low on rations and supplies. After a while, malaria and dysentery took its toll and reduced the fighting force of 19,000 Marines. John Basilone had to be thinking about promises made for supplies, and the broken promises to the troops.

In late October, 1942, the man known to his friends as *"Manila John"* Basilone would find himself in the fight of his life – one that would turn him into a war hero. **Bloody Ridge** was the key high ground above Henderson Field. He and the two machine gun sections under his command held off an attack by a far numerically superior Japanese force. He was one of only three Marines in that group to survive.

That territory had to be held to secure the airfield from which the American *Cactus Air Force was flying.* **Henderson Field** was important to Allied air efforts for the South Pacific. *Cactus Air Force* referred to the ensemble of Allied air power assigned to the island during the early stages of the Guadalcanal Campaign from August 1942 until December 1942, particularly those operating from **Henderson Field**. The term *"Cactus"* was derived from the Allied code name for the island.

Basilone's unit came under attack by a regiment of about 3,000 soldiers from the Japanese Sendai Division using machine guns, grenades, and mortars against the American heavy machine guns. The Sendai were experienced elite fighters like the Marines. Basilone commanded two sections of machine guns which fought for the next two days until only Basilone and two other Marines were left standing. The machine guns Basilone commanded were the M1917 Browning. It was a crew-served, belt-fed, water-cooled machine gun capable of 450 rounds per minute with a range over 3,500 yards. The M1917 weighed in at a hefty 47 pounds.

As in any long battle, ammunition became critically low. Basilone fought through hostile ground to resupply his heavy machine gunners with urgently needed supplies. He moved an extra gun into position and maintained continual fire against the incoming Japanese forces. He then repaired and manned another machine gun, holding the defensive line until relief arrived. When the last of the ammunition ran out shortly before dawn on the second day, Basilone, using his pistol and a machete, held off the Japanese soldiers attacking his position. By the end of the engagement, Japanese forces opposite the Marines' lines had been virtually annihilated.

"Valor in Action" was a painting by Marine Corps Artist Charles Waterhouse depicting Basilone (upper left), single-handedly holding off hordes of attacking Japanese with his Browning Automatic Rifle on *"Bloody Ridge"* at Guadalcanal.

In the **Battle of Bloody Ridge** a few Marines, and most notably John Basilone, held the high ground above **Henderson Field**. The following month after the decisive Naval Battle of Guadalcanal (November 12 – 15, 1942), the Japanese abandoned their attempts to retake Henderson Field, although scattered fighting would continue on Guadalcanal for a few more months.

For his own critical role in the Battle of Bloody Ridge, Sergeant John Basilone was awarded the Medal of Honor.

The President of the United States of America, in the name of Congress, takes pleasure in presenting the Medal of Honor to Sergeant John Basilone (MCSN: 287506), United States Marine Corps, for extraordinary heroism and conspicuous gallantry in action against enemy Japanese forces, above and beyond the call of duty, while serving with the First Battalion, Seventh Marines, FIRST Marine Division in the Lunga Area. Guadalcanal, Solomon Islands, on the night of 24 - 25 October 1942. While the enemy was hammering at the Marines' defensive positions, Sergeant Basilone, in charge of two sections of heavy machineguns, fought valiantly to check the savage and determined assault. In a fierce frontal attack with the Japanese blasting his guns with grenades and mortar fire, one of Sergeant Basilone's sections, with its gun crews, was put out of action, leaving only two men able to carry on. Moving an extra gun into position, he placed it in action, then, under continual fire, repaired another and personally manned it, gallantly holding his line until replacements arrived. A little later, with ammunition critically low and the supply lines cut off, Sergeant Basilone, at great risk of his life and in the face of continued enemy attack, battled his way through hostile lines with urgently needed shells for his gunners, thereby contributing in large measure to the virtual annihilation of a Japanese regiment. His great personal valor and courageous initiative were in keeping with the highest traditions of the U.S. Naval Service.

Beyond Belief: True Stories of Marine Corps Heroes

A Hero's Homecoming

Basilone's Medal of Honor was presented in Australia by Major General Alexander A. Vandegrift on May 21, 1943. News coverage of *"Manila John's"* heroic stand catapulted him into instant fame, something the young man tried to shy away from without much success. His photo and reports of his action was published in every major newspaper, as well as magazines, back in the United States.

As was common for those that received the Medal of Honor at that time, the War Department used the men for patriotic purposes at home. They were quickly returned stateside, in part to keep the recipient safe after going through hell, but also to be paraded around to speak at war bond drives and to promote recruitment. Most of these heroes disliked the "dog and pony show" their action and subsequent fame had brought them. In the latter months of 1943, Basilone was the best show in town.

A September 1943 parade in Raritan, New Jersey, drew a huge crowd. The parade made national news in Life Magazine and Fox Movietone News. After the parade, Basilone toured the country raising money for the war effort and achieved unprecedented celebrity status. Hundreds of War Bond tours and rallies took place in the United States. Hollywood stars and starlets were often the attraction and military heroes like Basilone were in demand. Over the course of the war, 85 million Americans purchased bonds totaling approximately $185 billion.

Such tours were indeed an important role thrust upon Medal of Honor recipients, and others who achieved fame for their combat roles during the war. They remained, nevertheless, a difficult adjustment for obscure Soldiers, Sailors, Airmen and Marines who were suddenly pulled from the war zone, where they had a sense of belonging among their comrades, and catapulted into the American

x

150

John Basilone (USMC)

spotlight. Ira Hayes, a Native-American Marine who years later would endure the *"dog and pony"* show in the closing days of the war as one of the Marines depicted in Joe Rosenthal's famous photo of the flag raising over Iwo Jima, was literally crushed by this unwelcomed duty.

The pressure continued even after the war, and he once noted, "I kept getting hundreds of letters. And people would drive through the reservation, walk up to me and ask, 'Are you the Indian who raised the flag on Iwo Jima?'" In fact, although he often spoke of his price in the Corps, he never talked about the event that made him famous. It drove him to drink to excess, eventually resulting in his premature death after an altercation on January 24, 1955, – so long-lasting was the pressure of being a *"war hero."* (It was later learned that Hayes was not the Native American depicted in the photo, but rather had participated in a second flag raising.)

Manila John, a good Marine, continued to follow orders despite his disdain for his new public role. He repeatedly requested to return to *"stay with my boys,"* but the Marine Corps denied each request, telling him he was needed more on the home front.

He was offered an officer commission, which he turned down. Later he was offered an assignment as an instructor, which he refused as well. Finally, his request to return to the fighting was approved. This time he did additional training on the west coast at Camp Pendleton. While at Pendleton, Basilone met and married Lena Mae Riggi, a sergeant in the Marine Women's Reserve serving as a field cook. They married in July 1944. Even his wedding turned into a *media circus*.

Marine Corps Gunnery Sgt. John Basilone and Lena Basilone on their wedding day July 10, 1944 at St. Mary's Star of the Sea in Oceanside, Calif. (Photo courtesy of St. Mary's Star of the Sea)

Beyond Belief: True Stories of Marine Corps Heroes

THE LAST STINT

Late in 1944, Gunnery Sergeant John Basilone finally received orders to return to the Pacific fight. The newlywed certainly knew what he was getting into — he was no longer the naive New Jersey boy looking for adventure and believing everything said by some slick military recruiter. But he was thrilled to at last going to be *"Staying with my boys."*

Returning to the fleet, Basilone was assigned to Company D, First Battalion, Twenty-Seventh Marine Regiment, FIFTH Marine Division. On February 19, 1945, the first day of the invasion of Iwo Jima, he was serving as a machine gun section leader. While the landing at Guadalcanal had been uneventful, even surprising to the Japanese, that was not the case on Iwo Jima. When the Marines landed, the Japanese concentrated their fire at the incoming Americans from heavily fortified blockhouses staged throughout the island.

Units were pinned down everywhere. Basilone flanked the side of the Japanese positions until he was directly on top of the blockhouse. He then attacked with grenades and demolitions, single-handedly destroying the entire strong point and its defending garrison.

Basilone then fought his way toward Airfield Number 1 and aided a Marine tank that was trapped in an enemy minefield under intense mortar and artillery barrages. He guided the heavy vehicle over the hazardous terrain to safety, despite heavy weapons fire from the Japanese. As he moved along the edge of the airfield, he was killed by Japanese mortar shrapnel or small arms fire.

His actions helped Marines penetrate the Japanese defense and get off the landing beach during the critical early stages of the Iwo Jima invasion. Basilone was posthumously awarded the Marine

John Basilone (USMC)

Corps' second-highest decoration for valor, the Navy Cross, for extraordinary heroism during the battle of Iwo Jima.

The President of the United States of America takes pride in presenting the Navy Cross (Posthumously) to Gunnery Sergeant John Basilone (MCSN: 287506), United States Marine Corps, for extraordinary heroism and devotion to duty while serving as a Leader of a Machine-Gun Section, Company C, First Battalion, Twenty-Seventh Marines, FIFTH Marine Division, in action against enemy Japanese forces on Iwo Jima in the Volcano Islands, 19 February 1945. Shrewdly gauging the tactical situation shortly after landing when his company's advance was held up by the concentrated fire of a heavily fortified Japanese blockhouse, Gunnery Sergeant Basilone boldly defied the smashing bombardment of heavy caliber fire to work his way around the flank and up to a position directly on top of the blockhouse and then, attacking with grenades and demolitions, single-handedly destroyed the entire hostile strong point and its defending garrison. Consistently daring and aggressive as he fought his way over the battle-torn beach and up the sloping, gun-studded terraces toward Airfield Number 1, he repeatedly exposed himself to the blasting fury of exploding shells and later in the day coolly proceeded to the aid of a friendly tank which had been trapped in an enemy mine field under intense mortar and artillery barrages, skillfully guiding the heavy vehicle over the hazardous terrain to safety, despite the overwhelming volume of hostile fire. In the forefront of the assault at all times, he pushed forward with dauntless courage and iron determination until, moving upon the edge of the airfield, he fell, instantly killed by a bursting mortar shell. Stouthearted and indomitable, Gunnery Sergeant Basilone, by his intrepid initiative, outstanding skill, and valiant spirit of self-sacrifice in the face of fanatic opposition, contributed materially to the advance of his company during the early critical period of the assault, and his unwavering devotion to duty throughout the bitter conflict was an inspiration to his comrades and reflects the highest credit upon Gunnery Sergeant Basilone and the United States Naval Service. He gallantly gave his life in the service of his country.

Beyond Belief: True Stories of Marine Corps Heroes

Basilone was one of only thirteen Marines in history to be awarded both of the highest valor awards a Marine could receive. He was also the second (of three) Medal of Honor recipients to be killed in combat after receiving the Medal of Honor. He was the only person ever to be subsequently killed in action in the same war in which he earned the Medal of Honor. His death solidified the military's penchant from removing Medal of Honor recipients from the battlefield in subsequent wars.

Basilone's wife Lena, originally from Oregon, remained in California after Johns' death and never remarried. She remained active with the Women's Marine Association and died in June 1999 at 86 years of age. She was buried at a VA National Cemetery in Riverside, California wearing her wedding ring, having turned down being interred at Arlington near her husband John because she didn't want to make a fuss.

In 1945, the U.S. Navy named a Gearing-class destroyer after John Basilone (DD/DDE-824; and it was christened by his widow. It served until 1977 when it was de-commissioned. In 2002 the U.S. Postal Service released a series of "Distinguished Marine" postage stamps. Included in the series was a postage stamp in memory and honor of Manila John Basilone. In 1922, a second destroyer (DDG-122) was commissioned.

John Basilone died while doing his duty to his utmost. On his left arm was a tattoo that read *"Death before Dishonor."* John lived by that motto. To this day, *"Manila John"* Basilone is one of the Marine Corps' unbelievable stories of heroism.

Gregory Boyington (USMC)

The Black Sheep Squadron

BY JIM FAUSONE

It may be polite to only focus on the positive exploits of Marine heroes, but to tell the true story it is important to recognize the faults and flaws that many of our Marine heroes had to overcome on the road to fame. Greg Boyington certainly had many faults and flaws. He also had the capacity to recognize his faults, if not overcome them, and learn from other men when given good advice. Those faults and flaws never stood in the way of him serving his country and meeting his duties as a United States Marine.

Colonel Gregory *"Pappy"* Boyington, USMC, was the *"bad boy"* hero of World War II that America needed in the Pacific Theatre. He led an ad hoc squadron of fliers known as the *Black Sheep*. The exploits of Pappy and his cohorts were captured in

Beyond Belief: True Stories of Marine Corps Heroes

Boyington's autobiography, **Baa Baa Black Sheep**, in 1958. He wrote well after World War II when he had time to reflect on his combat actions and time as a prisoner of war. But Boyington acknowledged the bad boy reputation was warranted, and maybe even cultivated. He didn't shy away from the bad boy reputation he had gained, and to some degree reveled in it. His story proves that there is hope for greatness, even by the screw ups, daredevils, and drunks.

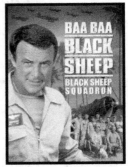

A television show in the 1970s made Pappy's Black Sheep wildly known to new generations. In 1970 Boyington and his squadron's unusual and often insubordinate antics were brought to life in a popular television show. Released as *"Baa Baa Black Sheep,"* with Robert Conrad staring as Boyington; it was re-named *"Black Sheep Squadron"* in its second and final season. The series itself was part military drama with an equal part of comedy, due in no doubt to Boyington's unusual but true-to-life characteristics. If some of the antics seem incongruous, those who knew *Pappy* Boyington knew that is was an uncannily realistic portrayal of an uncommon man and a unique Marine Corps hero.

THE PACIFIC NORTHWEST CULTURE

Gregory Boyington was born on December 4, 1912, in beautiful Coeur d'Alene, Idaho. The panhandle of Idaho has more in connection with Washington state than southern Idaho. It is dominated by a deep and pretty lake and is now considered up-and-coming. In the 1900s, it was very rural and known as timber country. He had Irish and Brule Sioux (a Lakota tribe) blood and genetics.

Native Americans have demonstrated their patriotism and war spirit defending the United States of America for decades before they were recognized as citizens. The Indian Citizenship Act of 1924 granted citizenship to the indigenous peoples of the United States. It was enacted partially in recognition of the thousands of Native Americans who served in the armed forces during World War I.

The Irish are also known for patriotism and a willingness to mix it up, particularly when alcohol is involved. An overly broad generalization, to be sure, but one has to wonder if Boyington's genetics may be a reason he was such a fighter and a drinker.

The family ultimately moved to Tacoma, Washington, where he was a wrestler at Lincoln High School. After graduation from high school in 1930, Boyington attended the University of Washington in Seattle, where he was a member of the Army ROTC. He was on the *Husky* wrestling and swimming teams, and for a time he held the Pacific Northwest Intercollegiate middleweight wrestling title. Wrestling was to be part of his life long after the war. He spent his summers working in Washington in a mining camp, a logging camp, and with the Coeur d'Alene Fire Protective Association in road construction.

He graduated college in 1934 with a bachelor's degree in aeronautical engineering. Aviation was clearly in his blood – he took his first plane ride when he was 6 years old. Boyington married in fall 1934 for the first time. His wife, Helen Clark, was 17 years old and bore him three children. Greg married Helen under his then name of Gregory Hallenbeck. He worked as a draftsman and engineer for Boeing in Seattle. His parents, the Hallenbecks, maintained an apple ranch in Okanogan, Washington.

BENDING THE RULES

Greg Hallenbeck had been a member of the Army ROTC program. He was commissioned a second lieutenant in the U.S. Army Coast Artillery Reserve in June 1934, after graduation, and then served two months of active duty with the 630th Coast Artillery at Fort Worden, Washington. In the spring of 1935, he applied for flight training under the Aviation Cadet Act, but he discovered that it excluded married men. Boyington had grown up as Gregory Hallenbeck, and assumed his stepfather, Ellsworth J. Hallenbeck, was his biological father. However upon receiving his birth certificate, he learned that his biological father was actually Charles Boyington, a dentist, and that his parents had divorced when he was an infant.

Greg really wanted to fly. Less than a year after being married, he used the name *"Gregory Boyington"* to enroll as a U.S. Marine Corps aviation cadet – there was no record of a Gregory Boyington being married. That also meant he could not claim any benefits of having a spouse or dependents at that time. But Greg wanted to fly, so he left his Army commission life behind.

By June 1935, he was in the U.S. Marine Corps Reserves on inactive status. He was assigned to Naval Air Station Pensacola for flight training. Boyington was designated a Naval Aviator on March 11, 1937, then transferred to Marine Corps Base Quantico for duty with Aircraft One, Fleet Marine Force. He was discharged from the Marine Corps Reserve on July 1, 1937, in order to accept a second lieutenant's commission in the Marine Corps the following day. He attended The Basic School in Philadelphia from July 1938 to January 1939. Upon completion of the course he was assigned to the Second Marine Aircraft Group at the San Diego Naval Air Station. He took part in fleet operations off the aircraft carriers *U.S.S. Lexington* and *U.S.S. Yorktown*. Promoted to first lieutenant on November 4, 1940, Boyington returned to Pensacola as an instructor in December.

Boyington was always looking to hop from one exciting possibility to the next. He wrote in his autobiography, *"I never completely got out of one situation before getting into another."* This was a challenge for the family and the three children he had with Helen. He was away from home a lot, even before the war, seeking the next adventure and paycheck. While he remained married for seven years, the financial burdens of family life always dogged him. Boyington, a father who was never around, claimed Helen neglected the children and they were placed with his parents. Their divorce naturally followed in 1941.

FLYING TIGERS

The next crazy opportunity came in August 1941. Boyington resigned his commission in the Marine Corps to accept a position with the **Central Aircraft Manufacturing Company** (CAMCO). CAMCO was a civilian firm that had been contracted to staff a Special Air Unit to defend China and the Burma Road from the Japanese. This later became known as the **American Volunteer Group** (AVG) or more commonly known as the *"Flying Tigers"* in Burma.

This was not about flying, fighting the Japanese, or defending the Chinese – but about money. Boyington was sure that between his well-known financial problems and drinking, he would be passed over for captain in the Marine Corps. Joining CAMCO was simply about a paycheck. Boyington, as always throughout his life, was in trouble with creditors and the IRS, and needed to make some quick cash. He was convinced that flying for CAMCO would lead to easy money. The group had contracts with salaries ranging from $250 a month for a mechanic to $750 for a squadron commander, roughly three times what they had been making in the US military. There was also a bonus to be paid for every Japanese airplane shot down.

The AVG was the brainchild of retired Army Air Corp Officer Claire Chennault. Recruited from civilians and from the active service ranks, 300 men were recruited by CAMCO – about 100 of whom were pilots from the Navy, Marines, and Army Air Corps. Active duty recruits were required to resign their commissions, as the pilots of the AVG would be required to serve as civilians in China, since the United States was not yet at war with the Japanese.

Boyington, and the others, were promised that upon resignation from AVG they could be reinstated with rank in the branch of service they had left. This 28-year old believed that bonus pay from shooting down ill-equipped Japanese planes would get him above water financially, and then he would return to the Corps with a clean slate. He claimed six air-to-air victories in his time with AVG, which would have given him the title "Ace," but ultimately he would only be officially credited with two. It was an issue that caused him considerable consternation throughout his career, and in retirement. Like most of military life, service with the AVG contained a lot of time waiting around. Boyington filled those hours arguing with his commanding officer, drinking copious amounts of whiskey, and enjoying the local women. Whether under the name Hallenbeck, or Boyington, it was who he was.

His escapades aside, during his time with the *Flying Tigers*, Boyington became an accomplished flight leader, but he was frequently in trouble with his commanding officer, Claire Chennault. This pattern would repeat itself during his subsequent military career.

Beyond Belief: True Stories of Marine Corps Heroes

In April 1942, he broke his contract with the AVG and returned on his own to the United States. The roughly eight months with the AVG did expose Boyington to real dog fights against Japanese pilots who were skilled, and he quickly learned that certain flying techniques could save your life. These were skills he would go on to employ and later add to his victory total. But while he became a better pilot, he did not become a better man.

BACK IN THE MARINES

While AVG was fighting in China, the United States declared war after the Japanese attack on Pearl Harbor on December 7, 1941. Boyington was itching to return to the fight with the Marines. His expectation was that the paperwork he signed prior to AVG was a golden ticket, but it was never going to be that easy. He sought reinstatement and was told to go back to Washington State and wait. Without a paycheck, clothes, or a purpose, the next three months found Boyington parking cars for 75 cents per hour — the same job he had in high school. After a fifth of bourbon he wrote a three-page letter for reinstatement and sent it to the Assistant Secretary of the Navy. That ranting letter may be lost to history, but it had the impact of getting him active duty orders and ultimately back in the fight in the Pacific.

THE SOLOMON ISLANDS

Major Boyington returned to the Marine Corps and was sent to the Solomon Islands where the Allies were stopping the Japanese advance, and attempting to turn the tide of the war, regaining lost territory. In late January 1943 the **Battle for Guadalcanal** wrapped up and *Operation Cleanslate*, the occupation of Russell Islands, was launched. United States forces saw the capture of these islands as the first step in the control of the Solomon Islands. It was the first stepping stone to push the Japanese army out of their strongholds in the region.

A major target in the Solomons was New Georgia, located 170 miles further north. Because of this, the Russell Islands had an advantageous position — at only 25 miles from Guadalcanal. Furthermore, once in U.S. possession, the Russells offered potential airfields, PT boat bases, and staging areas for future operations. The airfields became particularly important. Further, the Allies could simply not let the Japanese occupy the islands as they would pose a huge threat to Guadalcanal and American operations to the north. The Marine assault on the Russell Islands was not the grind of Guadalcanal, but the airstrips were important to the Allies.

As the air strike efforts jumped from island to island, providing transport support and other important assets, Boyington was still without a squadron or an opportunity to engage Japanese fighters. He seized on the opportunity to reconstitute a squadron that had been shut down because of a lack of planes, parts and pilots. Marine Fighting Squadron Two-Hundred Fourteen (VMF-214) was reconstituted in August 1942, on the island of Espiritu Santo in the New Hebrides. Its 27 pilots came under *Pappy* Boyington's command for the first time. At 31 years of age, older than his pilots, Boyington became known affectionately as *"Grandpa"* or *"Pappy."* *Pappy* Boyington's experience would make him an unusual and unorthodox commander – and certainly unforgettable.

Marine Attack Squadron Two Hundred and Fourteen - VMF 214 (*Black Sheep Squadron*) on Turtle Bay Fighter Strip, Espiritu Santo, New Hebrides, September 11, 1943. Giving instructions for flight. Note Major Gregory *"Pappy"* Boyington, (center). U.S. Navy photograph, now in the collections of the National Archives. (2016/06/28).

Beyond Belief: True Stories of Marine Corps Heroes

The VMF 214, known as the *Black Sheep*, got their hands on the Vought F4U F Corsair fighter. This beautiful and swift machine was a pilot's dream. It was fast and responsive and dove well when in a tight spot. The fighter's inverted gull wings gave the aircraft an unmistakably recognizable outline and was designed to provide ground clearance for the massive 13-foot propeller. This cobbled-together squadron, without the normal stateside training, found the Corsair ideal for their situation. Its 2,000 horsepower engine and top speed of 465 mph made it one of the fastest planes in theater. The Corsairs flown by VMF-214 were seldom flown by the same pilot every day. In fact, in a show of leadership that endeared him to his pilots, *Pappy* would always fly the plane in the poorest condition on every mission. The Black Sheep are credited with shooting down 97 Japanese aircraft and damaging another 103 during the squadron's two six-week tours of duty, making the Black Sheep one of the highest scoring flying outfits in the South Pacific at that time.

Marine Attack Squadron Two Hundred and Fourteen - VMF 214 (Black Sheep Squadron) on Turtle Bay Fighter Strip, Espiritu Santo, New Hebrides. They are shown before leaving for Munda, with an F4U in the background, 11 September 1943. Note, Major Gregory *"Pappy"* Boyington, 8th from left, front row. U.S. Navy photograph, now in the collections of the National Archives.

Gregory Boyington (USMC)

Boyington wanted to mix it up. He had command experience and age that should have resulted in a headquarters billet. Not *Pappy*.

In fact he regularly mixed it up with one of his group commanders, Colonel *Lard*, to the edge of insubordination. *Pappy* wrote about Lard, but acknowledged that his book and the TV show used the name *Lard* rather than his real nemesis at the time, Lieutenant Colonel Joseph Smoak.

The two had crossed paths back at flight school and the hostility intensified over time. Boyington saw *Lard* as an overweight, bureaucratic, paper-pusher. *Lard* sized Boyington up as a rule-breaking drunk. At one point, he ordered *Pappy* not to drink or he would be removed from flying. Once, when *Lard* removed *Pappy* from company squadron command, General James T. Moore interceded, countermanded the order, and chewed out Smoak. Many years later, in 2017, *Pappy* stated in a **History Net** interview, *"Lieutenant Colonel Joseph Smoak, operations officer of Marine Air Group 11, was a real by-the-book Marine, but unlike most of the characteristic backstabbers, he had pulled his time when it counted. He had served in China, and I respected him for that. I was simply the kind of officer he could not understand. I have no ill will toward him or anyone."*

Fate put in *Pappy*'s path, good men who kept him between the rails. Men like General *"Nuts"* Moore, Admiral Halsey, General Chesty Puller, and unnamed chaplains among them. Boyington reflected on the conversations with these men and many others in, **Baa Baa Black Sheep**. *Pappy* was a wildcard, but did listen to advice from those that he respected. His respect for *Nuts* was real and deep. He wrote, *"What I appreciated so much was that Nuts Moore told you the problem and then would sit back and listen while you told him how to go about getting it done."*

Boyington lived by the leadership principle, *"Never send somebody out on a mission that you, as squadron commander, would not go on yourself and always take the first of what promises to be ugly or bad missions."* This endeared him to the squadron, but put him constantly at risk. That stress played into the drinking, carousing and insubordination. But it also led to fast aerial combat pitting Corsairs against Zeros and *Pappy* against less experienced Japanese pilots. He racked up kill after kill. At times he worried he would not have another chance to mix it up.

After being denied four kills with the AFG, he had again, and officially, earned the title *"Ace."* As he approached World War II Ace Eddie Rickenbacker's record of 26 kills, the pressure of the media and press to predict when he would get that tie-breaking kill mounted. The original *"Fast Eddie,"* Rickenbacker was the United States' most successful fighter Ace in World War I and received the most awards for valor, including the Medal of Honor, by an American during the First World War.

Fate is a tricky thing, and karma is often a bitch. On January 3, 1944, on Bougainville, Major Boyington explained, *"I was to lead a fighter sweep over Rabaul, meaning two hundred miles over enemy waters and territory again."* With the protection of a wingman, Captain George Ashmum of New York City, *Pappy* splashed a Zero but in minutes the wingman was shot down. The two had been jumped by about 20 planes. *"I could feel the impact of enemy fire against my armor plate, behind my back, like hail on a tin roof. I could see the enemy shots progressing along my wing tips, making patterns"* recalled Boyington.

Boyington's Corsair engine went up in flames with no options – pulling up would direct the flames into the cockpit, and too low would leave him unable to bail out properly. He pulled the eject stick and flew through the canopy.

The chute popped, but did not have time to open, and then he was in the ocean submerging to avoid strafing by the Zeros. As he floated in the ocean, he took inventory of his injuries which included his left ear being almost torn off, shrapnel holes in his arms and shoulder, a left ankle shattered, and a large chunk of left-leg calf muscle missing. He was not thinking of the Ace record, but of surviving. He asked himself why a *Higher Power* would save a bum like him. After eight dangerous hours, he was recovered from the ocean by a submarine. As fate would have it, it was a Japanese submarine.

Gregory Boyington (USMC)

Five days after *Pappy* was shot down, the **Black Sheep Squadron** concluded their second combat tour in the Solomons, and the squadron was disbanded. The pilots were assigned to other squadrons and the legend of VMF-214 took on a life of its own. *Pappy* was assumed to be dead.

TWENTY MONTHS AS A PRISONER

When retrieved by the submarine, Boyington's emergency backpack was collected with his name stenciled on the pack. The Marine aviator **Ace's** reputation preceded him, and the Japanese knew who he was. He was to serve 20 months in two different camps on the mainland of Japan. Like all prisoners in Axis camps, he was starved, tortured, interrogated, and treated inhumanely.

OFUNA CAMP

The first prisoner of war camp was in a suburb of Yokohama at a Japanese naval camp known as Ofuna. This camp kept 70 - 90 *"special prisoners"* whom the Imperial Navy felt had military intelligence that could be extracted. Boyington spent March 1944 until April 1945 at Ofuna. At this secret intimidation camp, the prisoner names were never revealed to the Red Cross so the family back home did not know they were alive, and no communications or packages were received from the Red Cross. It was during this time he was shown a press release telling his story and announcing that he had been posthumously awarded the Medal of Honor and that his mother had christened a new carrier. He was pleased to hear about his mother and was shocked when the interrogator said Japan appreciated heroes and offered him a cigarette. There were small acts of kindness along with the brutal conditions that led to a badly healed ankle, beriberi, malnutrition, and losing 80 pounds − plummeting his weight to 110.

Over time, *Pappy* would be tasked with working in the camp kitchen with a civilian cook, preparing meals for the guards. This created the opportunity to steal food for himself and other prisoners. Two of the civilian cooks were aware of what was happening and either assisted or turned a blind eye. The additional food helped him and others regain weight, health and survive.

The President of the United States of America, in the name of Congress, takes pleasure in presenting the Medal of Honor to Major Gregory Boyington (MCSN: 0-5254), United States Marine Corps Reserve, for extraordinary heroism and valiant devotion to duty at the risk of his life above and beyond the call of duty as Commanding Officer of Marine Fighting Squadron TWO HUNDRED FOURTEEN (VMF-214), Marine Air Group ELEVEN (MAG-11), FIRST Marine Aircraft Wing, in action against enemy Japanese forces in the Central Solomons Area from 12 September 1943 to 3 January 1944. Consistently outnumbered throughout successive hazardous flights over heavily defended hostile territory, Major Boyington struck at the enemy with daring and courageous persistence, leading his squadron into combat with devastating results to Japanese shipping, shore installations, and aerial forces. Resolute in his efforts to inflict crippling damage on the enemy, Major Boyington led a formation of 24 fighters over Kahili on 17 October and, persistently circling the airdrome where 60 hostile aircraft were grounded, boldly challenged the Japanese to send up planes. Under his brilliant command, our fighters shot down 20 enemy craft in the ensuing action without the loss of a single ship. A superb airman and determined fighter against overwhelming odds, Major Boyington personally destroyed 26 of the many Japanese planes shot down by his squadron and, by his forceful leadership, developed the combat readiness in his command which was a distinctive factor in the Allied aerial achievements in this vitally strategic area.

OMORI CAMP

The special prisoners were moved out of Ofuna, an intelligence camp, to Omori, a labor camp. Omori prison camp was on an artificial island in Tokyo Bay, connected to the main city by a bamboo-slat bridge. This labor camp meted out physical punishment on a daily basis, and had some of the most feared guards in the country.

Gregory Boyington (USMC)

Other special prisoners at Ofuna and Omori with *Pappy* included former 1936 Olympic track athlete Louis Zamperini, an Army Air Forces Pilot. At the Berlin Olympics, Zamperini was a teammate of Jesse Owens and met Adolph Hitler. Louie was the subject of the bestselling book and hit movie, *"Unbroken."* He also struggled after the war and getting back to the United States, but ultimately Louie turned to religion  to find peace. He credits his wife with taking him to a Billy Graham revival that opened his heart and allowed him to release the hate and pain he held.

At Omori, the day involved picking up or breaking up rubble in the surrounding area of Yokohama. The prisoners were dressed in rags and lacked strength to efficiently perform such labor intensive work, but falling behind or taking a break resulted in beating and berating. Boyington always remembered the horrible conditions the ordinary Japanese citizens who he saw on the streets were in, and wrote that these civilians had treated the prisoners honorably.

It was at Omori that the imminent end of the war started to become clearer to the prisoners. As American B-29 planes flew over, the area was pounded. The prisoners rejoiced in the bombing, which they called *"Music"* so the guards would not punish the prisoners for their jubilation. As a new airframe, the B-29s had never been seen by the prisoners, but inspired awe and hope.

Even though the end was in sight, it became difficult for some prisoners to hang on. In August 1945, the atomic bombs dropped on Hiroshima and Nagasaki were unknown to the Omori prisoners. While Omori prison guards tried to explain what had occurred, it was incomprehensible to the prisoners. A guard with relatives in Nagasaki tried to explain it but he did not speak English, and *Pappy* wrote, *"I didn't fully believe it until after the war."* The lack of timely information was a byproduct of being a special captive.

On August 29, 1945, the special prisoners of Omori were released by way of Tokyo. The men were taken to a Tokyo POW Camp (Shinjuku) at Tokyo Bay Area 35-140, until September 12, and then flown to Hawaii before being transported to California. Their health and well-being were of major concern, along with military debriefing and attending to financial and legal matters.

Major Gregory *"Pappy"* Boyington, USMC, flying Ace, who was reported missing for 16 months, as seen after his rescue from prison camp hospital at Aomori near Tokyo. Shown: Commander Harold E. Stassen, right of the staff of Admiral William F. Halsey, USN, greets Major. Boyington who later received the Medal of Honor for his actions during the war. Photograph dated August 29, 1945.

AWARDS AND DECLARATIONS

Boyington learned he received the Medal of Honor while in captivity from the Japanese. The nation thought he died when his plane was shot down and presented his award posthumously. Boyington, recalling his bad-boy reputation and the embarrassment he had sometimes brought upon his commanders, later jokingly wrote that the Marines probably would not have granted the award if they had known he was still alive. After the war, in December 1945,

Gregory Boyington (USMC)

Boyington was also awarded the Navy Cross, which he considered a *"booby prize"* presented with a two minute ceremony.

The President of the United States of America takes pleasure in presenting the Navy Cross to Major Gregory Boyington (MCSN: 0-5254), United States Marine Corps Reserve, for extraordinary heroism and distinguished service in the line of his profession as Commanding Officer and a Pilot of Marine Fighting Squadron TWO HUNDRED FOURTEEN (VMF-214), Marine Air Group ELEVEN (MAG-11), FIRST Marine Aircraft Wing, during action against enemy aerial forces in the New Britain Island Area on 3 January 1944. Climaxing a period of duty conspicuous for exceptional combat achievement, Major Boyington led a formation of Allied planes on a fighter sweep over Rabaul against a vastly superior number of hostile fighters. Diving in a steep run into the climbing Zeros, he made a daring attack, sending one Japanese fighter to destruction in flames. A tenacious and fearless airman under extremely hazardous conditions, Major Boyington succeeded in communicating to those who served with him, the brilliant and effective tactics developed through a careful study of enemy techniques, and led his men into combat with inspiring and courageous determination. His intrepid leadership and gallant fighting spirit reflect the highest credit upon the United States Naval Service.

The words describing *Pappy* as a *"daring,"* *"tenacious,"* *"fearless,"* and *"effective tactician"* certainly captures the character of Marine Major Gregory Boyington. So would *"hard-headed,"* *"stubborn,"* *"daredevil,"* and *"drunk."* But as was noted in the outset of his story, in polite society one should ignore faults and flaws and only recognize heroism.

The following day, the Medal of Honor which had been issued two years earlier, posthumously presented to his *widow* by President

Franklin D. Roosevelt, was presented by then President Harry S. Truman.

Boyington felt the Medal of Honor ceremony with other recipients was appropriately solemn and dignified. President Truman told them all, *"I would rather have this honor than be President of the United States."*

Truman had served in the Missouri National Guard and in World War I and was sent to France with an artillery unit. *Pappy* probably did not know that Truman, at the end of World War I, had told his unit, *"Right now, I'm where I want to be — in command of this battery. I'd rather be here than the president of the United States."*

<u>FINAL YEARS IN THE MILITARY</u>

Boyington's faults and flaws were in remission for a while, as he strove to live up to the honor of his awards. He recognized that capture prevented him from drinking, and that it had been a terrific benefit to him both mentally and physically. He had every stated intention to stay sober.

In the Honolulu stopover, *Pappy* once again met up with Major General *Nuts* Moore, who tried to give him good advice about post-war fame and challenges. Moore was ending his career and had civilian opportunities. Boyington was considering staying in the Corps, but because of his physical condition and the fact he had been out of operations for over two years, his military future had an expiration date on it, even if he did not know it.

A war bond tour for the Marines did occur; Medal of Honor recipients were often put on parade. These month-long bond tours always became boring, tedious and stressful. As Boyington tried to envision a future, he had to again deal with financial hardships. Prior to the war he had placed his service pay in a trust for his children. He entrusted a female friend, a *"drinking gal,"* to manage it, only to learn upon return that it was not done well. Neither he nor the children were getting all the money due. He should have known you could not trust the promises of a drunk.

As a Medal of Honor recipient, Lieutenant Colonel Gregory Boyington was in demand for parades, speaking engagements, and meet and greets. With that demand came all the trappings of instant and temporary celebrity. There is a long list of MOH recipients that find the stress of such celebrity status to result in alcoholism and bankruptcy. *Pappy* had brushes with both prior to his celebrity status, and was pulled back into the bottle by his Medal of Honor fame and the pressure it placed upon his post-war life.

The expiration of his military career came before he expected. The Medical Board, probably prompted by enemies from within the Corps, scheduled a review of his physical condition to determine his ability to continue to serve. The combat injuries and the POW-caused medical conditions certainly provided good grounds for his ultimate medical retirement. He was promoted to *"bird"* or full Colonel prior to his medical retirement in August 1947. This was a graceful end to a military career of a Medal of Honor recipient and World War II Ace that was always precarious at best.

He was officially credited with two air-to-air victories with the AVG, and twenty-two with the Marine Corps, two shy of Eddie Rickenbacker's twenty-six. The privilege of breaking that record went to fellow Marine Corps fighter pilot Joseph Foss, who bagged his 26th victory flying out of Guadalcanal on January 15, 1943.

THE FINAL FOUR DECADES

One lesson learned from those awarded the Medal of Honor, and life in the Marine Corps, is that life goes on for the living long past the fleeting time when valor and heroism are demanded and *Semper Fi* is the daily motto.

Back in the civilian world at age 35, Boyington had to face the most frightening enemies of all, his own faults and flaws. His story did not have the happy ending of Louie Zamperini, who found God and a purpose in Christian ministry focused on at-risk youth, which he had once himself been. Louie received the Distinguished Flying Cross but did not carry the burden of alcoholism or multiple marriages during his 97 years of life.

Financial issues would haunt Boyington constantly. He held various sales and marketing jobs, each for a few years. Companies attracted to him were often financially flawed themselves, hoping his fame would make the difference. His well-known drinking exploits had him representing a brewery for a while. A drunk should not own a bar or sell for a brewery, but Greg Boyington had to make a living.

For many years he refereed professional wrestling matches in California and surrounding areas. His fame was promoted, the adulation of the crowds was stimulating, being around the brawling fighters felt natural, the money was easy, and he could do the job while stinking drunk.

Another fault or flaw he returned home to were his revolving marriages that cost him money and energy. Upon returning to the United States he married for the second time in 1946, this time to a 32-year old woman. He married for a third time at age 47 to a 33-year old woman. At age 66, he married a fourth and final time in 1978 to Josephine Wilson, then 51 years of age. That marriage lasted ten years until his death in 1988, from terminal cancer.

Josephine survived him for another four years, dying at the age of 62. One can only hope somewhere along that marital road *Pappy* had found true love, or something that resembled it. While talking about press celebrity, which was a part of his personal life, Boyington wrote: *"For all this was not sufficient for a man who just wanted to be wanted, and for some reason, or another, had felt that he never had been since childhood."*

Pappy had been a favorite target of the press in the late 1940s and 50s because of his many faults, flaws and marriages. But over time he fell out of regular negative press coverage and his image was burnished in the 1970s with the television release of *Baa Black Sheep*.

It helped tremendously that handsome and popular actor Robert Conrad played Boyington. Conrad found ratings success from 1976 to 1978 as legendary tough-guy and World War II fighter Ace *Pappy* Boyington in the series which is still in regular cable television rotation. The show's success led Conrad to win a **People's Choice**

Gregory Boyington (USMC)

Award for Favorite Male Actor and a Golden Globe nomination for his performance.

For a man that craved being wanted, that had to feel somewhat like vindication to Boyington, even if he criticized the show for its lack of authenticity and *"Hollywood hokum."*

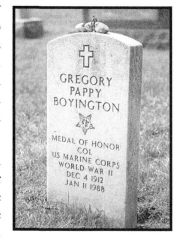

A decade after the television show ended, *Pappy*'s health finally caught up with him. His fourth wife Josephine was with him during hospice and at the end. He developed terminal cancer and died on January 11, 1988. He was buried with full military honors at Arlington National Cemetery.

Before his death Boyington had seen one child commit suicide. Another son graduated from the U.S. Air Force Academy in 1960 and retired from the U.S. Air Force as a lieutenant colonel. Boyington had many things to be proud of and many things to regret.

Colonel Gregory *"Pappy"* Boyington's life provides both inspiration and a cautionary tale. Greatness can be accomplished by those with faults and flaws. Overcoming those faults and flaws takes greatness. Friends and allies will often provide good advice that may be hard to hear and harder to live by. Only you can come to peace and understand that you are wanted.

John Peter Fardy (USMC)

Forgotten No More

BY JIM FURLONG

The birds sang happily as they chased one another through the trees. Otherwise, there was a stillness in the cemetery. The quiet foretold a typical hot, humid, August summer day at Holy Sepulcher Cemetery in suburban Chicago.

Up a slight hill and in the trees, a bagpiper wailed a wistful tune from his ancient instrument. *"O Danny Boy, the pipes, the pipes are calling."* The mourners stirred at the tune but remained respectfully silent.

As the piper finished his ballad, the birds in the trees resumed their calls to each other.

At that moment a young man appeared, a boy really − Shane Creedy, all of ten years old. Without amplification and a capella, in perfect pitch, he sang the *National Anthem,* and then *The Marine Corps Hymn.* But what he did next stunned those in attendance.

With all his heart poured into it, he sang:

> *"Ba dhúchas riamh dár gcine cháidh*
> *"Gan iompáil siar ó imirt áir*
> *"'S ag siúl mar iad i gcoinne námhad*
> *"Seo libh, canaídh Amhrán na bhFiann"*

Coming from the lips of the young man was the "Soldier's Song," the Irish National Anthem being sung in the ancient Gaelic.

> *"We're children of a fighting race*
> *"That never yet has known disgrace*
> *"And as we march, the foe to face*
> *"We'll chant a soldier's song"*

175

Beyond Belief: True Stories of Marine Corps Heroes

What was even as amazing – many of those in the crowd sang along in the ancient Gaelic. Men in their late 80's and early 90's were recalling the words from their long-ago childhood.

Who was this veteran being honored on this day by 80- and 90-year-old high school classmates? His name was John Peter Fardy, and he earned the Medal of Honor by his actions on May 6, 1945, nearly 66 years prior to this August 15, 2011, tribute on what would have been his eighty-ninth birthday.

So, who was John Fardy and why was this unknown guy included in the *Beyond Belief* series? Why is he included in a book with many Marine legends such as *"Manila John"* Basilone, Greg *"Pappy"* Boyington, and Evans Carlson, to name a few. It's a little more complicated than that, and has two starting points.

The second starting point is one of the most intriguing. In the year 2000, the Marine Corps started a project it called *Semper Fidelis – A psychological study of heroic bravery*. It was finished but never published. The study tried to focus on the characteristics of (at the time) 182 Marine Corps Medal of Honor Recipients since World War I. It had columns for name (obviously), hometown, education, siblings, and many other characteristics trying to narrow down the question – *"What is a hero?"*

It is fitting that the last bit of data gathered was a column with a record of tributes accorded those recipients. *"Google searches were conducted for all recipients. Five web sites sources were initially heavily relied upon: the United States Marine Corps Headquarters History and Museum Division, "Who's Who in Marine Corps History;" medalofhonor.com; Americans.net; C. Douglas Sterner's HomeofHeroes.com, and arlingtoncemetery.org."*[19]

Since Pearl Harbor, the Medal of Honor has been awarded to 82 Marines during World War II, 42 for actions in Korea, and 58 Marines received the award during the Vietnam."

"Across the United States, memorials and tributes abound for more than 100 Marine Medal of Honor recipients…

---

[19] Barrett, Terence W., PhD, *The Search for the Forgotten Thirty-Four,* Printed by CreateSpace. Publication Funded by Aftermath Research, Fargo, ND.

John Peter Fardy (USMC)

"Statues or monuments have been dedicated to twenty-three Marine recipients in their hometowns and war memorials or plaques to nine others. The Navy has commissioned fifty-five ships in the name of Marine Corps Medal of Honor Recipients. Fourteen public schools, seven VA Hospitals/Medical Centers or Clinics, six Veterans Nursing Homes, at least one Federal Building, six U.S. Post Offices, fourteen Marine Camps and bases, forty-one American Legion Posts/VFWs/AMVETs/Marine Corps Detachments, Reserve Centers, and Associations, one Disabled American Veterans Chapter, thirty-five buildings/halls/rooms, one National Guard Armory, one museum, and five airports have been named after them.

"Nationwide, names of Marine recipients has been dedicated to twenty-two streets/avenues/drives/roads, either highway, thirteen highway bridges and exchanges, three memorial pavilions and highway rest areas, fourteen parks and playgrounds, ten athletic fields and one college campus."[20]

But what was most surprising was not that most had received well deserved accolades and recognitions, but that thirty-four such heroes had received absolutely no recognition. Zero. Zilch. Certainly, the actions of these thirty-four heroic Marines deserved at least some recognition. Certainly, their actions exemplified *"gallantry and intrepidity,"* and rose to the level of being *"beyond the call of duty."* Their actions had demonstrated extraordinary courage and involved great personal risk which, for many of these thirty-four, resulted in their deaths'.

Armed with these names, Terence W. Barrett began researching their backgrounds for the book **The Search for the Forgotten Thirty-Four Honored by the U.S. Marines, Unheralded in Their Hometowns?** When the editor of this series, Doug Sterner, released the names of potential subjects for this **Beyond Belief** book about Marines, he cautioned his potential authors *"Please don't go for the low-hanging fruit, our Marine MOH recipients have been highly covered."* Of course, Fardy's name was not on the list of potential subjects. I highly recommend Dr. Barrett's book. The fact that

---

[20] Ibid.

Beyond Belief: True Stories of Marine Corps Heroes

almost 20% of the Marines earning the Medal of Honor since the beginning of World War II have gone unrecognized beyond the award is almost . . . well, *Beyond Belief.*

But Fardy is even more unique in some respects. Like the other thirty-three, there are no streets named after Fardy. There are no boulevards, highways, interchanges, or rest areas named for him. No Federal Buildings, Post Offices, Recruit Depots, Marine Corp Camps, or even mess halls or classrooms in these Camps named for Fardy. Schools, libraries, parks, or even playgrounds in his hometown do not carry his name.

The post-World War II housing boom hit the suburban Chicago community of Park Forest, about 25 miles south of downtown. It had streets in a new housing subdivision named after World War II Medal of Honor recipients, but Fardy's name was not included. Perhaps the fact that the Gaelic pronunciation of Fardy's name is "Far-*DAY"* caused concern for a developer a long way from the city center. But seriously?

Was Fardy's family called to the White House for a big ceremony with the President of the United States? No. The award was presented to the family by the Marine Corps League. Fardy's heroic actions came on May 6, 1945, two days before VE Day on May 8, about five weeks before VJ Day. After nearly four years of war, perhaps the country wanted to move on and put the war behind. I almost get that.

But what would happen next is the biggest slight of the hero, in my opinion. In 1949 Fardy's body was removed from its burial site on Okinawa and reinterred at Holy Sepulcher Cemetery in suburban Chicago. John Fardy gave his life for his Country –

heroically. But even his headstone did not indicate that he had ben awarded his country's highest honor, the Medal of Honor.

John Peter Fardy (USMC)

THE FIRST STARTING POINT

The first starting point for this story though, innocently enough, starts on a fall day in 1936. The annual ritual of class photos was taking place in the courtyard (now known as the John Peter Fardy Medal of Honor Memorial Courtyard) of Leo High School on West 79th Street in Chicago.

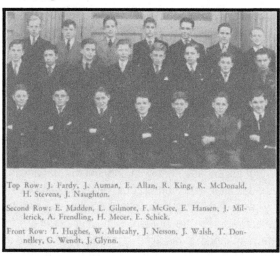

Top Row: J. Fardy, J. Auman, E. Allan, R. King, R. McDonald, H. Stevens, J. Naughton.

Second Row: E. Madden, L. Gilmore, F. McGee, E. Hansen, J. Millerick, A. Frendling, H. Mecer, E. Schick.

Front Row: T. Hughes, W. Mulcahy, J. Nesson, J. Walsh, T. Donnelley, G. Wendt, J. Glynn.

What makes this photo possibly unique among all class photos anywhere is, seen in this photo there is both a Medal of Honor recipient AND a Navy Cross recipient (this country's second highest award for heroism) – literally standing shoulder to shoulder. Top Row far left is John Fardy and standing next to him is Joseph Auman. Interestingly there is another person of some note in the photo. Bottom row second from right is George Wendt, Sr. Many will remember his son, George Wendt, Jr., who for many years played the beloved Norm Peterson in the television show *CHEERS*).

JOSEPH M. AUMAN

Private Joseph Martin Auman was born at Chicago, Illinois, January 4, 1922. He enlisted in the Marine Corps on August 27, 1940, at Chicago, soon after graduating from Leo High School. After duty at San Diego, Private Auman served at Guadalcanal where he was killed in action November 12, 1942. When his company was forced to make a temporary withdrawal, Private Auman, with utter disregard for his own personal safety, manned a machine gun and covered the retirement. Steadfastly remaining at his exposed position. he continued to fire his gun until killed by the enemy. For his gallant devotion to duty for his country, Private Auman was posthumously awarded the Navy Cross.

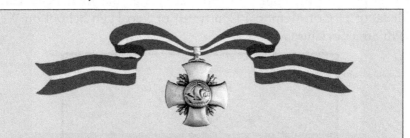

The President of the United States of America takes pride in presenting the Navy Cross (Posthumously) to Private Joseph M. Auman (MCSN: 293089), United States Marine Corps, for extraordinary heroism and devotion to duty while serving with Company E, SECOND Marine Raider Battalion during an engagement with the enemy Japanese forces at Asamana, Guadalcanal, Solomon Islands, on 11 November 1942. When his company was forced by overwhelming enemy fire to make a temporary withdrawal, Private Auman, with utter disregard for his own personal safety, manned a machine gun and covered the retirement. Steadfastly remaining at his exposed position, he continued to fire his gun until killed by the enemy. His dauntless courage and outstanding devotion to duty were in keeping with the highest traditions of the United States Naval Service. He gallantly gave up his life in the defense of his country.

Private Auman was a member of *"Carlson's Raiders,"* the Second Marine Raider Battalion. Another member of Auman's Company E was another Leo High School graduate named Lawrence *"Larry"* Spillan. Larry was a year younger than Joe Auman, but Joe's brother William was in his same graduating class. The Auman brothers and Spillan were known friends so it is probably no coincidence that Joe Auman and Larry Spillan were both *Carlson's Raiders,* and had participated in both the Makin Atoll Raid and The Long Patrol.

The Long Patrol began on November 6, 1942, in the search for Japanese fleeing from the north on Guadalcanal. On November 11, the fifth day of the patrol, the Raiders encountered the enemy.

John Peter Fardy (USMC)

"The patrols encountered nothing until 1000 hours, when E Company ran into a determined Japanese defense. Corporal John D. Bennett was leading his men across a field of Kunai grass when an unseen machine gun shattered the air with its hammering. Bennett was killed immediately along with several others while fellow Marine Private Pete Arias and two other survivors hit the dirt. Another fire team under Private Darrell Loveland tried to advance but was also pinned in the field. Small arms fire, mortars, and grenades pelted the Marines. Arias was pinned down only 20 yards from a Japanese machine gun. Fortunately, the enemy could not see him. Other Marines were not so lucky. Private James Van Winkle was hit three times as he tried to get to cover. Captain Throneson radioed Carlson that his company was engaged."[21]

"The Marines tore into their enemy with BARs and chattering .30-caliber machine guns. Pfc. Jesse Vanlandingham recalled, "It was like shooting birds. The guys in the front lines were mowing them down." Caught in the water, many Japanese troops never even had the chance to fire back. Still, the seasoned enemy veterans reacted quickly, setting up a machine gun of their own on the far bank. It drew Marine fire, but determined Japanese soldiers kept manning it. Each time the shooter was killed, another Japanese would take his place. Finally, several Marines led by Lieutenant Cleland Early crept close enough to throw grenades, silencing the machine gun for good. Checking the position, Early was almost killed when he turned over an enemy body and exposed a grenade the man was holding. Luckily the young Marine only took some fragments in one hand."[22]

"HE KNEW HE WOULD DIE... BUT HE KEPT FIRING."

"Within a short time, the expected counterattack happened, as two Japanese companies moved on Washburn's flank at 1130 hours. Washburn pulled his company back into the jungle a short distance and radioed a report to Carlson. The Japanese, believing they had repulsed a small enemy patrol, resumed crossing the

---

[21] Miskimon, Christopher, *Carlson's Long Patrol: Marine Raiders at Guadalcanal,* Warfare History Network Magazine, Late Fall, 2012.

[22] Ibid

river; some even paused to bathe. The Marines were not finished yet, though. Washburn reorganized his men and sent two platoons into a new attack while a third moved around to the north for a flank attack of its own.

"Having let their guard down, the Japanese were completely surprised, and many were killed in the Marines' deadly crossfire. As before, however, they recovered quickly and fought back, sending more mortar fire crashing into the American positions. Small attacks and counterattacks went back and forth in the humid, hot jungle. Marine Lieutenant Robert Burnette used his deadly shotgun to kill a Japanese only 10 yards away. Machine guns ripped from both sides, and grenades tore through foliage and human flesh alike. This went on for some six hours until the Marines began running out of ammunition. Now the greater enemy numbers started to tell. Washburn decided to pull back rather than risk being outflanked. The Japanese were slowly surrounding them.

"A trail going north through a gully provided the Raiders with a way out. Washburn placed a machine gun at its mouth to cover the retreat then pulled his platoons out one at a time. A young Marine, Private Joseph Auman, manned the gun and lay down covering fire as his Raider brethren escaped the Japanese trap. Before the 20-year-old Marine could make his escape, he was overwhelmed and killed. "He knew he would die," said Private Lathrop Gay. "But he kept firing." Auman was awarded a posthumous Navy Cross for his sacrifice, which allowed his company to fight again."[23]

In the same action, the same Company E, and within minutes of each other, Leo High School lost two graduates as Lawrence *"Larry"* Spillan was also killed in action. Further, later in the war in the Pacific, Joe Auman's brother and Larry Spillan's friend, Army Private First Class William Auman was killed on Okinawa on April 30, 1945, while serving with the 17th Infantry Regiment.

Back home in Chicago, the Auman family hung a flag in their front window with two Gold Stars — a flag no parent wants to be

---

[23] Ibid

authorized. Each gold star represents a son or daughter killed in service to their county — proof of the family's price paid in the cause of freedom.

JOSEPH M. AUMAN, (APD-117) TROOP TRANSPORT

The Navy, desperate to raise the morale on the home front, decided to name five ships after five Raiders who were killed in **The Long Patrol**. Among them was a destroyer named after Joseph Auman, but it was ultimately redesignated as a fast, troop transport.

The *U.S.S. Joseph M. Auman* (APD-117) was laid down on November 8, 1943, as DE-674 by Consolidated Steel Company, Orange, Texas, and launched on February 5, 1944. It was sponsored by Mrs. Bernard Tommey, aunt of Private Auman; reclassified APD-117 on July 17, 1944; and commissioned on April 25, 1945, with Lieutenant Commander H. A. Steinbach in command..

Following shakedown out of Guantanamo Bay, Cuba, *Joseph M. Auman* departed Norfolk, Virginia, on July 9, 1945, reaching San Diego on July 24 via the Canal Zone. She conducted more intensive training with the San Diego **Shakedown Group**, then embarked **Underwater Demolition Team No. 7** and carried them to Yoriage Beach, Shiogama, Japan for reconnaissance of landing beaches. After completing the mission, she returned the demolition group to San Diego on October 13.

She departed San Diego on October 20 and steamed to Manila Bay, Philippine Islands, where she embarked 100 Navy passengers and carried them to Samar. From Samar the fast transport loaded cargo and delivered it to Shanghai, China, on December 4. *Joseph M. Auman* continued to carry cargo and passengers in the Pacific until she returned to the United States and was decommissioned at Green Cove Springs, Florida, on July 10, 1946, joining the Atlantic Reserve Fleet. She remained in the Reserve Fleet until struck from the Navy

Beyond Belief: True Stories of Marine Corps Heroes

List on December 12, 1963, and sold to the government of Mexico. She now serves the Mexican Navy as Tehuantepec (B-5).

Private Auman's actions were certainly worthy of recognition and naming a naval vessel after the Marine Raider is fitting. It is still puzzling why there were no such tributes for his friend and Marine Corps comrade, John Fardy.

JOHN PETER FARDY

John Peter Fardy was born in Chicago, Illinois, on August 15, 1922. He was the youngest child of Martin and Mary Fardy, and the sole son with two older sisters, Mary Therese and Anne. He attended Catholic schools in Chicago, where he was known as *"Whitey"* for his nearly-white-blonde hair.

After graduating from Leo High School in 1940, unlike his classmate Joseph Auman who joined the Marine Corps, Fardy elected to pursue higher education. After taking a course in typing at the **Fox Secretarial College,** he entered the **Illinois Institute of Technology** in 1941 to major in mechanical engineering. He left the university after one year and went to work at the **Cornell Force Company.**

On May 8, 1943, he was inducted into the Marine Corps. Following **Boot Camp** at the **Marine Corps Recruit Depot,** San Diego, California, he requested and was assigned to the **Japanese Language School,** and was promoted to private first class in July, two weeks before entering the language school. A month later he was transferred to **Camp Elliott,** San Diego, where he trained as an automatic rifleman in a Marine Corps infantry battalion.

THE WAR IN THE PACIFIC

After the Pearl Harbor attack on December 7, 1941, with the U.S. Navy weakened, Japan continued its land grab and expanded its area of influence deep into the South Pacific, Southwest Pacific, and even parts of the Indian Ocean. Japan controlled Manchuria and virtually the entire Chinese mainland coastal area. In early 1942 the Japanese captured the Philippine Islands, forcing General Douglas

184

MacArthur to move his Pacific Theatre headquarters from Manilla to Australia. Then the Korean Peninsula fell.

The Japanese moved fast and deep. After they captured major territory in New Guinea and the Solomon Islands, the United States was forced to alter critical supply routes to Australia. In fact, Australia felt very threatened, as indeed it should have, as New Guinea was just a few hundred miles from the north coast of Australia.

The onslaught of expansion continued. What we know today as Indonesia, the Netherlands East Indies, fell to the Japanese. Malaysia, Singapore, and other British colonies came under the control of Japan, and French Indochina (Vietnam) was occupied. The tiny and ancient kingdom of Siam (Thailand), fell to the Axis powers as did Burma.

The news coming out of the Pacific in 1942 foretold a disaster in progress. Something had to be done to stop the Japanese onslaught and it had to be done fast.

In the **Battle of Coral Sea** in early May 1942, the United States began to gain traction in the war in the Pacific. Coral Sea was, at best, a draw but it was the first time that the United States had thwarted an attempt by Japanese forces to take territory. This was quickly followed in June 1942 by the **Battle of Midway** which would forever go down in the annals of American Naval History of a victorious battle of epic proportions. These actions were all naval battles – ships and aviators. That changed on August 7, 1942, when U.S. Marines launched the amphibious invasion of Guadalcanal in the Solomon Islands, east of New Guinea.

In 1942 as the Japanese continued taking island after island in the Southern and Central Pacific, concern among Allied commanders grew. It was feared that as the Imperial Japanese Navy continued to land soldiers in the southern Solomon Islands, a British protectorate, the next steps might be an invasion of Australia. The Japanese dominance in the Pacific also threatened the Hawaiian Islands and possibly the West Coast of the United States.

After the victory at Guadalcanal the United States and its Allies spent 1943 retaking islands previously lost to Japan. The ultimate goal

Beyond Belief: True Stories of Marine Corps Heroes

of this new ground war was to use the reclaimed islands as stepping-stones to reach and recover the Philippine Islands, and then mount continued invasions of the Japanese home islands. It was in this environment that Private First Class John Fardy became a part of the war in the Pacific.

In Sand Diego, Fardy was assigned to the 29th Replacement Battalion and was deployed on October 28, 1943, to Nouméa, New Caledonia, where he was sent to the 27th Replacement Battalion which was preparing to ship out to join the FIRST Marine Division. Sent on to Goodenough Island, D'Entrecasteaux Islands in December, he was attached to Company C, First Battalion, First Marines, with which he would serve and fight for the next eighteen months.

From Goodenough Island he deployed with his regiment to Finschaffen, where he remained until Christmas Day 1943. On December 26 the FIRST Marine Division landed on Japanese-held Cape Gloucester, New Britain, and Private First Class Fardy was in the midst of war, fighting to capture two enemy airdromes on an island few people had ever heard of. The landings were the second amphibious landing of the FIRST Marine Division, after the earlier August 1942 landings at Guadalcanal. By January 16, 1944, their mission accomplished, the FIRST Marine Division pulled back to the Russell Islands for three months of training before their next combat operations.

Thereafter, the island-hopping campaign moved into a fast pace throughout the Southwest Pacific. After practice landings at Guadalcanal, which was now firmly in American control, on September 15, 1944, the FIRST Marine Division landed on Peleliu. Major General William Rupertus, the commander of the FIRST Marine Division, predicted that the island would be secured within four days. It was not to be – two months of bitter fighting in the coral hills overlooking a strategic airport that was the objective to be taken by the Marines and the Army's 81st Infantry Division, followed.

The Japanese holding Peleliu fought like cornered animals, ruthlessly resisting in their heavily-fortified positions to the end – *"death before dishonor."* Casualties were high on both sides – the battle for Peleliu resulted in the highest American casualty rate of all amphibious operations in the Pacific. More than 1,700 Marines (70% casualty rate) of Colonel Lewis B. *"Chesty"* Puller's First Marine Regiment, were killed in the action. The National Museum of the Marine Corps would

subsequently call the battle for Peleliu *"the bitterest battle of the war for Marines."*

The First Marine Regiment was literally decimated, and were pulled out and retuned to the Russel Islands in October. They were replaced at Peleliu by the Fifth Marine Regiment, and subsequently the Seventh Marine Regiment. By the time the fighting ended in late November, the FIRST Marine Division suffered 6,500 casualties (33% of the Division), and was so badly depleted that it remained out of action until the invasion of Okinawa on April 1, 1945.

While the First Marines were rebuilding after the losses at Peleliu, on December 21, 1944, John Fardy was promoted to corporal. A veteran of two very bitter and hard-fought amphibious assaults and subsequent campaigns, he was battle-tested and was made a squad leader in preparation for the next invasion and battle.

OKINAWA

By February 1945, while much of the attention was diverted to the Philippine Islands where General MacArthur was keeping his promise to return, the FIRST Marine Division had rebuilt sufficiently to begin training for its next mission. Practice amphibious assault landings were made at Baniki in the Russell Islands, Guadalcanal, and on Ulithi Atoll in the Caroline Islands.

Beyond Belief: True Stories of Marine Corps Heroes

The target of the next operation was the Japanese island of Okinawa, only 340 miles away from the Japanese mainland. In preparation, the U.S. Army's 77th Infantry Division captured the surrounding smaller islands by March 26, 1945, paving the way for the largest amphibious assault of the Pacific War.

Operation Iceberg, the amphibious assault and subsequent fighting to take control of Okinawa, began on Easter Sunday, April 1, 1945. Over the weeks that followed, a massive armada of landing craft ferried members of the FIRST, SECOND, and SIXTH Marine Divisions (88,000 Marines) ashore, along with soldiers of the XXIV Army Corps (7th, 27th, 77th, and 96th Infantry Divisions). In all over the 82-day battle, they numbered hundreds of thousands of American Soldiers and Marines.

As at Peleliu, the Japanese firmly resisted, defending every ridge and valley, and reinforcing the defenses around **Kadena Airfield**, the prime target of the American forces. The enemy knew that in American hands, that airfield would provide U.S. Army Air Forces with a highly valuable airfield from which they could launch bombing missions against the Home Islands and their capitol city of Tokyo.

The FIRST Marine Division landed on L-Day (Landing Day – April 1, 1945) on the northern tip of Okinawa, fighting alongside the SIXTH Marine Division to clear the northern half of the island. This was accomplished in the first few weeks, and on May 1 the Division was sent couth to relieve the Army's 27th Infantry Division.

Six days later, Company C, First Battalion, First Marines were advancing against a strongly fortified and fanatically defended Japanese position when Corporal Fardy's squad was sudden taken under heavy small arms fire.

Corporal Fardy temporarily deployed is men along a convenient drainage ditch for protection. As they returned fire on the enemy, the Japanese threw a grenade that landed among the Marines in the ditch. With no

time to throw it out, Corporal Fardy selflessly threw himself on the grenade, shielding his comrades from death or injury. The valiant fighter from Chicago, who had survived three harrowing amphibious assaults over 18 months of combat in the Pacific, survived the blast and was taken to a field hospital for treatment. He died of his wounds the following day, having sacrificed his life for his friends.

Initially, Fardy was buried in an American Cemetery in Okinawa. His family did not receive many details of how he died – only that he was wounded and later succumbed to his wounds.

The Marines of his squad who survived only because of Corporal Fardy's selfless action would not forget. They urged their chain of command to recommend Fardy for the Medal of Honor, which they did. The process of awarding the Medal of Honor, which includes witness statements and forensic evidence, began.

Over five years during World War II, President Harry Truman presented 85 Medals of Honor, summoning living heroes to the White House to receive the award. He did not, however, relish giving the Medal of Honor posthumously to the families of the deceased. He adhered to a *"definite policy"* of not presenting posthumous Medals of Honor to the next of kin at the White House.

As a result, a little more than a year after their son's heroic actions, Martin and Mary Fardy accepted the Medal of Honor at ceremonies conducted by the Marine Corps League's Chicago Detachment on September 15, 1946.

The President of the United States of America, in the name of Congress, takes pride in presenting the Medal of Honor (Posthumously) to Corporal John Peter Fardy, United States Marine Corps, for conspicuous gallantry and intrepidity at the risk of his life above and beyond the call of duty as a squad leader, serving with Company C, First Battalion, First Marines, FIRST Marine Division, in action against enemy Japanese forces on

Okinawa Shima in the Ryukyu Islands, 7 May 1945. When his squad was suddenly assailed by extremely heavy small arms fire from the front during a determined advance against strongly fortified, fiercely defended Japanese positions, Corporal Fardy temporarily deployed his men along a nearby drainage ditch. Shortly thereafter, an enemy grenade fell among the Marines in the ditch. Instantly throwing himself upon the deadly missile, Corporal Fardy absorbed the exploding blast in his own body, thereby protecting his comrades from certain and perhaps fatal injuries. Concerned solely for the welfare of his men, he willingly relinquished his own hope of survival that his fellow Marines might live to carry on the fight against a fanatic enemy. A stouthearted leader and indomitable fighter, Corporal Fardy, by his prompt decision and resolute spirit of self-sacrifice in the face of certain death, had rendered valiant service, and his conduct throughout reflects the highest credit upon himself and the United States Naval Service. He gallantly gave his life for his country.

After the war ended, *"Funeral Ships like the USAT Cardinal O'Connor began transporting the thousands of repatriated war dead from the Pacific back to the United States in October 1947. John Peter Fardy was brought home from Okinawa to Chicago for reburial on American soil in early April 1949. The Chicago Detachment of the Marine Corps League ensured military honors were extended to him."*[24]

On Thursday, April 7, 1949, the temperatures rose into the mid-50's and the winds picked up into what Chicagoans refer to as a *lazy wind – "It's too lazy to go around you, so it goes through you."* Additionally, light rain showers fell for a time during the services.

John Fardy's funeral procession began from the family home on Calumet Avenue on Chicago's South Side, and proceeded nine miles to the Southwest to 6001 West 111th Avenue in Alsip, Illinois. It turned and traveled through the gates of the Archdiocese of Chicago's **Holy Sepulcher Cemetery**. Beyond the front gate the cars turned left at the first road inside the gates and proceeded to the eastern end of Section 23. John Fardy, hero of the battle for Okinawa, was finally home – his final resting place in Grave 3, Lot

---

[24] Barrett, Terence W., PhD, *The Search for the Forgotten Thirty-Four,* Printed by CreateSpace. Publication Funded by Aftermath Research, Fargo, ND.

John Peter Fardy (USMC)

16, Block 3. There was nothing on his headstone to indicate the high honor he had received, only his name, home state, his identity as a corporal in the 1st Marines, 1st Marine Division in World War II, his date of birth, and date of death.

About 62 years later, a remarkable chain of events resulted in the Leo High School Alumni Association being informed that a terrible oversight had occurred on Fardy's headstone. Headstones of those who served in the military are usually engraved with medals the service member had earned such as the Purple Heart and valor medals such as the Bronze Star through the Medal of Honor – particularly those headstones provided by the Veterans Administration. But this was not the case for John Peter Fardy. For sixty-two years people by the thousands had no doubt walked past his resting place near the entrance to one of Chicago's largest cemeteries, oblivious to the fact that a hero was buried there.

The **Leo Alumni Association** contacted this author, knowing that I was a decorated Vietnam Veteran and was active in Veterans causes. I assembled a small committee to figure out what needed to be done, including football coach and teacher Michael Holmes (Class of '76) and Mark Lee (Class of '85). Mark's brother Eric was a former Marine who gave his life about a decade earlier while serving the citizens of Chicago as a police officer. Any costs incurred would be borne by the **Alumni Association**, so we sought the advice of Alumni officers, John Gardner (Class of '75), a 25th Infantry Division Vietnam Veteran, and Alumni officer James Farrell (Class of '61), and Richard Furlong (Class of '59).

We contacted the **Veterans Administration Headstone Division.** Quite frankly they were not very helpful – Corporal Fardy had his headstone and essentially that was that.

The committee then considered engraving the existing headstone. We contacted a memorial company near the cemetery. **Maurice Moore Memorials** indicated that they could engrave the medal and the inscription *"MEDAL OF HONOR"* in-situ on the existing headstone. However, before we could engrave the headstone, we needed the permission of Fardy's descendants.

Author and researcher Dr. Terence Barrett was kind enough to provide the obituary for Fardy's sister, Mary Therese Martin.

However, there are literally hundreds, if not thousands, of Martins in the Chicago area alone, not even considering the possibility that they might have moved. The committee was starting to feel it was hopeless to get the permission to engrave Fardy's headstone when someone suggested checking the **Leo Alumni Association Directory**. Sure enough, hiding in plain sight was John Martin, Leo Class of 1967, born in 1949 right about the time Fardy's body was being interred at Holy Sepulcher Cemetery.

A call was made to John Martin who graciously consented to the engraving. The committee also mentioned that it would like to rededicate the grave after the engraving had been finished. John said he was certain that his brothers and sisters as well as his cousins from the Thometz family (Anne's children) would participate in the rededication.

JOHN FARDY'S LEGACY PRESERVED

During the rededication ceremony, several of Fardy's nieces and nephews privately shared their thoughts on their heroic uncle. John Martin told me that he was told by his mother that John Fardy was just an *"ordinary guy."* I recalled a quote I once heard from Ralph Waldo Emerson, the esteemed American poet and philosopher who said: *"A hero is no braver than an ordinary man, but he is brave five minutes longer."*

John also gave me an indication of just how much esteem John Fardy was held in by **Leo High School**. John Martin also went there and recalled that on his (John Martin's) first day of school, one of the teachers, a Brother Coogan, said to John that he knew who his uncle was and what he had done, and should John Martin ever have any school problems that he should come to him (Brother Coogan).

John Hanlon graduated with John Fardy in the Class of 1940. John recalled Fardy as just one of the guys. He was neither an exceptional student nor an exceptional athlete. In his Senior Yearbook Fardy had one student activity listed – Public Speaking.

Fardy's niece, Mimi Dillon, recalls her mother Therese (Fardy's oldest sister), and has faint recollections of her stories of John, but it wasn't until she was older that she came to realize the enormity of what he had done. She recalled that her husband Tom was an ROTC

John Peter Fardy (USMC)

graduate and was stationed at Fort Huachuca, Arizona. Her grandmother, (Fardy's mother) came to visit them at the base housing they were in. When word got out that the mother of a Marine Medal of Honor recipient was at the base, it was a big deal. She recalls that six Marines in Dress Blues came to visit her grandmother at the Dillon house on base. She recalled the Marines brought her mother candy and flowers, and her mother was extremely proud and very touched by the Marines' act of kindness. Fardy's mother, Mary, died peacefully three days after that visit.

Ms. Dillon also recalled an event at the Palmer House in Chicago that was attended by Marines from all over the country. She thought it might have been veterans of the Okinawa battle, but she was very young at the time. One speaker specifically mentioned Fardy and said nobody in the room would be alive if it wasn't for John Fardy.

She said John's family was planning a big welcome home party at the St. Clotilde Church, when news of John's death arrived, and left them stunned. The welcome home party became a memorial service.

WHY SHOULD WE AS A NATION HONOR OUR HEROES

I asked to include this chapter in *Beyond Belief* because to me at least, it was beyond belief that a hero such as John Fardy didn't even have mentioned on his grave headstone the fact that he earned a Medal of Honor.

I don't think any person ever gets up in the morning and says to themselves, *"you know, I think I'll become a hero today."* In fact, it's the circumstances that seek out the hero and the individual's character allow him to act that way.

This author is a disabled veteran. I'd like to think that the day I earned my award every other soldier in my squad would have done the same thing. There was an unspoken rule among soldiers in harms way – *I'll cover your six (back) if you'll cover mine.*

But its fair then, to ask why we as a Nation should honor our heroes. I think we are proud as a nation that we have such sons and daughters as John Fardy – a hero walking among us brings us a certain sense of pride in ourselves. Further, we learn the personal

Beyond Belief: True Stories of Marine Corps Heroes

characteristics of heroes so that the person they are, can teach us what kind of person has the potential to be heroically brave under difficult circumstances.

Finally, it is hoped heroes will also provide encouragement to others active in the Armed Services who put themselves in harms way on behalf of their fellow servicemembers and their Nation.

THE REDEDICATION CONCLUDES

At the gravesite, the rededication continued. Father Thomas Mescall (Class of '65) offered a prayer for the assembled. The Master of Ceremonies said a few words and asked John Fardy's nephew and namesake, John Martin, to read the actual citation. Then guest speaker, Dr. Terence Barrett stepped forward to speak to the assembled. He emphasized how John Fardy went to an academically challenging high school. He was not the high achieving valedictorian or anything near that. But he rose to the challenge of academics. He worked hard and got his diploma. And he took that work ethic with him into the Marine Corps and onto the battlefield.

After Dr. Barrett's remarks, behind the crowd, the Honor Guard was called to attention to begin the volley for the 21-gun salute. The Honor Guard that day were Marines from Chicago's Reserve Detachment, the Second Battalion of the Twenty-Fourth Marines, FOURTH Marine Division. They rendered the 21-gun salute, an ancient custom that is reserved for people of high respect. It predates the United States and many countries have adopted its use – namely to honor someone of significance.

Tom Day Plays Taps in honor of John Peter Fardy. (Photo by Charles Furlong)

Immediately after the 21-gun volley, in full Marine Class A uniform, Tom Day, founder of **Bugles Across America**, stepped forward, snapped to attention, and brought the gleaming chrome instrument to his lips. As he played *Taps*, tears

194

started forming at the eyes of many of the assembled. Then that beautiful melody faded into the distance.

The Non-Commissioned Officer in Charge (NCOIC) stepped forward. There was no flag-draped coffin, so he carried a flag with only 48 stars since Fardy's actions occurred before Alaska and Hawaii entered the Union. Two other members of the Honor Guard unfolded the flag and began the process of folding the flag for presentation to the family. The flag folding ceremony holds a particular meaning.

THE FLAG ITSELF

The portion of the flag denoting honor is the canton of blue containing the stars representing states our veterans served in uniform. The field of blue dresses from left to right and is inverted only when draped as a funeral cloth over the casket of a veteran who has served our country honorably in uniform. In the U.S. Armed Forces, at the ceremony of retreat, the flag is lowered, folded in a triangle and kept under watch throughout the night as a tribute to our nation's honored dead. The next morning it is brought out and, at a ceremony of reveille, flown high as a symbol of belief in the resurrection of the body.

MEANING BEHIND THE 13 FOLDS

The flag-folding ceremony represents the same religious principles on which our great country was originally founded.

1. The first fold of our flag is a symbol of life.
2. The second fold is a symbol of our belief in eternal life.
3. The third fold is made in honor and remembrance of the veteran departing our ranks, and who gave a portion of his or her life for the defense of our country to attain peace throughout the world.
4. The fourth fold represents our weaker nature; as American citizens trusting in God, it is Him we turn to in times of peace, as well as in times of war, for His divine guidance.
5. The fifth fold is a tribute to our country. In the words of Stephen Decatur, "Our country, in dealing with other countries, may she always be right, but it is still our country, right or wrong."

6. The sixth fold is for where our hearts lie. It is with our heart that we pledge allegiance to the flag of the United States of America, and to the republic for which it stands, one nation under God, indivisible, with liberty and justice for all.

7. The seventh fold is a tribute to our <u>armed forces</u>, for it is through the armed forces that we protect our country and our flag against all enemies, whether they be found within or without the boundaries of our republic.

8. The eighth fold is a tribute to the one who entered into the valley of the shadow of death, that we might see the light of day, and to honor our mother, for whom it flies on Mother's Day.

9. The ninth fold is a tribute to womanhood. It has been through their faith, love, loyalty and devotion that has molded the character of the men and women who have made this country great.

10. The 10th fold is a tribute to father, who has also given his sons and daughters for the defense of our country since he or she was first born.

11. The 11th fold represents the lower portion of the seal of King David and King Solomon and glorifies the God of Abraham, Isaac and Jacob.

12. The 12th fold represents an emblem of eternity and glorifies God the Father, the Son and Holy Ghost.

13. The 13th and last fold, when the flag is completely folded, the stars are uppermost, reminding us of our national motto, "In God We Trust."

AFTER THE FOLDING CEREMONY

After the flag is folded and the end tucked it, it looks like a cocked hat, reminding us of the soldiers who served under General George Washington, and the Sailors and Marines who served under Captain John Paul Jones during the American Revolution. It was their service and sacrifice that preserves for us today, more than two centuries later, the right, privileges, and freedoms that we enjoy.

The NCOIC then steps forward with the folded flat to present it to the next of kin. In the memorial for John Fardy, the flag was presented to John Martin, the eldest child of Therese, and Anne Thometz McGuire, the eldest child of Anne.

John Peter Fardy (USMC)

(Photo by Charles Furlong)

As the flag is presented the NCOIC says: *"On behalf of the President of the United States, the United States Marine Corps, and a grateful nation, please accept this flag as a symbol of our appreciation for your loved one's honorable and faithful service."*

The service has concluded, and the assembled crowd appears ready to leave when spontaneously those in the crown begin placing the American flags that they held in their hand around the headstone with the newly engraved Medal of Honor on it.

This ceremony was done not to just honor John Peter Fardy for his heroism but to honor all those in the Armed Services who have given the ultimate sacrifice for the Cause of Freedom

Semper Fidelis

Descendants of John Fardy are all smiling with pride for their Uncle. *(Photo by Charles Furlong)*

Beyond Belief: True Stories of Marine Corps Heroes

Guy "Gabby" Gabaldon (USMC)

The Pied Pier of Saipan

By Scott Baron

By early 1944, American forces in the Pacific theater of war had vastly improved their ability in making amphibious landings, however the Japanese had simultaneously improved their ability to defend their islands, resulting in greater and greater number of casualties.

Saipan, in the Marianna Islands, would put the Marines ability to the test. It's capture was considered essential to victory in the Pacific.

The envisioned full-scale invasion of the Japanese mainland, with its estimated one million American casualties, would require airfields within range of the mainland from which to launch B-29 **Superfortress** bombers, with an operational range of 1,500 miles (2,400 km), to support the invasion, and Saipan fit the bill.

The invasion of Saipan would involve 535 ships and 127,570 personnel, primarily troops of the SECOND and FOURTH Marine Divisions. Two days prior to the invasion, on June 13, 1944, the guns aboard seven battleships and eleven destroyers shelled Saipan and a sister island, Tinian, expending 15,000 16-inch and 5-inch shells, and 165,000 other shells.

The following day, eight older battleships and eleven cruisers replaced the more modern *fast* battleships and continued bombarding the island.

At 0700 hours on June 15, 1944, 300 LVTs (Landing Vehicle Tracked) began landing Marines of the SECOND and FOURTH Marine Divisions on the west coast of Saipan, taking the Japanese high command by surprise. The had expected the landings further south.

199

Beyond Belief: True Stories of Marine Corps Heroes

By 0900 hours, 800 Marines were ashore. A naval force of eleven ships, comprised of two battleships (*U.S.S. Tennessee* and *U.S.S. California*), two cruisers (*U.S.S. Indianapolis* and *U.S.S. Birmingham*) and seven destroyers, provided fire support for the invasion and by nightfall, the Marines had established a beachhead, six miles long by a half-mile deep. That night, a Japanese counterattack failed, with heavy casualties.

The following day, June 16, the Army's 27th Infantry Division landed and advanced to the airfield at As Lito, and a nighttime counterattack again failed, with the Japanese abandoning the field on June 18.

On June 19 - 20, the **Battle of the Philippine Sea**, nicknamed the *Great Marianas Turkey Shoot*, took place — the largest, and last carrier-to carrier-battle of the Second World War. The disastrous loss by the Japanese of three fleet aircraft carriers and between 550 - 645 aircraft eliminated any possibility of resupply or reinforcement of the Japanese garrison on Saipan, sealing their fate.

Thus began a twenty-four-day battle (June 15 - July 9) that would pit Marine Lieutenant General Holland *"Howling Mad"* Smith and approximately 71,000 troops landed on the island against approximately 31,000 troops of the Japanese 31st Army under the command of Lieutenant General Saito Yoshitsuga.

Surrounded and cut off, the Japanese refused to surrender, choosing to fight to the last man from caves, and in the mountainous terrain. In desperation, at dawn on July 7, the Japanese launched a *"Banzai charge,"* hoping to drive the American invaders back into the sea, and *"for the honor of the*

Emperor" They suffered a loss of over 4,000 soldiers and civilians that had joined the charge.

In the close quarters combat that made up most of the fighting for the island, Americans suffered 2,949 killed or missing, and another 10,364 wounded, compared to Japanese losses of 29,000 killed (of which 5,000 were suicides) and only 2,100 prisoners taken.[25]

The battle for Saipan included many legendary stories of courage and valor, among them, the **Navajo Codetalkers**, who used their native language to direct naval gunfire onto targets and frustrated Japanese attempts at eavesdropping on sensitive communications. It also included 800 African-American Marines who unloaded food and ammunition on the beach under fire, the first Black Marines to see combat in World War II.

Four Marines would be awarded the Medal of Honor for their actions on the island, all of them posthumously.

On June 16, Gunnery Sergeant Robert H. McCard, Fourth Tank Battalion, FOURTH Marine Division, courageously exposed himself to enemy guns when his tank was put out of action bringing all the tank's weapons to bear on the enemy, until the severity of hostile fire caused him to order his crew out the escape hatch while he covered them, killing sixteen of the enemy, sacrificing himself to ensure the safety of his tank crew.

On June 25, Private First Class Harold G. Epperson, First Battalion, Sixth Marines, SECOND Marine Division, while fighting in the defense of his battalion's position and maintaining a steady stream of devastating fire against rapidly infiltrating enemy, a Japanese soldier, assumed to be dead, sprang up and hurled a powerful hand grenade into the emplacement. Determined to save his comrades, Private First Class Epperson unhesitatingly threw himself on a grenade to contain the blast, saving the other members of his squad.

---

[25] Figures vary depending on the source.

Beyond Belief: True Stories of Marine Corps Heroes

On July 7, Private First Class Harold C. Agerholm, Fourth Battalion, Tenth Marines, SECOND Marine Division, disregarded heavy enemy fire and, as his citation recounted, *"appropriating an abandoned ambulance jeep, repeatedly made extremely perilous trips under heavy rifle and mortar fire and single-handedly loaded and evacuated approximately forty-five casualties."* He was killed by a sniper as he tried to help two other wounded men.

On July 8, Sergeant Grant F. Timmerman, Second Tank Battalion, Sixth Marines, SECOND Marine Division, fearlessly covered an open tank hatch with his own body to prevent an enemy grenade from killing his crew and the grenade exploded on his chest, killing him instantly. Although two members of the crew received slight wounds from the grenade, none were killed.

As American forces advanced and made gains for control of Saipan, an estimated 22,000 Japanese civilians died on the island. The majority committed suicide by jumping from cliffs later named *Suicide Cliff* and *Banzai Cliff*. Many jumped while holding babies and small children. Often it was a family suicide − youngest children were pushed by the eldest, then mothers pushed the eldest, and finally, distraught fathers pushed the mothers and then jumped after them.

Civilians were encouraged by Japanese propaganda to commit suicide rather than be captured by the Americans, who they were told were committing atrocities including rape and torture. It was believable because, in fact, Japanese soldiers had long been doing just

Guy *"Gabby"* Gabaldon (USMC)

that among the civilian populations of territory they had controlled by invasion and force, going back to the infamous **Rape of Nanking**, China, over six weeks from December 1937 to January 1938. Estimates vary with rapes committed, numbering perhaps more than 80,000. Civilian deaths, often by torture, ranged from 40,000 to perhaps as high as 300,000, making it one of the worse massacres of World War II. The brutality was unbelievable – Japanese soldiers were even known to use their bayonets to open the womb of pregnant Chinese women, and then toss the unborn child into the air and then catch them on the bayonets of their rifles. They were also known to have done this with living infants.

Brutal treatment of civilians by the Japanese continued, although usually not to the same degree, throughout China during World War II, especially in the aftermath of the 1942 **Doolittle Raid**, as well as in the Philippine Islands, and other islands and territories the Japanese Army gained control of. Thus the propaganda fed the Japanese civilians of islands now being invaded by Americans was believable, and Japanese civilians on Saipan willingly went to their self-inflicted deaths rather than live under the new occupiers.

Operating by himself, to prevent this useless waste of life by Japanese soldiers and civilians, was a streetwise, Japanese-speaking eighteen-year old Mexican-American private first class from the barrios of East Los Angeles, who would become famous as *"The Pied Piper of Saipan."* Credited with capturing over 1,000 Japanese soldiers and 500 civilians on Saipan, Guy Gabaldon holds the distinction of probably capturing more enemy soldiers than anyone else in American military history.

GUY GABALDON

Born one of seven children in a Mexican-American family in East Los Angeles on March 22, 1926, Guy Louis Gabaldon, trying to escape the gangs, made friends with Nisei (first generation Japanese-American) twins Lane and Lyle Nakano. Impressed with their self-discipline and honesty, he was taken in by their family when he was twelve years old,

Beyond Belief: True Stories of Marine Corps Heroes

and he attended Japanese language and culture classes with the family's children, where he learned to speak what he called *"backstreet"* Japanese.

After Pearl Harbor was attacked on December 7, 1941, his adopted family, along with all Japanese-Americans on the west coast, were ordered to relocate, many of them becoming interned in **American Relocation Camps** that were little more than concentration camps. His Nisei *"brothers"* enlisted in the 442d Regimental Combat Team (RCT), an all-Nisei unit of the U.S. Army for service in Europe, and his parents and sister were interned at the *Heart Mountain Relocation Camp* in Wyoming.

"I wanted to go with them" Gabaldon later recounted, *"but they wouldn't let me."* So, at age 15, he moved to Alaska and found work in a cannery. He wanted to enlist in the Navy and serve aboard submarines, but at 5'3", and with a perforated eardrum, the Navy wasn't interested. He enlisted in the Marines after turning 17, on March 22, 1943 – the recruiter, aware of the Corps need for Japanese speaking Marines, overlooked his size and eardrum..

After basic training at Camp Pendleton, San Diego, California, Private Gabaldon was trained in heavy weapons (mortars), and was sent to **Enlisted Marine Japanese Language School** at Camp Elliott, also at San Diego. There he qualified as a scout/observer and translator-Japanese.

After training in amphibious landings, Gabaldon was assigned to the Headquarters and Service Company, Second Marine Regiment, SECOND Marine Division, which sailed from San Diego to Hawaii on December 23, 1943 aboard the *S.S. Young America,* arriving at Pearl Harbor on December 30.

After more amphibious training in Hawaii, the SECOND Marines embarked aboard the *U.S.S. Feland* on May 30, landing on Saipan on June 15, 1944, the first day of battle. When they landed, the diminutive Gabaldon was only an 18 year old kid.

During the early days of the campaign, Gabaldon found his small size an advantage in the close-in fighting required in jungle warfare, and earned respect among his comrades as a fierce and daring combatant.

Guy *"Gabby"* Gabaldon (USMC)

But, from almost his first night on the island, Gabaldon began going on unauthorized, solo patrols – leaving his position to scout out the enemy lines. With his knowledge of the language he decided to try to talk some Japanese soldiers into surrendering. Gabaldon's method was to approach a Japanese cave, shoot the guard, and yell to the Japanese inside that they were surrounded.

That first night, Gabaldon returned with two prisoners but, instead of praise, his commanding officer threatened him with a court-martial for leaving his lines and ordered him not to do it again. Disobeying his orders, Gabaldon made another trip the next night and came back with 50 prisoners. Acknowledging his success, his commanders granted Gabaldon authority to come and go as he pleased, or as he put it, to be a *"lone-wolf operator."*

Gabaldon entered caves, pillboxes and the jungle, often under direct fire, to persuade the Japanese troops and residents to surrender. Working alone, at great personal risk, he would speak to them in Japanese, working to convince them that the island was secured and that *"fighting to the last man,"* as the Japanese Code of Bushido *(death before dishonor)* demanded, would be a senseless loss of life.

An American Soldier meets and attempts to get a Japanese family to come out of hiding in their cave refuge.

As he recounted in a September 5, 2006, interview on **National Public Radio's** *All Things Considered; "My ability to speak Japanese (was) very limited, but it wasn't difficult to say raise your hands and come on out. At night, I'd usually go over to the caves. Saipan is just full of caves, and I'd get to one side of the mouth of a cave, and I'd say 'you are completely surrounded. I've got a bunch of Marines here with me behind the trees. If you don't surrender, I'll have to kill you,' and usually it worked - not always. I'd have to throw grenades in and kill, and I'd get maybe 10, 15, 20 at a time, and one day I got 800."*

Beyond Belief: True Stories of Marine Corps Heroes

That day was July 8, 1944. Cut off behind enemy lines a day earlier, Gabaldon had witnessed Japanese troops and civilians massing for a Banzai charge, a suicidal assault on July 7, the largest of the war with more than 4,000 Japanese killed. Following the charge, Gabaldon found himself trapped behind the lines. In an 1998 interview with *War Times Journal*, he remembered.

"It was in the morning of 8 July that I took two prisoners on top of the Banzai Cliffs. I talked with them at length trying to convince them that to continue fighting would amount to sure death for them. I told them that if they continued fighting, our flame throwers would roast them alive.

"I pointed to the many ships we had lying off shore waiting to blast them in their caves. 'Why die when you have a chance to surrender under honorable conditions? You are taking civilians to their death which is not part of your Bushido military code.

"The big job was going to be in convincing them that we would not torture and kill them, that they would be well treated and would be returned to Japan after the war. I understood that their Bushido Code called for death before surrender, and that to surrender was to be considered a coward. This was going to be a tough nut to crack.

"It was either convincing them that I was a good guy or I would be a dead Marine within a few minutes."

"I knew that there were hundreds of die-hard enemy at the bottom of the cliffs and if they rushed me I would probably kill two or three before they ate me alive . . . I finally talked one of my two prisoners to return to the bottom of the cliffs and to try to convince his fellow survivors that they would be treated with dignity if they surrendered.

"I kept the other one with me, not as a hostage, but because he said that if he went to the caves with my message and they did not buy it, off with the head. I couldn't help agreeing with him. The one that descended the cliff either had lots of guts or he was going to double-cross me and come back with his troops firing away. Who was the prisoner, me or the Japs? "

Guy *"Gabby"* Gabaldon (USMC)

"The Japanese soldier returned with about a dozen men, including an officer, all of them armed."

"They (weren't) pointing their weapons at me, but on the other hand, they didn't have to. If I go to fire they would have the drop on me. They'd chop me down before I fire a round."

Once the officer was convinced that his men would receive medical care and be well-treated, he went back to the caves, then returned with a group of fifty men, explaining that there were hundreds of people down below. Some were wounded, others were civilians. Then, as Gabaldon remembered *"They start coming up. The lines up the trails seem endless."*

Fortunately, to Gabaldon's relief, others had seen the large number of Japanese surrendering to him and he was soon joined by *"hundreds of Marines,"* and he would be credited with capturing over 800 prisoners in a single day.

Overall, Gabaldon would be credited with capturing 1,500 Japanese soldiers and civilians over the course of the campaigns on Saipan and Tinian. He also witnessed the suicides of dozens of Japanese civilians.

He landed on Tinian, where he saw combat and captured additional soldiers and civilians, and then returned to Saipan where he was ambushed and wounded by machine-gun fire while

A Japanese POW and his family pose with Gabaldon (Right)

engaged in fighting Japanese guerillas on the island. In the course of his mission, he was forced to kill 33 enemy soldiers, and was twice wounded.

He returned to San Francisco aboard the *U.S.S. Tryon*, (APH-1), arriving on March 11, 1945. Hospitalized in Oceanside, California,

Beyond Belief: True Stories of Marine Corps Heroes

while recovering from his wounds he was honorably discharged from the Marines as a private first class on November 10, 1945.

His company commander, Captain John Schwabe, stated that Gabaldon's actions resulted in obtaining vital intelligence which shortened the period of combat, resulting in the significant saving of life. He recommended Gabaldon for the Medal of Honor. He was awarded the Silver Star.

In June 1957, Gabaldon was a guest on the NBC television show *This is Your Life*, and in 1960 the Hollywood movie, *From Hell to Eternity*, brought to the big screen an account of the young Marine who captured so many and saved so many lives. Gabaldon was played by Jeffery Hunter, a blue-eyed, tall Caucasian.

The resulting publicity resulted in Gabaldon being awarded the Navy Cross, the second highest award for valor, on December 20, 1960.

Gabaldon (R) with Hollywood actor Jefferey Hunter on set of the movie about his WWII exploits.

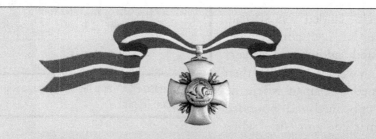

The President of the United States of America takes pleasure in presenting the Navy Cross to Private First Class Guy L. Gabaldon (MCSN: 517054), United States Marine Corps Reserve, for extraordinary heroism and devotion to duty while serving with Headquarters and Service Company, Second Marines, SECOND Marine Division, in action against enemy Japanese forces on Saipan and Tinian, Mariana Islands, South Pacific Area, from 15 June to 1 August 1944. Acting as a

Guy *"Gabby"* Gabaldon (USMC)

Japanese Interpreter for the Second Marines, Private First Class Gabaldon displayed extreme courage and initiative in single-handedly capturing enemy civilian and military personnel during the Saipan and Tinian operations. Working alone in front of the lines, he daringly entered enemy caves, pillboxes, buildings, and jungle brush, frequently in the face of hostile fire, and succeeded in not only obtaining vital military information, but in capturing well over one thousand enemy civilians and troops. Through his valiant and distinguished exploits, Private First Class Gabaldon made an important contribution to the successful prosecution of the campaign and, through his efforts, a definite humane treatment of civilian prisoners was assured. His courageous and inspiring devotion to duty throughout reflects the highest credit upon himself and the United States Naval Service..

Many felt that Gabaldon's actions justified the award of the Medal of Honor, and that he was passed over because he was Hispanic. Efforts were made by some to have the government acknowledge Gabaldon's contribution with the award of the Medal of Honor, but as of 2016, were still unsuccessful.

Following his Honorable Discharge, Gabaldon returned to Boyle Heights and married June, a girl from the neighborhood, with whom he had six children before divorce ended the marriage. He moved to Mexico and tried his hand at fishing, learned to fly, and started a successful import-export business. He also met and married Ohana Suzuki, with whom he had five more children.

In the mid-1970s, Gabaldon and Ohana moved to Saipan where he worked as police chief, giving tours, and as a drug-abuse counselor. He also wrote his autobiography, **Saipan: Suicide Island**, published in 1990.

After two decades on Saipan, Gabaldon returned to California in 1995 and moved to Florida in 2003. In 2000, Marine Corps General James L. Jones upgraded Gabaldon's rank from private first class to corporal.

"He told me to keep my nose clean and maybe in another 50 years, I'd be a sergeant," Gabaldon said.

Beyond Belief: True Stories of Marine Corps Heroes

Gabaldon passed away in Old Town, Florida, of heart disease on August 31, 2006, at the age of 80. He was buried with full military honors at Arlington National Cemetery, Section 8AA, Row 19, Site 1. Gabaldon was survived by his wife, Ohana and nine of his eleven children.

Sources

Burbeck, James. Interview with Guy Gabaldon, War Times Journal September 19, 1998 http://www.wtj.com/articles/gabaldon/

Goldstein, Richard. *Guy Gabaldon, 80, Hero of Battle of Saipan, Dies* New York Times, Sept. 4, 2006

Hoeferlin, Collin. *Guy Gabaldon* – Marineparents.com, Sept 2016 https://marineparents.com/marinecorps/guy-gabaldon.asp

Kakesako, Gregg. *'Pied Piper' returning to Saipan-The Chicano recipient of the Navy Cross will revisit the site of a historic WWII battle* Honolulu Star Bulletin, June 6, 2004

Guy Gabaldon, from East Los Angeles Kid to Pied Piper of Saipan – WWII History Archives, June, 2016 http://ww2awartobewon.com/wwii-articles/guy-gabaldon-pied-piper-saipan/

Rasmussen, Cecilia. The Pied Piper of Saipan' Stood Tall During WWII, Los Angeles Times, Nov. 13, 2005

Jack Lucas (USMC)

The Youngest Marine

BY KEVIN MANSFIELD

Even as a child, Jack Lucas was a remarkable man. At the age of seventeen, Jack was the youngest Marine in history to earn the Medal of Honor. This came as the result of his heroic and unselfish actions on Iwo Jima in 1945. He hated bullies. He hated injustice. He loved his country. And above all else, he loved HIS Marines.

Jacklyn Harold Lucas was born on Valentine's Day 1928 in Plymouth, North Carolina. His father passed away when he was 11 years old. That left him as the man of the house with his mother (pictured with young Jack) and his four-year-old brother. Without an actual

Beyond Belief: True Stories of Marine Corps Heroes

father-figure to keep him in line, his mother sent him to **Edwards Military Institute** in Salemburg, North Carolina. He did well with the structure at the military school and became cadet captain.

He was a 13-year-old cadet at **Edwards** on December 7, 1941, when word of the attack on Pearl Harbor came over the radio. He always had a strong sense of patriotism and the Japanese attack on his country fueled an obsession within him. He wanting to join the military, immediately, and to *"go kill Japs."* He had an uncle who had served in the Marine Corps, and that was the branch Jack wanted to be part of. However, being underaged did not work in his favor.

Jack tried to get his mother to sign papers stating that he was old enough to join the Marines. She refused, which prompted him to rely on his own resourcefulness. When his mother remarried, Jack was stubborn to resist the authority of his stepfather. Neither he nor his stepfather cared for each other.

Soon thereafter, after Jack forged his mother's signature on the papers to enlist, and his stepfather was plenty willing to drive him to the recruiting station in Norfolk, Virginia. Even though he was only fourteen, Jack was big for his age, standing 5'8" tall and weighing 180 pounds. Jack and his stepfather convinced the recruiters that he was old enough to join, and he arrived at the Marine Corps Recruit Depot, Parris Island, South Carolina, on August 7, 1942.

Jack excelled in boot camp, largely due to his experience at **Edwards Military Institute**. The drill instructors used him to drill the other recruits. Jack thought it lucky that his comrades didn't realize they were being drilled by a fourteen-year-old.

Following boot camp, Jack was assigned with his fellow Marines to various training duties in Florida, and soon found himself attending school as a machine gunner at Camp Geiger, North Carolina.

He finished at the top of his class from machine gun school. In fact, he did well enough that when he received subsequent orders after school, he was assigned to remain at Camp Geiger to be an instructor. It was an assignment that didn't fit Jack's plans for getting into the fight in the Pacific. He disregarded his orders and, instead, hopped on the train to California with the rest of his unit.

Jack Lucas in 1942 as a 14-year-old Marine Private.

When he arrived at Camp Elliott. his name wasn't on the muster roster. He explained to his Sergeant that this wasn't something a private should be trying to figure out or even worry about. His sergeant simply picked Private Jacklyn Harold Lucas up on their rolls and notified Camp Geiger that Private Lucas was now in California. Once again, Jack's resourcefulness and his determination to fight allowed him to forge his own destiny.

Jack's unit sailed from California and arrived in Hawaii in early November of 1943. His unit was at Camp Caitlin on Oahu, preparing for what would be the invasion of Tarawa. But when his unit departed Hawaii, Jack was not among them. As it turned out, Jack had written a letter to a girl in North Carolina, and in that letter, he mentioned that he was fifteen (older even, than he was at the time.). He didn't count on the fact that censors were reading outgoing mail, and when they did, the Marine Corps learned that Jack was underage. For that reason, he was denied the opportunity he so wanted – ship out with his unit to *"Kill Japs at Tinian."*

Further, his irate commander was prepared to discharge Jack from the Marine Corps. Jack countered this threat by telling the colonel that if he was sent back home, he'd just join the Army and use his Marine Corps training there. The Colonel relented from his plans to discharge the young Marine, but he made it clear that he wouldn't allow Jack into combat. Jack remained on Oahu with the Marine Corps, but he was assigned the unpleasant duty of driving a trash truck. It was certainly an assignment that wasn't part of Jack's plans to avenge the attack on Pearl Harbor.

Once again, Jack's resourcefulness gave him an idea. He had noticed that Marines who caused problems had a tendency of being shipped out to combat. It was the military's way of getting rid of their troublemakers. He figured that if caused enough trouble for the Marine Corps in Hawaii, he'd get himself shipped out from trash duty so he could do the job that he'd enlisted to do.

Jack found himself in the brig seventeen times for fighting and other offenses. His idea to *"fight his way into the fight"* wasn't going as planned and he figured it was time for a change of plans. He had shaped his own destiny in North Carolina by getting on the train without orders to do so. Getting out of Hawaii wouldn't be as simple.

It was January of 1945. There were several vessels at Pearl Harbor that were preparing to ship out to battle. Jack blended in with a group of Marines returning from liberty and took a boat to a ship that was carrying men from the FIFTH Marine Division. That ship was the *U.S.S. Deuel*. Jack knew that his first cousin, Sam Lucas, was with the FIFTH Marine Division. In what he described as being divine intervention, he discovered that his cousin was on that very ship. He found Sam and they visited for a while. When Sam told Jack that it was time to go back to the docks, Jack informed him that he planned to stay on the ship and was going with him. From that point on, Jack was AWOL (absent without leave), a criminal offense. But he once again succeeded in doing things his own way.

With the help of his cousin, Jack was able to stow away on the *Deuel* as it headed west from Oahu. One of several hundred Marines on the ship, he managed to blend in without it being discovered that he wasn't supposed to be there in the first place. It was pointed out that after 30 days of being AWOL, Jack would be classified as a deserter. He didn't want that. After 29 days on board, he turned himself in to Captain Robert Dunlap.

Jack Lucas (USMC)

Captain Robert H. Dunlap was the Commanding officer of Company C, First Battalion, Twenty-Sixth Marine Regiment. Dunlap would himself receive the Medal of Honor for his actions on February 20 and 21, 1945, at Iwo Jima.

Robert Dunlap

Jack, listed as AWOL, turned himself in to Captain Dunlap on February 8, 1945. He was still sixteen years old. The battalion commander, however, was impressed with Jack's enthusiasm and his desire to fight. Short of being listed as a deserter, he was assigned to Captain Dunlap's company. It was also the same company in which his cousin Sam was serving.

In an armada of more than 500 ships, the *U.S.S. Deuel* was part of the invasion force that was to land on the Japanese island of Iwo Jima. The first wave of Marines landed on the island around 9:05 a.m. on the morning of February 19, 1945. Jack landed on Red Beach One at around 3 p.m. on the same afternoon. Five days after his seventeenth birthday, Jack was finally in the fight.

Around noon of his second day on Iwo Jima, Jack was part of a four-man fire team that was engaging Japanese forces in the vicinity of **Airfield One**. They were firing on enemy soldiers in a trench when his rifle jammed. When he looked down to clear the malfunction, he saw two enemy grenades at their feet in the trench. Not knowing how long they had been there, he knew there was probably not enough time to pick up the grenades and throw them back at the enemy. So Jack did what he thought needed to be done. He shouted a warning of *"grenade"* to his teammates and pushed the nearest Marine out of the way. He forced one grenade into the soft, black sand with his weapon, and then threw himself on top of it while pulling the second grenade underneath his body.

The explosion that followed blew him into the air while creating more than 250 wounds to his body. Less than 24 hours after landing on Iwo Jima, Jack's fight with the Japanese was over.

Jack believed that if he hadn't responded to the grenades in the way he did, all his fire team would have at least been seriously wounded, which would have allowed the enemy soldiers to enter their trench and finish them off.

His teammates left him for dead as they didn't expect anyone to survive such a blast. They didn't have time to check on him anyway, as they were still actively engaged with the enemy. Jack later attributed his survival after the explosion to a silent prayer for God to save him. Although badly wounded, he never lost consciousness. Had he lost consciousness, he would have choked on his own blood, as he had a punctured lung among his many other wounds. He was also fortunate that only one of the grenades exploded beneath him.

After the explosion, Jack laid on the ground for an undetermined period, hoping that someone other than the Japanese would find him. When another Marine unit moved forward, all he could do was to move the fingers on his left hand as a signal that he was still alive. A Marine did find him and called a Corpsman up to tend to his wounds. The Corpsman provided life-saving treatment as well as protecting Jack from the enemy. A team of stretcher bearers managed to get him back to the beach, where he would await evacuation for more advanced medical treatment.

Jack eventually ended up on a hospital ship off shore where surgeons provided expert treatment of his wounds. From there, he travelled to Guam, Hawaii, and then to San Francisco. His final convalescent destination was Charleston, South Carolina. He received several surgeries along

Jack Lucas (USMC)

the way and, in September 1945, he received a medical discharge from the Marine Corps.

While in the hospital in Charleston he heard rumors that he was going to receive a medal. He didn't know a lot about medals at the time, so he wasn't sure what that was all about. When he received a call from Washington, D.C. on behalf of the President telling him that he was to receive the nation's highest military award, he started to understand that what he did at Iwo Jima was certainly a big deal.

On October 5, 1945, Jack joined a group of 13 other Sailors and Marines at the White House to receive the Medal of Honor from President Truman. He was only 17 years old. When hanging the Medal of Honor around the neck of a new recipient, it was common that Harry Truman to tell them, *"I would rather have that medal than to be president of the United States."*

With an impetuous bravado that was typical of Jack Lucas, when Truman told him about rather having the medal than be president, Jack responded *"Sir, I'll swap you!"* Obviously, the president didn't take Jack up on his offered swap. But it would have been interesting if he had!

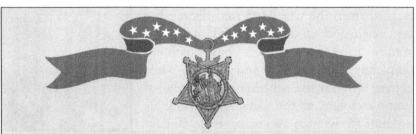

The President of the United States of America, in the name of Congress, takes pleasure in presenting the Medal of Honor to Private First Class Jacklyn Harold Lucas, United States Marine Corps Reserve, for conspicuous gallantry and intrepidity at the risk of his life above and beyond the call of duty while serving with Company C, First Battalion, Twenty-Sixth Marines, FIFTH Marine Division, during action against enemy Japanese forces on Iwo Jima, Volcano Islands, 20 February 1945. While creeping through a treacherous, twisting ravine which ran in close proximity to a fluid and uncertain frontline on D-plus-1 day, Private First Class Lucas and three other men were suddenly ambushed by a hostile patrol which savagely attacked with rifle fire and grenades. Quick to act when the lives of the small group were endangered by two grenades which landed directly in front of them, Private First Class Lucas unhesitatingly hurled himself over his comrades upon one grenade and pulled the other under him, absorbing the whole blasting forces of the explosions in his own body in order to shield his companions from the concussion and murderous flying fragments. By his inspiring action and valiant spirit of self-sacrifice, he not only protected his comrades from certain injury or possible death but also enabled them to rout the Japanese patrol and continue the advance. His exceptionally courageous initiative and loyalty reflect the highest credit upon Private First Class Lucas and the United States Naval Service.

Medal of Honor recipients during and after World War II were like present day rock stars. Having that kind of instant fame thrown upon you is overwhelming. But those pressures didn't keep Jack from handling things his own way. After all, he'd been playing by his own rules his whole life. He wasn't going to let a bit of notoriety stop him from continuing to do that.

Before leaving his mother to join the Marine Corps after the 8th grade, he promised her that he'd finish school when he returned from the war. He loved his mother very much and would never fail to keep a promise to her. It was a busy path to completing high school and college while keeping up with the schedule of a Medal of Honor recipient at the same time. And his weakness for women also managed to take up a lot of his time. In 1956, he finally completed his business degree from **High Point University** in North Carolina. A promise made was a promise kept.

Along the path towards keeping the promise to his mother, Jack married in 1952. Jack and his wife had three sons. But by 1961, Jack had a yearning to go back into the military. This time he chose to join the Army. According to Jack, he only had one fear and that was the fear of heights. So, he decided to conquer this fear by joining the paratroopers. The Marine Corps had few opportunities for people jumping out of airplanes, so Jack went into the Army instead. He completed his initial training requirements and was stationed with the 82d Airborne Division at Fort Bragg, North Carolina.

While at Fort Bragg, one of his jumps didn't go as planned. His unit was conducting a night drop from 1,200 feet. Jack was the last paratrooper out of the plane, but his main chute didn't open correctly. So, he deployed his reserve chute, which became entangled with the main chute. After unsuccessful attempts to get his chutes to open, all he could do was pray and try to relax so he could hopefully roll upon hitting the ground. On this airplane jump, he was the last man out and the first one to hit the ground. Fortunately, he survived.

Jack was still quick to think with his fists, and he was frustrated with the Army's refusal to send him to combat in Vietnam. After four years in the Army, he decided to leave the service. A friend helped get him into the meat business which provided him a good means to support his family. His new business ventures required a lot of traveling and he still hadn't recovered from his weakness for women. Jack ended up divorced from his first wife and shortly afterwards he was married to his second wife in 1968.

The meat business was doing well for Jack. By 1977 he had five shops in the Washington, D.C. area, along with a ranch in Maryland. But everything wasn't as good at home as he would have liked. One June evening Jack received a cryptic call from the Maryland State Police about needing to meet with him in person regarding a customer complaint. A customer complaint didn't seem like something the state police would handle but he agreed to meet with them to figure out what was going on. Much to his surprise, the trooper informed him that there was a threat on his life. What was even more shocking was the revelation that the person who wanted him dead was none other than his wife.

Jack knew there were problems between the two of them, but he never dreamed that this kind of betrayal was possible. The state trooper explained that there was a plot to hire a hit man to kill Jack and make it look like a suicide. They wouldn't have known about the details except that their informant was an acquaintance of Jack's and he wanted nothing to do with the plot. Their plan was for the informant to go back to the wife and tell her that he changed his mind. He would then bring a hit man into the plans – unknown to her, the hit man would be an undercover officer. The sting operation was successful in capturing the participants in the murder plot and they were all arrested and convicted.

The disappointment over his wife's treachery was very hard on Jack. Of course, his second marriage came to an end. He walked away from his business ventures, purchased some property, and moved into a mobile home there. One night the mobile home caught fire. Jack was able to get out of the blazing structure but he lost everything that was inside. After the fire he went through the ashes. As luck would have it, he found his Medal of Honor. The ribbon was gone but that was easy enough to replace.

After the fire, a friend offered to let Jack put up a tent on his property, giving him a new place to stay. A few weeks after living there, the police found marijuana growing nearby. As if Jack hadn't already been through enough, the police suspected that he had something to do with it and he was arrested. As soon as they realized he hadn't been there long enough to be responsible for the plants, the charges were dropped.

After the marijuana incident, Jack received an invitation to visit Hattiesburg, Mississippi. He soon decided that Hattiesburg would be his new home and he remained there for the rest of his life. In 1998, he met a woman named Ruby and his life was never the same. The two married and he found the love of his life who would remain beside him until his passing in 2008.

Jack had always relished life as a recipient of the Medal of Honor. Being the caretaker of the nation's highest military award opened a lot of doors for him. He enjoyed the camaraderie of his fellow recipients and it was a brotherhood that so few have ever known. The recipients are typically some of the humblest Americans you will ever meet. They are quick to tell you that they wear **The Medal** for everyone who served with them, and they all agree that there are so many others who performed heroic acts without recognition.

Jack never lost his gruff exterior and was never one to stop living by his own rules. At one Medal of Honor Society convention, he decided to take his rented motorcycle for a spin through the hotel lobby. He told of another occasion where another recipient was boasting about his own heroics and was talking about how tough he was. Jack didn't take kindly to this because he felt they were all heroes, and it was out of line to imply that one recipient was more heroic than the others. So, he slapped the braggart and knocked his hearing aid across the room. It was never a good idea to get on Jack's bad side. Maybe there were limits to his appreciation of others. But you always knew where you stood with Jack Lucas.

In 2006, Jack completed his memoirs, appropriately titled **Indestructible**. He was excited that the book allowed him to share his story with others. He enjoyed traveling with Ruby and signing copies of his book for people. **Indestructible** was documentation of his legacy. He had spent many years talking to people about patriotism and the importance of serving others. With the publishing of his book, his story could be told long after his passing.

Jack was diagnosed with leukemia in April 2008. On so many occasions, fate had tried time and again to end his life. He had survived the Japanese on Iwo Jima, a hitman contract, and even a fall from 1,200 feet. – but this time he was facing something that even he couldn't beat.

After two months of treatment, things became unbearable for Jack. With Ruby by his side, he was taken off dialysis. Six hours later, just after midnight on June 5, 2008, the **Indestructible Marine** had lived through throwing himself ton two grenades, was gone. In his last moments, Ruby told him, *"Jack, you know you're dying."*

Jack raised his head and said *"I ain't dead yet."* On the surface it might have seemed to be the last words of a tough guy who didn't know how to quit. But maybe Jack knew that he and his legacy would never die.

What a glorious legacy he did leave behind. Fourteen years after Jack's death, Ruby still receives calls from people who want to talk about the Marine hero who influenced so many. The three members of his fire team on Iwo Jima all lived into their 80's because of Jack's unselfish actions in 1945. Twice every year, on Veterans Day and Memorial Day, members of the Marine Corps League in Hattiesburg hold a small ceremony at the cemetery where they change out the flags on Jack's grave.

A stretch of road in Forrest County, Mississippi, has been named the **Jack Lucas Medal of Honor Memorial Highway.** A guided missile destroyer, the *U.S.S. Jack H. Lucas* is due to be commissioned by the Navy in 2023. At the Mississippi Armed Forces Museum in **Camp Shelby,** there is an exhibit detailing Jack's service, and where his medal is currently displayed. His medal is slated to be inherited by his great-grandson upon his 25th birthday. It is hoped that thereafter **The Medal** will remain with the family in the future.

His black marble headstone at the Highland Cemetery in Hattiesburg seems more like a monument than a grave marker. On the reverse of the headstone is engraved the following tribute: *"What we have done for ourselves dies with us. What we have done for others remains and is immortal."* Jack made a difference to so many people.

His headstone also lists his wife Ruby, who one day will be reunited with him.

For the rest of his life, you could see the scars and the black volcanic ash that remained under his skin. His experience on Iwo

Jima was still visible on his body, but being a Marine was in his DNA. He always had time for another Marine. The fact that they wore the **Eagle, Globe, & Anchor** was all he needed to know.

And they weren't just Marines. He always referred to them as HIS Marines. We will always be HIS Marines. Semper Fi.

Beyond Belief: True Stories of Marine Corps Heroes

Charles Abrell (USMC)

The Ultimate Sacrifice

By Adam Ballard

The Korean War, a conflict that would come to be known as *"The Forgotten War,"* it is where Americans would witness some of the most arduous and bitter fighting conditions, in history. The thousands of men and women who served and sacrificed on the Korean Peninsula demonstrated the upmost of devotion to mission and to their brothers-in-arms. Of 1,789,000 men and women who served in Korea, more than 30,000 were killed in action, and more than 100,000 suffered combat wounds.

One of the most striking examples of how bitter the fighting in Korea was, and how sacrificial the valor displayed, is the fact that a stunning 73% of the Medals of Honor awarded in the Korean War were posthumous awards.

War	Total MOHs	Posth.	% Posth.
World War I	132	42	32%
World War II	473	273	58%
Korean War	147	108	73%
Vietnam War	266	164	62%
Totals All Wars	3,534	654	19%

Of a total of 42 United States Marines who earned Medals of Honor in Korea, 28 did not survive to wear their award. Among them is the name of one U.S. Marine whose valor should never be forgotten. Corporal Charles Abrell was a veteran of the Inchon Invasion that broke the back of the North Koreans, and the Chosin Reservoir battle in North Korea, both in the first six months of the war. Then, in the summer of 1951, was awarded the Medal of Honor for actions eleven months after the war began.

Beyond Belief: True Stories of Marine Corps Heroes

CHARLES ABRELL

Charles Gene Abrell was born August 12, 1931, in the family home in the small town of Terre Haute, Indiana. His father, Charles E. Abrell was a truckdriver and laborer. His mother, Bernice O. Abrell, was a housekeeper.

Much of Charles childhood and upbringing can only be described as an enigma. Having struggled during and after the **Great Depression**, his parents moved from job to job, and eventually made their way to Las Vegas, Nevada. There, Charles made his decision to join the United States Marine Corps, still listing Terre Haute, Indiana, as his home of record.. He went on to graduate from **Marine Corps Recruit Depot**, Parris Island, South Carolina, and was subsequently stationed at **Camp Lejeune**. Serving as a rifleman, he was promoted to corporal, and was sent to Camp Pendleton, California. There, he served with the FIRST Marine Division until he was deployed on August 17, 1950, to serve in the Korean War.

INCHON

The Korean War began at 4:00 a.m., on the morning June 25, 1950, when nearly 100,000 soldiers of the North Korean People's Army (NKPA) invaded across the 38th Parallel which was the tenuous border between Communist North Korea, and the Democratic Republic of South Korea. They were supported by tanks and 130 aircraft. Unprepared to meet such a surprising attack, the South Korean Army and small detachments of American forces were overwhelmed. The Republic of Korea (ROK) Army was nearly destroyed, and the South Korean capitol city of Seoul, just 50 miles below the 38th Parallel, felt to the invaders within days.

American and South Korean forces retreated to the city of Pusan at the southern coast of South Korea, where they defended their small perimeter. Even when the U.S. Army's 24th Infantry

Charles Abrell (USMC)

Division arrived to help defend the Pusan Perimeter only six days after the invasion began, the outlook was grim

Throughout the months of July and August the United States moved quickly to shore up defenses at Pusan with supplies and an infusion of new troops. Throughout the period, from his headquarters in Japan, Army General Douglas MacArthur had been named by the Joint Chiefs of Staff as Commander in Chief of the United Nations Command (UNC). He was eager to mount a counter-invasion to infuse massive amounts of United Nation's forces into South Korea to turn the tide of the war.

His controversial plan was not to send more troops across the small expanse of the Sea of Japan to Pusan, but rather to circumvent the Korean peninsula and sail north to land at Inchon, just below the 38th parallel and less than 20 miles west of Seoul, which was now solidly under North Korean control.

The senior military leaders were justified in their opposition to that daring plan. Inchon's long, narrow channel with no beaches, dotted with islands that further restricted ship movement, and above all tides that, at thirty-two feet, were one of the two highest in the world, Inchon had what experts called *"the look of a place created by some evil genius who hated the Navy."* At low tide, mud flats extended anywhere from one thousand to six thousand yards, meaning that landings were only possible during high tide.

The Joint Chiefs of Staff, however, approved MacArthur's planned invasion early in the war. The course of events in and around Pusan delayed implementation and changed the schematics of what was originally planned to commence on July 22 with an assault by the Army's 1st U.S. Cavalry Division. The 1st Cavalry was thrown instead into battle east of Taejon, and General MacArthur turned his attention to the First and Fifth Regiments of the FIRST Marine

Beyond Belief: True Stories of Marine Corps Heroes

Division to lead the Inchon invasion, along with the men of the sole reserve unit in Japan, the Army's 7th Infantry Division.

In retrospect, MacArthur's most ardent detractors will admit that the surprise amphibious assault at Inchon, dubbed *Operation Chromite*, was a stroke of military genius. In a matter of days, the highly successful operation broke the back of the North Korean invasion of the South and liberated the capitol city of Seoul.

Actually, *Operation Chromite* was planned and proposed in early July when the war in Korea was barely a week old. It was typically *MacArthuresque*—transporting a large force completely around the enemy to land behind them, thus blocking supply routes and cutting off any retreat. The harbor at Inchon afforded all strategic requirements:

D-Day was September 15, 1950. Nearly 70,000 American Soldiers and Marines approached Inchon in a task force of 320 warships supported by four aircraft carriers. At 5:00 a.m. Marine Corsairs struck the small island of Wolmi-do, followed within an hour by the initial Marine landing. Half an hour later the small island at the approach to Inchon was under American control and 108 enemy had been killed, 136 captured. Marine casualties were light with only seventeen Americans wounded.

The landings at Inchon was Corporal Abrell's baptism of fire. He was assigned to Second Battalion, FIRST Marine Division as part of Regimental Combat Team 1, whose role in this three-pronged attack was to land at and secure **Blue Beach**. On the opening day of the invasion, First Lieutenant Baldomero Lopez (pictured) became the first Marine of the Korean War to earn the Medal of Honor. It was posthumously awarded.

As the battle began, the combined North Korean gun fire quickly overwhelmed their amphibious assault and sank one of their Landing support Ships. Under the command of Colonel Lewis

"Chesty" Puller, the Marines seized the initiative, pushed through the overwhelming fire, and secured **Blue Beach**. Stunned and surprised with the American resolve, most of the North Koreans surrendered almost immediately upon Marines' advance up the beach. As the FIRST Marine Division continued to secure the landing zone and surrounding areas, they met little resistance and took few casualties. In the late hours of the first day, and the early hours of the second, the FIRST Marine Division headquarters had been secured and Corporal Abrell and the rest of the Division began to march inland.

Soon, Corporal Abrell found himself in a battle that would earn him his first Purple Heart – the **Second Battle of Seoul**. On September 25 at approximately 7:00 a.m., the FIRST Marine Division began its assault on Seoul. There they encountered extremely dense North Korean defenses. Barricades, snipers, machine guns, and anti-tank weapons could be found around every corner and at every major intersection. Casualties multiplied as the Division engaged in laborious house-to-house fighting. Major Edwin Simmons, with Third Battalion, FIFTH Marines was quoted in saying; *"It's like attacking up Pennsylvania Avenue towards the Capitol in Washington, D.C."* After two more days of fighting, Seoul was officially retaken and returned to control of the South Korean government.. Corporal Abrell's wounds from that battle were relatively minor, and he was quickly patched up and on the move again. Leaving Seoul behind, he joined his Marines as they began to march north – into North Korea.

If the Inchon Landing was, perhaps, General Douglas MacArthur's greatest stroke of tactical genius, what followed thereafter may have been his worst.

The divided peninsula of Korea rests between the Sea of Japan and the Yellow Sea. It's only neighbor sits along the north-east boundary of North Korea. That border is the Yalu River, and that neighbor is the Chinese Manchuria. Fearful of an American sweep into the north following the successful landing at Inchon, the Chinese government issued a warning that if General MacArthur sent his troops north of the 38th parallel, they would be met by soldiers of the Chinese Army. Military planners doubted that the threat was real,

Beyond Belief: True Stories of Marine Corps Heroes

and sent the Allied forces north to neutralize the forces of North Korea and insure that a repeat of the June 25 invasion would not occur. On October 9, 1950 the first elements of American military units crossed the 38th parallel to take the battle home to the North Koreans. Five days later two Chinese Armies consisting of 12 Divisions (120,000 soldiers) crossed the Yalu River undetected.

For weeks the Chinese soldiers moved into the rugged mountains of North Korea, traveling only under cover of night and camouflaging their positions during the day. As MacArthur's forces moved north in a two-prong front, the EIGHTH Army moved toward the Yalu River from the western side of the peninsula and the TENTH Army on the eastern coast. The Americans didn't realize a well hidden, massive force was waiting to pounce on them. On October 25 the hidden enemy attacked, surprising the forces of the ROK army. In three days they destroyed four ROK regiments.

Still, American war planners were hesitant to believe the Chinese Force was more than just a few scattered units of North Korean soldiers, and committed the men of the EIGHTH and TENTH Armies to an offensive campaign to end the war and, as General MacArthur promised, get American soldiers *Home by Christmas.*

While the EIGHTH Army was moving up the western edge of North Korea, on the east coast. the port city of Wonsan was taken, followed by the city of Hungnam. From there, members of the FIRST Marine Division moved northwest on the Military supply Route (MSR) to the vital Chosin Reservoir. The village of Koto-ri was almost mid-way from Hungnam to the north edge of the reservoir, and the 4,200 Marines of the FIRST Marine Regiment set up there. The FIRST Marine Division Headquarters was established at Hagaru-ri, a small village at the southern tip of the reservoir. By November 27, 3,000 Americans inhabited Hagaru-ri, most of them engineers, clerks, and supply personnel.

Charles Abrell (USMC)

The combat troops, warriors of the Fifth and Seventh Marine Regiments, moved 12 miles northwest to the village of Yudam-ni. From here they were to travel west, crossing the rugged mountains to link up with the EIGHTH Army. That was the plan, but the plan hadn't factored in two unexpected obstacles:

- Between 120,000 and 150,000 well hidden Chinese Communist soldiers, and

- The worst winter weather conditions in 100 years.

THE CHOSIN RESERVOIR

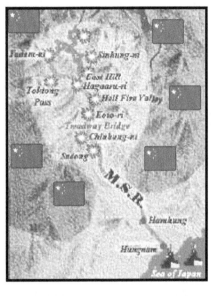

The Chosin Reservoir is a manufactured lake located in a northeastern part of the peninsula. The **Battle of the Chosin Reservoir** would primarily focus around the 80-mile-long road that connected the Reservoir with the city of Hungnam. This road would go on to serve as the only retreat route for U.N. forces in the area. The battle was fought over some of the roughest terrain and during one of the harshest winters on the Korean peninsula; with temperatures dropping to nearly -40 degrees due to a Siberian cold front blowing into the area. Weapon lubrication froze to a jelly like substance, vehicles would not start, and Medics and Corpsman had to defrost morphine syringes in their mouths before administering them to wounded Marines. However, against all odds, they prevailed.

One can only guess how cold it became in the high Taebaek mountains around the Chosin Reservoir during the winter of 1950. At one regimental headquarters the thermometer fell to minus 54 degrees. American Marines shivered in their foxholes, while vehicle drivers were forced to run their engines 24-hours a day. If the engine were shut down, chances were high that it couldn't be restarted. A rare hot meal could quickly freeze in the time it took a Marine to move from the serving line to a place where he could sit down to eat it. Then, to add to the misery, the Chinese launched their surprise attack.

The *"Home by Christmas"* offensive officially began on November 24, the day after Thanksgiving. In the west the EIGHTH Army began their drive to the Yalu River, only to be surprised by an unbelievable swarm of hidden Communist soldiers. Within days the CCF (Chinese Communist Forces) destroyed the ROK II Corps, leaving the EIGHTH Army without flanking cover or general support. The badly battered EIGHTH Army was ordered to fall back, a 275 mile withdrawal that in six weeks cost 10,000 casualties.

On the eastern slope of the Taebaek Mountains, most of the Marines were unaware of what was happening in the west, or just how badly outnumbered and surrounded they, themselves, were. Corporal Abrell and his Marines were digging in – establishing fighting positions and headquarters at the Chosin Reservoir.

The first indication of what the Marines were facing came on the morning of November 27 as two companies of the FIFTH Marines began the push from Yudam-ni westward. Before noon they ran into an enemy roadblock. Unaware of the numbers of enemy around them, the Marines engaged the Chinese, destroying the road block. Then enemy fire began to rain on them from all directions. The Marines knew they were in for a fight, one that lasted for nearly four hours. Then, when the firing subsided, the Marines attempted to dig in. The intensity of the battle convinced them that they were facing more than straggling units of North Korean soldiers. They knew the enemy would attack again, in force, under the cover of darkness. They did!

That night an estimated 120,000 Chinese soldiers from the Chinese Peoples Volunteer Army began to attack the U.N. Forces. Quickly becoming overwhelmed, the FIRST Marine Division Headquarters, which was established in the town of Yudam-ni; was cut off from the main body of the FIRST Marine Division, which was itself cutoff from other U.N. support units located further north. This effectively left the entire FIRST Marine Division without support or instruction.

Charles Abrell (USMC)

Hoping to destroy the Marines positions quickly, the Chinese began rushing them in waves of thousands. This forced the Marines to dig into the frozen soil in order to hold their positions. With waves of attackers still coming, close quarters and hand-to-hand combat quickly enveloped the lines as the Chinese continued to storm the position in what seemed like endless waves.

Despite the enemy's superior numbers, the Marines successfully held their positions. When day broke on November 28, the American Forces and the Chinese were locked in a stalemate on an auxiliary road between Hagaru-ri and Yundam-ni. As two more days of strenuous fighting went on, some units, such as Fox Company, Seventh Marines, which was located near the Toktong pass, were still completely cut off. However, the

Marines of Company F, Seventh Marines move up Fox Hill. From its heights they look down on the MSR as 8,000 Marines moved from Yudam-ni to Hagaru-ri.

FIRST Marine Division Headquarters was able to successfully reestablish communication with higher echelon forces.

Facing insurmountable odds of well-trained Chinese soldiers, General MacArthur ordered a withdrawal of U.N. forces. Acting on these orders, the commanders, Colonel Raymond L. Murray of the Fifth Marines and Colonel Homer L. Litzenberg of the Seventh Marines, issued orders to break out from their still surrounded positions.

Their mission was to move the bulk of the Division from Yundam-ni to Hagaru-ri. Dismayed by the unfathomable concept of Marines retreating, the commander of the FIRST Marine Division, Major General Oliver P. Smith famously remarked *"Retreat, Hell! We're not retreating, we're just advancing in a different direction.."* Knowing the only road back to Hagaru-ri and subsequently Koto-ri had already been cut off by the Chinese, the Marines had to retake that strategic position before a withdrawal could happen.

Staged behind a single M4A3 Sherman tank, and with orders in hand, the convoy began to move south towards the still stranded Fox Company. As these Marines began their departure, they faced some of the most ferocious attacks from the Chinese troops. The assault forced the Marines to dig into their position, further slowing their advance. Fortunately, air support supplied by the First Marine Air Wing allowed the Marines to continue their progress. Recapturing several key positions, this continued to facilitate the Marines' movement south.

Soon thereafter, the Fifth and Seventh Marines successfully relived the tattered remains of Fox company, who had suffered grievous losses at the hands of the Chinese. Summoning their last remaining strength these Marines fought to secure Toktong pass and they reached Hagaru-ri the next day, December 2.

Beginning December 6, after a badly needed rest and resupply, the Fifth and Seventh Marines continued their breakout towards Koto-ri. After having successfully recaptured key terrain features along the route, the Chinese forces attempted one last major offensive to stop the withdrawal. The battered Marines repulsed each wave of the attack, and successfully inflicted heavy casualties on the enemy forces. On December 7, what remained of the Marine column reached Koto-ri and established a defensive position.

Only fragments of two U.N. divisions stood between Koto-ri and the evacuation port of Hungnam. The Chinese troops began to dig into an area known as Funchilian Pass. Here, they emplaced obstacles, destroyed bridges, and occupied key terrain overlooking the route. In response to their actions, the First Battalion, First Marines attacked the Chinese defenders. The Marines were successful in destroying the enemy positions, however the Chinese fought to the last man.

Through the combined efforts of U.S. Marine and Army Engineers, the bridges leading to Hungnam were repaired and the U.N. forces proceeded to the evacuation point. Thereafter the only notable engagements were small fire fights breaking out from survivors of the desolated Chinese divisions that once defended the area. What would happen next would come to be known as *"The greatest evacuation movement by sea in U.S. Military history."* The Marines, vastly outnumbered and fighting not only a massive and well trained Chinese Army as well, withdrew.

Although difficult to account for his movements during the battle, Corporal Abrell's unit was critically involved in some of the most brutal fighting of the battle. After arriving at Hungnam port on December 11, the FIRST Marine Division was gradually evacuated to South Korea. Here, they faced further combat, albeit light combat, against North Korean forces during the Battle of Wonju. In total, the FIRST Marine Division reported 17,833 Casualties.

At the Chosin reservoir, despite their best efforts, the Chinese forces had failed to crush the indomitable FIRST Marine Division. The Marines came out unashamed, bringing their equipment, their wounded, and most of their dead. They would live to fight another day, and continue the gallant legacy of the United States Marine Corps. At the Chosin Reservoir, outnumbered Marines established their own legacy . . . not one of retreat — but one of surviving against incredible odds through leadership, teamwork, and the highest degree of brotherhood.

For their heroic leadership, Colonels Murray and Litzenberg were awarded Distinguished Service Crosses by the Army. Murray also earned a Gold Star in lieu of a second award of the Navy Cross. Major General Oliver P. Smith also received a Distinguished Service Cross for his heroic leadership at the Chosin Reservoir. Incredibly, of the 42 Medals of Honor awarded to Marines in the Korean War, 9 were awarded for actions in a span of 7 days at the Chosin Reservoir.

Beyond Belief: True Stories of Marine Corps Heroes

CHOSIN RESERVOIR MARINE MEDALS OF HONOR

Staff Sergeant **Robert S. Kennemore**  E/2 7th Marines Nov. 27 & 28, 1950	Private **Hector A. Cafferata, Jr.**  F/2 7th Marines Nov. 28, 1950	Captain **William E. Barber**  F/2 7th Marines Nov. 28 – Dec. 2, 1950
Private First Class **William B. Baugh**  **Killed in Action** G/3 1st Marines Nov. 29, 1950	Major **Reginald R. Myers**  HQ/3 1st Marines Nov. 29, 1950	Captain **Carl L. Sitter**  G/3 1st Marines Nov. 29 & 30, 1950
Staff Sergeant **William G. Windrich**  **Killed in Action** I/3 5th Marines Dec. 1, 1950	Lieutenant Colonel **Raymond G. Davis**  HQ/1 7th Marines Dec. 1 - 4	Sergeant **James E. Johnson**  **Killed in Action** J/3 7th Marines Dec. 2, 1950

Charles Abrell (USMC)

Corporal Abrell participated in sporadic fighting following his service at the Chosin Reservoir. But his next, and final major combat experience in Korea was from May 20 to June 10, 1951, during the U.N. counter offences near the Hwacheon Reservoir. By this time, he was a seasoned combat veteran of many battles over nearly a year in Korea.

BATTLE OF HWACHEON RESERVOIR

After the stunning repulse of the United Nations forces' advance into North Korea, both of the EIGHTH U.S. Army in the west along the border with China, and on the east coast at the Chosin Reservoir, the UN forces retreated back to the south. There they held tenuously near the Demilitarized Zone at or above the 38th Parallel, to reinforce from the heavy losses sustained, and to reorganize. In April, General Maxwell Taylor, now commander of U.N. Forces in Korea, along with EIGHTH

Army commander General James Van Fleet, launched *Operation Courageous*, an effort to trap large numbers of the Chinese People's Volunteer Army (PVA) and NKPA between the Han and Imjin River's north of Seoul.

The United Nations Command initiated *Operation Dauntless* to solidify the ground gained, as well as effort to advance the U.N. lines to positions ten to twenty miles north of the 38th parallel, along a line called *"Line Kansas."* Operation Dauntless and *Operation Rugged* (April 1 – 21, 1951) generally succeeded until the Chinese brought a halt to the U.N. advance with their own Spring Offensive.

The Chinese were now fully vested in the war in Korea, and the combined PVA and NKPA offensive was launched on April 20, moving massive forces on the roads above Yanggu and Inje, east of the Hwacheon reservoir on the edge of *Line Wyoming*. The area was defended by the 6th ROK Division, the U.S. Army's 6th Infantry Division, and the FIRST Marine Division.

On the night of April 21, the PVA 40th Army struck in force, decimating the 6th ROK Division, which literally dissolved By 1:30 a.m. the following morning, the FIRST Marine Division headquarters learned that the ROK lines had been breached, leaving the Marines' flank dangerously exposed.

What remained of the ROK 6th Division fled in full retreat, and the Marine flank was not only dangerously exposed, but the Division's MSR and all crossing points of the Pukhan River were at risk of falling to the enemy. Veterans of the Division's winter battles in North Korea's Chosin Reservoir would later compare the battle of the Hwacheon Reservoir to what they had faced, and struggled to survive, the previous November – minus the sub-zero weather.

When night fell on April 22, the communists began their attack on the positions held by the FIRST Marine Division. Marine Private First Class Herbert Littleton of Napa, Idaho, was serving with an artillery forward observer team of Company C, First Battalion, Seventh Marines when a numerically superior communist force launched their attack. Moving to an advantageous position to call in artillery fire against the enemy force, when a grenade was thrown into his position he covered it with his own body, saving the other members of his team from severe injury or death, becoming the twentieth Marine to earn the Medal of Honor in the Korean War. It was awarded posthumously, his citation noting that his actions enabled the rest of his team to repulse the enemy attack.

The following night under the cover of darkness, the communists overran an outpost of Company G, Third Battalion, First Marines. Technical Sergeant Harold *"Speedy"* Wilson braved the enemy fire to assist survivors back to the line and direct their treatment. Although wounded by gunfire in the right arm and left leg, he continued his valiant actions, rallying his men to resist. Wounded again in the head and shoulder, he refused medical attention and continued to lead and to fight. When he could no longer use either arm to fire his weapon, he re-supplied his men with rifles and ammunition taken from the wounded. When the enemy attack intensified, he requested reinforcements, directing their fire until blown off his feet by a bursting mortar round. *"Dazed and suffering from concussion, he still refused medical aid and, despite weakness from loss of blood, moved from foxhole to foxhole, directing fire, resupplying ammunition, rendering first aid, and encouraging his men. By his heroic actions in the face of almost certain death, when the unit's ability to hold the disadvantageous position was doubtful, he instilled confidence in his troops, inspiring them to rally repeatedly and turn back the furious assaults. At dawn, after the final attack had been repulsed, he personally accounted for each man in his platoon before walking unassisted 1/2 mile to the aid station for treatment."*

For his actions that night, Technical Sergeant Wilson was awarded the Medal of Honor.

The eight-day Battle of the Hwacheon Reservoir pitted 400,000 United Nations forces against more than 700,000 PVA and NKPA troops. Although the enemy suffered more than 110,000 casualties (some estimates went as high at 160,000) in comparison to 14,000 U.N. casualties, in the face of still overwhelming odds, the U.N. troops pulled back to the *No Name Line*, yielding more than 30 miles of territory to the enemy.

During the first two weeks in May, General Van Fleet focused on solidifying and fortifying the *No Name Line*. Meanwhile, despite the heavy casualties sustained at the Hwacheon Reservoir, Chinese Chairman Mao Zedong insisted on mounting a second phase of the Spring Offensive. More than 150,000 communists began attacking ROK and TENTH Corps in the east at the Soyang River.

The Communist's plan was to attack below the Soyang River in the Taebaek Mountains. The hope was to sever the lines between six ROK divisions in the east, from the remainder of the EIGHTH Army, and totally destroy the ROK defenders. While this area would bear the brunt of the communist attack, the PVA and NKPA would supplement their offensive in the east with secondary attacks across the entire front

Beyond Belief: True Stories of Marine Corps Heroes

BATTLE OF THE SOYANG RIVER

Arrayed against this Chinese Second Spring Offensive was the FIRST Marine Division, located centrally on the Korean Peninsula, South of the 38th Parallel. The Division was assigned to advance toward the Munsan-Chuncheon segment of *Line Topeka.*

From there, they were to encircle PVA and NKPA forces fighting laterally of them to capture all road junctions in vicinity of the Hwacheon Reservoir. Advancing rapidly, the Division and its adjacent units had all reached *Line Topeka* by the evening of May 23. Having experienced a large amount of success in their advance, the FIRST Marine Division was relived by the south Korean Royal Marines in order to allow them to prepare for an attack on the Chuncheon-Hwacheon axis road complex, on the western end of the Hwacheon Reservoir. Their mission was to lead the advance in order to facilitate follow-on forces occupation of what was identified as a critical area of control.

Over the next several days, the Marines were faced with extremely rough terrain and grueling climbs – more Marines were killed or wounded by the environment than the still retreating Chinese troops. Continuing the slow advance, the FIRST Marine Division had only moved several miles by the evening of May 24. In order to continue their drive forward, the Marines were assigned a regiment named *Task Force Gerhart* to follow and support their efforts of seizing an area that was believed would be the enemy forces' primary withdrawal route.

Still slowed by the sporadic enemy contact, the FIRST Marine Division was ordered to accelerate its advance, as commanders were still hopeful of dispatching large groups of enemy troops expected to pass through the area. Their next objective was to seize the town of Yanggu. By May 27 further support efforts were allocated in order to advance the movement and free up combat power of the FIRST Marine Division.

On May 29, Private First Class Whitt L. Moreland of the First Battalion, First Marines was engaged with the enemy near Kwagch'i Dong, while serving as an intelligence scout. He voluntarily accompanied a rifle platoon in an assault against a strongly defended enemy hill position and, after it was taken and secured, he led a party forward against an enemy bunker 400 meters to the front. When the enemy began raining grenades on the advancing Marines, he *"kicked several of the grenades off the ridge line where they exploded harmlessly and, while attempting to kick away another, slipped and fell near the deadly missile. Aware that the sputtering grenade would explode before he could regain his feet and dispose of it, he shouted a warning to his comrades, covered the missile with his body and absorbed the full blast of the explosion."*

For his sacrificial actions, he was posthumously awarded the Medal of Honor.

It wasn't until June 1 that the FIRST Marine Division was eventually able to seize and move through Yanggu. By June 4, the First Marine Division and Korean Royal Marines were ordered to advance toward *Line Kansas.*

Moving under some of the most difficult combat conditions, U.N. forces faced steep ridges, narrow fronts, and difficult climbs that further slowed the already exhausted troops. Furthermore, logistical resupply was stalled due to one-lane roads, and bridges that required significant engineering work before trucks could traverse them. However, the most difficult obstruction was the Chinese and North Korean defenders.

The enemy was well organized and emplaced in fortified positions across every ridgeline. The communists were noted as being significantly more aggressive and insistent in their fighting – not giving an inch of ground; and when positions were lost, they quickly organized a counterattack to recapture or destroy the occupying Marines. On June 9, identifying the threat, the Commander of the FIRST Marine Division committed all his Marines, to include his reserves, in order to destroy the bitter resistance they were facing. It was under such combat conditions, after nearly a year of fighting from Inchon to the Chosin Reservoir, to the Hwacheon Reservoir, and then the return to that area in the Taebaek Mountains, that Corporal Charles Abrell made his ultimate sacrifice.

On June 10, 1951, while assigned as a Fireteam Leader in Company E, Second Battalion, First Marines, Corporal Abrell and his

Beyond Belief: True Stories of Marine Corps Heroes

comrades began to assault on of the many heavily defended ridgeline positions occupied by the North Korean soldiers. While fully suppressed on the side of a hill by withering machine gun fire, Corporal Abrell noticed the devastating casualties being generated by this single enemy position. Knowing the risk to his Marines, Corporal Abrell rushed forward from covered position to covered position in order to reach the assaulting squad, which was pinned down by the machinegun fire. Instructing the Marines to follow his assault, Corporal Abrell single-handedly charged up the hill towards the enemy bunker.

As he stormed the emplacement, he received two more wounds before he reached their position. Astonishingly, Corporal Abrell proceeded to pull the pin on a hand grenade and throw himself bodily into the bunker with the armed grenade still in his grasp. The explosion killed the entire six-man enemy gun crew, as well as himself. This action directly influenced his platoon's success that day and further allowed his company to advance and capture the entire ridgeline, successfully destroying each enemy position they encountered. For his actions he became the 23d Marine to earn the Medal of Honor during the first eleven months of the Korean War.

The President of the United States of America, in the name of Congress, takes pride in presenting the Medal of Honor (Posthumously) to Corporal Charles Gene Abrell (MCSN: 1082642), United States Marine Corps, for conspicuous gallantry and intrepidity at the risk of his life above and beyond the call of duty while serving as a Fire Team Leader in Company E, Second Battalion, First Marines, FIRST Marine Division (Reinforced), in action against enemy aggressor forces on 10 June 1951, near Hangnyong, Korea. While advancing with his platoon in an attack against well-concealed and heavily fortified enemy hill positions, Corporal Abrell voluntarily rushed forward through the assaulting squad which was pinned down by a hail of intense and accurate automatic-weapons fire from a hostile bunker situated on commanding ground. Although

Charles Abrell (USMC)

previously wounded by enemy hand grenade fragments, he proceeded to carry out a bold, single-handed attack against the bunker, exhorting his comrades to follow him. Sustaining two additional wounds as he stormed toward the emplacement, he resolutely pulled the pin from a grenade clutched in his hand and hurled himself bodily into the bunker with the live missile still in his grasp. Fatally wounded in the resulting explosion which killed the entire enemy guncrew within the stronghold, Corporal Abrell, by his valiant spirit of self-sacrifice in the face of certain death, served to inspire all his comrades and contributed directly to the success of his platoon in attaining its objective. His superb courage and heroic initiative sustain and enhance the highest traditions of the U.S. Naval Service. He gallantly gave his life for his country.

The FIRST Marine Division, as well and the United Nations' Forces reached and gained full possession of their objectives – the Chinese *Spring Offensive* was stopped with heavy losses. On July 10, cease-fire negotiations began, and the war entered a two-year stalemate. Sporadic fighting would continue two more years until the Korean Armistice Agreement was signed on July 27, 1953, a year and one month and two days after it began.

Nineteen more Marines would earn Medals of Honor in the last two years of the war, more than half of them awarded posthumously. More than 33,686 U.S. military personnel were killed during the war, including 4,267 United States Marines. Nearly 25,000 Marines suffered combat wounds and were awarded Purple Hearts.

On September 4, 1952; Corporal Abrell's Medal of Honor was posthumously presented to his mother by secretary of the Navy Dan Kimball. Her son was laid to rest at Westlawn Cemetery in Farmersburg, Indiana.

At the Vigo County Courthouse lawn in Terre Haute, Indiana, a hometown hero is remembered by a bronze larger-than-life statue.

Beyond Belief: True Stories of Marine Corps Heroes

Donald Dunagan (USMC)

A Marine's Secret Past

By C. Douglas Sterner

The men and women who enter service in the branches of our military forces come from wide-ranging backgrounds. They include highly educated college graduates, high school graduates from valedictorians to those who struggled to barely pass their classes, and even high school dropouts. They come from backgrounds of wealth, or hard-working blue collar workers, even general laborers, as well as the shiftless and unemployed. The ranks of U.S. Army Soldiers, Navy Sailors, Marines, and Coast Guardsmen truly represent a cross-section of America. Some enlisted out of a patriotic desire to serve. Others found military service an option to overcome their backgrounds and current, often hopeless, life situations.

Especially during the periods from World War I, through the Vietnam War, when the demand for recruits was high and recruiting standards were more lax than in recent years; some entered military service with troubled backgrounds. Not a few who had run afoul of the law were given the choice by a judge – join the military or go to jail.

As a result, many of the men and women who swore the oath and donned the uniform of our branches of military service, brought with them secrets from their past making their best efforts to hide from their recruiters, their commanders, and their comrades in uniform.

When Donnie Dunagan was drafted into the Marine Corps in 1952 at the height of the war in Korea, he brought with him a secret. It was one he tried to hide from every one throughout his 25-year-career as a Marine Corps Infantrymen and subsequently as a Marine Corps officer. It was a secret he even kept from his wife when he married. During two tours of duty, perhaps the thing he feared most was that one day the men he commanded in battle, might learn about his secret past.

EARLY LIFE AS A STREET PERFORMER

Donald *Donnie* Roan Dunagan was born at sea while his parents, Mr. and Mrs. W. F. Dunagan were en route from Ireland to the United States. When the ship docked at Galveston, Texas, a stranger offered the family a ride to San Antonio. There he received a second birth certificate listing his date of birth as August 16, 1934. An earlier birth certificate recording his birth at sea two or three days earlier had been issued by the ship's Captain Roan, whose surname became Donnie's middle name.

When his father received the offer of a job in Memphis, Tennessee, paying twenty cents an hour, the family promptly relocated. The Dunagans lived in abject poverty on that meager salary, thankful for what they had during the depression years. They had immigrated to escape even worse conditions in poverty-stricken Ireland. As he began to talk, Donnie spoke not only English, but at age 13 months learned to count in Spanish from a neighbor. From his parents and friends, he also learned German and French.

He recalled that his mother would walk with him to *"two to three ding-dings"* to watch a street performer named Sam, who with his Victrola, would dance and entertain small crowds for pennies and nickels. Donnie began to teach himself, at that young age, to both sing and dance as well, and found himself following Sam's example – becoming part of *"Ding-dings,"* a street act with Sam.

Decades later in an interview with **San Angelo Lifestyles**, he recalled. *"I later learned that Sam was related to a famous Vaudevillian performer on Broadway, Peg Leg Bates, and someone in this fancy car (that pulled up during one performance), knew him. The person in the car handed something to Sam and the crowed cried out, 'a double sawbuck' ($10)."* Sam ran off with the money while Dunagan continued to dance by himself, but returned minutes later and handed his mother half of it, having ostensibly made change. Donnie recalled that this five dollars enabled his family to pay rent, and still have left over change.

This was Donnie's first opportunity to contribute meaningfully to his impoverished family's economic needs. Soon thereafter, with a home-made top hat and tap shoes stuffed with tissues so they would fit his small feet, he entered a talent show. Dancing his way through the tune of *"A Tisket, a Tasket,"* he won first place, and the prize of $100 – equivalent to two-and-a-half years' salary for laborers like his father. He later learned that his mother had sold her wedding ring in order to buy the tap shoes and costume that he wore for the contest.

The family returned home exuberant, to find a talent scout for movie giant RKO, who had been in the audience, waiting for them. Dunagan recalled, *"I, like most people of the day, had never seen a movie, so my dad was suspicious."* After a conference call from the talent scout's hotel room later that day, Mr. Dunagan was convinced, and soon the family was on their way to Hollywood. Dunagan later told **San Angelo Lifestyles***: "We went from maybe eating one meal a day to being on a train that had a dining car. It was there that I ate ice cream for the very first time and it's my vice to this day."*

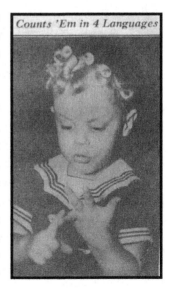

Counts 'Em in 4 Languages

Beyond Belief: True Stories of Marine Corps Heroes

His Hollywood audition was announced in *The Express* on September 12, 1937, under a headline that read, *"Boy, 3, Prepares for Film Career in Four Tongues."* They further noted that he was, *"judged in a recent local beauty show to rank 100 per cent in beauty, 100 per cent in personality, and 100 percent in health."*

HOLLYWOOD CHILD STAR

For his screen test, his mother curled his hair, which Donnie hated, but which, with his performance, with a goat no less, garnered him a contract and a job in the 1938 movie *Mother Carey's Chickens."* The following year he was performing in his second motion picture, *"Son of Frankenstein,"* with veteran actors Basil Rathbone, Boris Karloff, and Bela Lugosi. Dunagan played the role of the young son of Baron Wolf von Frankenstein and his wife Elsa (Josephine Hutchinson).

Also in 1939 he had roles in *"Fixer Dugan," "Terry Kennedy," "The Forgotten Women"* and *"Tower of London."* In 1940 he had an uncredited role in *"Vigil in the Night,"* and the following year he performed in *"Meet the Camp."* In 1942 he had one final role, and then retired from acting.

When Dunagan entered into contract with RKO, as a minor, his contract had to be approved by the Los Angeles Superior Court. It stipulated that his parents set aside half of his salary in a trust fund. Nevertheless, the child actor's success was ample enough that the remaining half of his salary enabled his family to, for the first time in their lives, live comfortably. Donnie Dunagan was the first person to benefit from the new law, passed after the parents of child actor Jackie Coogan (*"The Kid"* 1921), squandered his earnings. Like Coogan's parents, Donnie's parents also overspent the half of their son's earnings that enabled them a lifestyle they had never before known.

"We'd gone from a one-room tenement to a house in Beverly Hills, and it was too much, too quick," Dunagan recalled in an

interview in **The Guardian**. *"The family just ruptured, and I was then farmed out to a bunch of people."*

Tension mounted in the family and ultimately the couple fell apart, and then divorced. Both died premature deaths not long afterwards and Donnie became an orphan. In 1945 when he was ten years old, Donnie was placed in an orphanage in San Antonio, Texas.. Later he returned to Los Angeles to live at an orphanage operated by Father Howard, an early mentor he came to dearly love.

Father Howard died when Donnie was fourteen years old, and he ran away from the orphanage. Thereafter he was on his own and living in a boarding home, working at a menial, low-paying job as a lathe operator. He had made a decision at age nine not to talk about his film career, and began focusing on the future. By age 17 he was hoping to become a doctor and worked hard to hopefully get a football scholarship to attend college. However, when he turned 18, he received a letter from **Uncle Sam**.

MARINE CORPS SERVICE

In 1952 Dunagan received his draft notice to appear for a physical. Instead, in January 1943 he enlisted in Marine Corps for service as an enlisted Infantryman. It was a good fit.

He brought with him a secret from his past that he dearly hoped his new *brothers-in arms* would never find out. Acknowledging his secret, he later told **The Guardian**, *"You have to understand what it's like in the Marine Corps, or in the CIA, or FBI. Those were the best men I ever met in my life, but they would never talk about their past, or boast about their achievements . . . only tacky men did that."*

Of course, in Dunagan's case, he had an ulterior motive for hiding the secret from his own past.

Beyond Belief: True Stories of Marine Corps Heroes

"Standing in the line for medical doctors at a table," he recalled, *"lots of you −, from behind me came a 6'3" or taller Marine First Sergeant − World War II type − Marine Recruiter. He is not supposed to be in there . . . (it was) against strong regulations.*

"'Son, are you Doonagan (miss-spoken)?' he inquired. I replied that I was. 'Son," he went on, *'The Marines have a foot ball team and boxing teams. Do you still do both?' I replied that I did. 'Come with me, Son, and you get paid for doing that stuff you do now for free!!! Paid!!!'*

"Ha, living in a boarding house since age 14 and school, and for free!!! Paid! Ha. I went right with him, kind of covert out the rear door. That was when I realized that this big guy may not be OK in the recruit room. One day later the Los Angeles recruiting command put me on a trail with a clip board and told me to keep under order with the, I think 15 to 17 new enlistments in San Diego. It was my first leadership challenge . . . great fun life."

Over the years that followed Dunagan continued to perform well in the Corps, and gain additional stepping stones in leadership,. After **Boot Camp**, having tested 167 on the **Stanford Test**, he was trained as a Drill Instructor through a special program, reportedly becoming the youngest DI in Marine Corps History.

Excitedly, the young Marine sewed his new Private First Class stripes on his uniform before reporting to DI School. In his haste, they were, by his account, *"about 30 percent crooked."*

Reporting to the school, he was met by the First Sergeant of the legendary DI School. *"You can't be a DI,"* he shouted angrily, directly into the young man's face. *"Look at you (shirt). You are even a 'Crooked PFC'."*

"I got teased for that for months," he remembers.

The negative reception aside, the following year at age 20, he became the Corps' youngest Senior Drill Instructor. *"Years later when I was a hyper young Gunnery Sergeant, before officer promotions,"* he recalled, *"that old World War II 'Top Sergeant' and I became real close friends."* A year after becoming a DI, at age 20, he was the youngest Senior Drill instructor in the Marine Corps.

Donald Dunagan (USMC)

Promoted thirteen times in the first 21 years of his career, he was a senior sergeant at age 21, and later a *Mustang* – a commissioned officer who had come up through the ranks. Following his time as a Drill Instructor he attended the Army's counterintelligence training in Maryland. *"Credentialed, armed, and in civilian clothes,"* he recalled in a 2001 interview with the Carlsbad Current Argus, *"I was engaged in some of the most interesting and risky counter intelligence operations."* Still doing his best to hide the secret from his past that haunted him, he served as an in-the-field counterintelligence agent, all over the world.

On loan to the Army, he was twice cited by the Secretary of the Army. His first was for designing a show-box-size detect system to expose wire taps and induction taps. He was cited a second time, prior to his Vietnam War service, for leading in other intelligence actions.

In 1967 Dunagan deployed as a Marine combat leader to Vietnam, with the Third Battalion, Fifth Marines as the Combat Intelligence Patrol Leader Officer.. Serving through the infamous Tet Offensive of 1968. He subsequently served a second combat tour – and was medically evacuated from both tours from serious combat wounds. He was awarded three Purple Hearts for wounds in combat, and a Bronze Star for Valor, and a Navy Commendation Medal for Valor. *"I have some holes in my body that God didn't put there,"* he says. *"I*

Dunagan being awarded the Bronze Star Medal

got shot through my left knee. Got an award or two for saving some lives over time."

Dunagan recalls how his close friend, Major General Kenneth J. Houston would sometimes introduce him to audiences, ribbing him about his two medical evacuations, when Major Dunagan was giving presentations. Houghton had been Dunagan's Regimental Commander in Vietnam and began with the words: *"and here is this*

Beyond Belief: True Stories of Marine Corps Heroes

Marine Dunagan guy . . . (I) sent him to Vietnam a couple of times and he just came out early, kind of the easy way for him."

Following the Vietnam War, by 1977 Dunagan had risen to the rank of major. He was selected for the National War College in Kansas, a major stepping stone to future promotion, perhaps even to flag rank. A required physical involved a hearing test, which Dunagan failed. Angrily, he opted to retire after a quarter-century of honorable Marine Corps service. Years later physicians found a benign tumor inside his hearing tract that had impeded his hearing. After it was removed he had no further issues with his hearing. He said, *"I have not forgiven Navy doctors in San Diego for the poor examination error terminating my growing and wonderful career in the Marines."*

In numerous interviews, Dunagan later recalled one interesting incident as his retirement date neared. Major Dunagan was summoned to the office of a Marine Corps General with whom he served and who now instructed him to *"audit the auditors."*

"General, when do you think I'm going to have time to do that?" Dunagan recalled saying in an interview for NPR in 2015. *"He looked at me, pulled his glasses down like some kind of college professor. There's a big red, top-secret folder that he got out of a safe somewhere that had my name on it. He pats this folder, looks me in the eye, and says, 'You will audit the auditors. Won't you, Major Bambi'."*

Dunagan blanched – the secret he had tried so hard to hide for twenty-five years was known to this Marine general.

MAJOR BAMBI

Donnie Dunagan's last movie before retiring, the one he had a major role in, in 1942, was the Walt Disney animated feature **"Bambi."** Dunagan had been personally selected by Disney to do the voice for the movie's namesake. (Dunagan did the voice for 70% of the movie, although an older child actor was brought in to do the voice for the latter part of the movie when Bambi was older.)

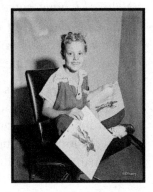

Donald Dunagan (USMC)

"This may sound corny to any reasonably intelligent person," Dunagan would later remark. *"I would not have made it as a very young first sergeant, CWO gunner, a regular line lieutenant, company commander, or field grade officer with the nickname 'Bambi'."*

In another interview he noted, *"(In) 1975 I found out that Disney was re-releasing. I was an operations officer and a commander out in San Diego and I was afraid that they were going to show the film where we were stationed. I could just hear all the boys calling home to their mothers and saying, 'Hey mom, guess who my commanding officer is – Major Bambi'."*

Dunagan's secret remained hidden from all but the general and one other, for decades.

Donald Dunagan went on to successful civilian careers. He managed offices for national life insurance companies and designed the first pet health insurance company in the United States, which he later sold to the Veterinarian's Association. He served as CEO and CFO of major, close-held corporations. On loan from the Defense Department, he was trained and hired by the Nevada Gaming Commission to inspect game tables and slot machines. Still, he is quick to point out regarding his multiple successes, "nothing can displace the adventures, hyper challenges, and respect for live that my Marine Corps years loaded me with.

On September 4, 1992, in New Mexico, he married Dana J. Flanders. The wedding date had been carefully chosen – it was an unforgettable date in 1967 when he had been part of a horrible battle in which one of his close friends was killed in action. Dunagan had known Navy Chaplain, Lieutenant Vincent Robert Capodanno before the two served together in Vietnam with the Fifth Marines. *"Father Capodanno was killed by an AK-47 while crawling around under intense close fire, trying to save lives of several of our troops, including a couple of my Scout*

Dunagan (Left) with Father Capodanno (Right) in Vietnam.

lads," he recalled. *"I wrote the next day, on grim brown ammunition type paper, on of several recommendations for the Medal of Honor. So, me and my lady savor the September 4 date for strongly extra reasons."*

When he married he said nothing to his wife about his past, including his role as the voice of Bambi. Three years after they were married, she happened to find a trove of old newspaper stories her husband had hidden away for decades. There, she learned her husband's secret.

MAY 31, 1940

To Be Heard But Not Seen

Disney Picks Donnie For 'Bambi' Model

Donnie Dunagan, 5-year-old grandson of Mr. and Mrs. Thomas E. Johnson, 1270 Carr, was picked yesterday by Walt Disney to impersonate "Bambi" in the full-length Disney cartoon of the same name.

Little Donnie, who has previously appeared in "Mother Carey's Chickens," "Son of Frankenstein" and other pictures, will not be seen on the screen in "Bambi," but he will serve as model for the tiny deer hero of the popular fairy tale.

His eyes, the expression of his face and the manner of his walk will be captured by the Disney artists for "Bambi" and he will also supply the voice, it was stated in Hollywood after the contract was signed.

Donnie has not been active in movie work for the past several months because of a measles attack, but he has completely recovered and is now on daily duty at the Disney studio.

Donnie Dunagan

In March 2005 Dunagan finally allowed an in-depth interview with Terry Pace of the **Times Daily**; his secret was out at last. Two months later he presented an after-dinner speech for a charity organization in his and Dana's hometown of San Angelo, Texas. Soon after the dinner he was contacted by KLS-TV, and as a result of their coverage, the Disney Corporation learned that Donny Dunagan was alive and well in Texas. They had long thought he had died.

"I got a call from a wonderfully grisly old Sergeant in North Dakota," Dunagan recalled. *"He told me, 'We could've handled Frankenstein. We called you worse than that and you know it*

Donald Dunagan (USMC)

wouldn't have mattered because you got us home sir. But we wish we knew about Bambi; we would've beaten you up about Bambi.'"

Speaking engagements quickly piled up and his mailbox began filling with fan letters. Despite his penchant for avoiding the spotlight, in his newly found fame he found a new mission. *"It's the letters mostly from young children and their many drawings and requests for advice and thanks for helping the homeless in the area from Texas, and the warmest thoughts one could savor that I treasure more than four rows of medals,"* he told the **San Angelo Lifestyles.** *"I was in the Marine Corps for twenty-five years, but I've been able to do more good in my life with Bambi."*

In 2017 Disney celebrated the 75th anniversary of *"Bambi,"* and Dunagan became even more in demand. He was at last reunited with Peter Benh, who at age four did the voice for **Thumper** in the movie. It was the first time the two had seen each other since the screening for the film in 1942.

Finally accepting his role as the embodiment of Bambi, Dunagan now talks more openly about his own part in the historic classic. He unashamedly recalls how difficult was the scene in the movie when Bambi's mother is killed by a hunter. *"They told me to call out 'Mother . . . Mother,' And I did,"* he told **Chicago Parent.** *"The film makers made me repeat this several times, and I didn't get it right until they told me that my mother was in the studio and was in danger. They told me to call out to her, and I really thought that she was in danger, so it sounded more authentic."*

He recalled that scene again in his interview with **San Antonio Lifestyles,** relating it to his experience in Vietnam in September 1977 when he had been shot for the second time in combat. *"I'm down and two other lieutenants are down,"* he recalled. *"There are a bunch of kids fighting who have a right to go home but we're outnumbered. One of them stands over me and says, 'Skipper, get up, get up, we need you."* Flashing back to 1942 he recalled similar dialogue when Bambi's father says, *"Bambi, get up, you must get up."*

255

Beyond Belief: True Stories of Marine Corps Heroes

"The Marine was telling me to get up just like the movie where the dad was telling Bambi to get up. For me, that was the most significant scene in Bambi, and my own life."

"I am proud as punch – and I don't use that word easily – to be associated with such a beautiful story," Dunagan says unapologetically. *"I was a highly accomplished shooter in the Marine Corps, and at other places and times – I worked at it. I was often invited to go on hunting trips in Montana or the Dakotas. Most often it was deer – and I couldn't do it. I just couldn't do it. I've done a lot of shooting, but I've never shot an animal – not one."*

Acknowledgements:

My sincere thanks to Donnie Dunagan for graciously affording me an interview for this story, and for his review of the finished work for accuracy. Today, he and Dana make their home in San Angelo, Texas.

Donald Dunagan has an amazing life to look back on, and a wealth of life experience that are hard to image. If he has slowed down any at age 88, he hasn't slowed much. As a speaker he is much in demand. He is also unabashed about his role as the voice of Bambi, answering fan mail that still arrives in his mailbox, signing posters, and promoting the wonderful Disney classic that he once did his best to hide from.

SOURCES

Brooks, Xan, *"How Bambi Fought the Viet Cong,"* The Guardian, February 16, 2005, https://www.theguardian.com/film/2005/feb/16/features.xanbrooks

Tatsch, Sabrina Forse, *"Gift of a Warrior with the Heart of Bambi,"* San Angelo Lifestyles, www.sanangelolifestyles.com/2019/03/21/190998/grit-of-a-warrior-with-the-heart-of-bambi

"Maj. Bambi: Meet The Marine Who Was Disney's Famous Fawn," National Public Radio, July 31, 2015, www.npr.org/2015/07/31/427821763/major-bambi-meet-the-marine-who-was-disney-s-famous-fawn

Clyde L. Bonnelycke (USMC)

Hero in Two Branches of Service

By C. Douglas Sterner

The Army established the Citation Star in World War I, which in 1932 became the Silver Star, the Army's third highest award for combat heroism. Until the Navy authorized the Silver Star in August 1942, it remained an Army-only award. The only Marines to receive a Silver Star prior to that date were Marines serving with the Army in World War I who received Army awards, and some of the earliest World War II Marine Corps recipients. Since the end of World War II, only 141 Marines earned an Army Silver Star, most of them during the Korean War when Marine and Army units had combined operations. Since Korea, only 17 Marines have received the Silver Star from the Army, including two Marines who received Army Silver Stars in OEF in Afghanistan.

Among these rare heroes, one Marine stands apart. He may be the only Marine in history to receive the Silver Star from the Navy as a Marine Corps Infantryman, and then receive an Army award as a U.S. Army soldier – TWICE!

On January 19, 1968, Sergeant Clyde L. Bonnelycke was a Marine Corps platoon sergeant serving with Company C, First Battalion, Third Marines, in support of a vastly outnumbered friendly unit north of the Cua Viet River in Vietnam. Upon arriving at the battle site near the DMZ, the Marines were pinned down by a heavy volume of small arms and automatic weapons fire from numerous fortified hostile positions.

Realizing the extreme danger, Sergeant Bonnelycke charged twenty-five meters through fire-swept terrain to reach an enemy bunker. Ignoring the hail of fire that surrounded him, he attacked the bunker, threw a grenade into it, and enabled his platoon to continue its attack and defeat the enemy.

Sergeant Bonnelycke was submitted for a Silver Star award, but his tour of duty in Vietnam, and his Marine Corps enlistment ended, without any further word on his nomination.

After returning home from Vietnam in the summer of 1968, Bonnelycke and accepted his honorable discharge after more than ten years in the Marine Corps. But civilian life didn't suit him. After a few weeks of rest as a civilian, he enlisted again, this time in the Army, and volunteered for another tour of duty in Vietnam. Instead, he was assigned to the 3d Infantry Division in Germany; a major disappointment for him. *"I wanted to go back where the fighting was at,"* he says. While serving in Germany, now as an Army Infantryman, the Navy finally found him and presented him with the Silver Star he had earned on January 19, 1918.

The President of the United States of America takes pleasure in presenting the Silver Star (Navy Award) to Sergeant Clyde L. Bonnelycke (MCSN: 1806071/ASN: 1806021), United States Marine Corps, for conspicuous gallantry and intrepidity in action while serving as a Platoon Sergeant with Company C, First Battalion, Third Marines, THIRD Marine Division in connection with operations against insurgent communist (Viet Cong) forces in the Republic of Vietnam. On 19 January 1968, Sergeant Bonnelycke's platoon was assigned to assist a friendly unit which had become heavily engaged with numerically superior enemy force north of the Cua Viet River in Quang Tri Province. Upon reaching the unit, the

Marines became pinned down by a heavy volume of small arms and automatic weapons fire from numerous fortified hostile positions. Realizing the seriousness of the situation, Sergeant Bonnelycke unhesitatingly exposed himself to the intense fire and fearlessly maneuvered across twenty-five meters of fire-swept terrain toward an enemy bunker. Upon reaching the hostile emplacement, he boldly threw a hand grenade into it, silencing the enemy fire and enabling his unit to continue its attack. His heroic actions and determined efforts inspired all who observed him and were instrumental in his unit accounting for twenty-three enemy soldiers confirmed killed. By his courage, aggressive fighting spirit and steadfast devotion to duty in the face of great personal danger, Sergeant Bonnelycke contributed immeasurably to the accomplishment of his unit's mission and upheld the highest traditions of the Marine Corps and the United States Naval Service.

After numerous requests for reassignment, U.S. Army Sergeant Bonnelycke finally got his wish. He returned to Vietnam in 1969 as a Platoon Sergeant with Company C, 2d Battalion (Airmobile), 8th Cavalry Regiment, 1st Cavalry Division. On July 13, 1969, in Tay Ninh Province, the point element of his platoon was ambushed and numerous men were wounded.

Realizing that there was no base of fire from which a counter attack could be launched, he moved to his wounded machine gunner and picked up the weapon. Laying down an effective base of fire, he enabled his platoon to mount their attack.  When Sergeant Bonnelycke had expended all his ammunition, he immediately seized several grenades and engaged an enemy bunker, silencing it with accurate throws. His actions allowed five members of the platoon to be evacuated and caused the enemy ambush to be broken.

For his actions that day, Army Sergeant Bonnelycke became, perhaps, the only Marine in history to receive a Silver Star while wearing the uniform of a

Beyond Belief: True Stories of Marine Corps Heroes

Marine Infantryman, and then again from the Army as an Army Soldier. By the time the medal was awarded, Bonnelycke had been promoted to Staff Sergeant.

The President of the United States of America, authorized by Act of Congress, July 8, 1918 (amended by act of July 25, 1963), takes pleasure in presenting a Bronze Oak Leaf Cluster in lieu of a Second Award of the Silver Star to Sergeant Clyde L. Bonnelycke (MCSN: 1806071/ASN: 1806021), United States Army, for gallantry in action while engaged in military operations involving conflict with an armed hostile force in the Republic of Vietnam. Sergeant Bonnelycke distinguished himself by exceptionally valorous action on 13 July 1969, while serving as the Platoon Leader of the Second Platoon, Company D, 2d Battalion (Airmobile), 8th Cavalry Regiment, 1st Cavalry Division (Airmobile), during a search and clear mission in Tay Ninh Province, Republic of Vietnam. Moving down a trail the point element was ambushed with mines, machine-guns, and small arms fire. The initial contact inflicted numerous wounds upon the members of Sergeant Bonnelycke's platoon. Realizing that there was no base of fire from which a counter attack could be launched, he moved to his wounded machinegunner and picked up the weapon. Laying down an effective base of fire, he enabled his platoon to mount their attack. When Sergeant Bonnelycke had expended all his ammunition, he immediately seized several grenades and engaged an enemy bunker, silencing it with accurate throws. His valorous actions allowed five members of the platoon to be evacuated and caused the enemy ambush to be broken. His gallant action is in keeping with the highest traditions of the Military Service, and reflects great credit upon himself, his unit, and the United States Army.

But Staff Sergeant Bonnelycke wasn't done.

Exactly one month after earning his first Army Silver Star, on August 12, 1969, Staff Sergeant Bonnelycke earned a second Silver Star from the Army, his third award, making him one out of about

150 of the more than three million Sailors, Soldiers, Airmen, and Marine who earned three or more Silver Stars.

When the base came under an intense rocket, mortar, and ground attack, Staff Sergeant Bonnelycke left the safety of his bunker and went to a bunker which had suffered a direct hit. Pulling the wounded personnel to safety, he raced to the berm and placed suppressive fire on the enemy with a machine gun. When he ran out of ammunition he made his way to another gun, where he continued his suppressive fire. Disregarding his wounds, he continually made his way back to the berm placing effective fire on the enemy, and helped carry wounded personnel to safety.

The President of the United States of America, authorized by Act of Congress, July 8, 1918 (amended by act of July 25, 1963), takes pleasure in presenting a Second Bronze Oak Leaf Cluster in lieu of a Third Award of the Silver Star to Staff Sergeant Clyde L. Bonnelycke (MCSN: 1806071/ASN: 1806021), United States Army, for gallantry in action while engaged in military operations involving conflict with an armed hostile force in the Republic of Vietnam. Staff Sergeant Bonnelycke distinguished himself by exceptionally valorous actions on 12 August 1969, while serving as a Platoon Sergeant with Company D, 2d Battalion (Airmobile), 8th Cavalry Regiment, 1st Cavalry Division (Airmobile), in Tay Ninh Province, Republic of Vietnam. When the base came under an intense rocket, mortar, and ground attack, Staff Sergeant Bonnelycke left the safety of his bunker and went to a bunker which had suffered a direct hit. Pulling the wounded personnel to safety, he raced to the berm and placed suppressive fire on the enemy with a machine gun. When that ran out of ammunition, he made his way to another gun, where he continued his suppressive fire. Disregarding his wounds, he continually made his way back to the berm placing effective fire on the enemy, and helped carry the wounded personnel to safety. His gallant action is in keeping with the highest traditions of the military service and reflects great credit upon himself, his unit, and the United States Army.

Beyond Belief: True Stories of Marine Corps Heroes

Today the humble hero, who retired as a Master Sergeant after 10 years as a Marine and 19 years of Army service, lives in Texas. His comrades, family, and close friends know of his awards, but even the man himself did not realize the historic nature of his service.

When I interviewed him the first time more than ten years ago, and told him that I can find no record of any other man earning a Silver Star while serving as a Marine Corps Infantryman, and then again as an Army Soldier, his reply was simply, *"Really? Can I hand the phone to my wife and have you tell her that?"*

I did.

Carlos Hathcock (USMC)

Marine Sniper

By Jim Fausone

Every military has trained and deployed snipers to strike the enemy at long distance since the incorporation of long rifle use. The term sniper puts fear in human beings. The stories of snipers find their way into books and films. This is the story of a U.S. Marine Corps sniper that achieved legendary results in Vietnam. When young Carlos Hathcock took up hunting in the early 1950s as a little boy it was unfathomable that he would become a feared and renowned sniper in Vietnam.

YOUNG HUNTER

Carlos Norman Hathcock, II was born in Little Rock, Arkansas, on May 20, 1942. He grew up in the small city of Wynne with fewer than 8,000 residents, in northeast Arkansas. Wynne was a bit of an accident; the settlement started in 1882 because of a train derailment which left a box car off the track, it becoming the first building in the city. The advent of interstate roads in the 1920s and 30s put Wynne on the map with U.S. Route 64. Later the north–south Arkansas Highway 1 was built through town making it an important highway crossroads for several decades, in addition to being a railroad town. Now, however, Interstate 40 has largely diverted long-distance travel away from Wynne. Hathcock's upbringing in his hometown was not about the roads and rail, but about the hills and country.

The outdoors would have been his refuge away from a hardscrabble life. His parents separated and he moved in with his grandmother for the first 12 years of his life. His life lessons were that of a country boy roaming the woods with his dog. Young Carlos, like most boys his age, played Army in the fields around the house. His father and namesake had been in World War II and brought back an old Mauser rifle as a souvenir. It was the perfect prop to march around and play soldier against make believe enemies. Mauser, originally Königlich Württembergische Gewehrfabrik (**Royal Württemberg Rifle Factory**), is a German arms manufacturer. Their line of bolt-action rifles and pistols have been produced since the 1870s for the German armed forces. Even if he did not know it, Carlos had his hands on a classic marksman's rifle.

As he grew older, he visited family in Mississippi, where again an outdoor lifestyle was foremost. He went from make believe to learning to hunt with a single shot 22-caliber rifle made by J.C. Higgins. J.C. Higgins sold sporting goods, including rifles, through **Sears Roebuck and Company** for many years. These low priced rifles gave a lot of bang for the buck, and were made by numerous manufacturers that included just about every major gun company of the time like **Savage, Mossberg, Marlin, Iver Johnson, Hi Standard,** and **Winchester.** Carlos had a reliable 22-caliber rifle to hunt small game. As a single shot, bolt action rifle, it required a skilled shooter. He was not shooting just for fun but to bring food home for the family. This was the start for the future Marine marksman.

JOINING UP - EXPERT MARKSMAN

Carlos, at an early age, wanted to be a Marine. Upon reaching the age of 17, he enlisted. It was May 1959, and the Corps would be the focus of his adult life. Training at Parris Island was as rigorous and transformative as you can imagine. Then, as today, every Marine is first a rifleman, trained to follow orders and uphold the Constitution. Marines trained and prized marksmanship, holding regular pistol and rifle competitions. With his experience, Carlos qualified as an expert marksman at basic training, and this gave rise to his place among the Corps' elite rank of shooters.

Carlos Hathcock (USMC)

Hathcock married Josephine Bryan Winstead on November 10, 1962, in North Carolina. They had one son, Carlos Norman Hathcock III, who also later joined the Marine Corps.

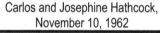

| Carlos and Josephine Hathcock, November 10, 1962 | Carlos II with Son, Carlos III Hathcock |

Hathcock would then go on to become a member of the Marine Corps Rifle Shooting Team. As such, he participated in prestigious competitions. This was target shooting with no one shooting back. Carlos would break virtually every record previously held and receive numerous awards, most notably the 1965 Wimbledon Cup U.S. Long Range High-Power Championship.

The **Wimbledon Cup** is a marksmanship trophy that was established in the 1870s by the British. In America, it was awarded annually during the **National Rifle & Pistol Matches** which are held at Camp Perry, Ohio, and it has become the most prestigious prize in U.S. long-range rifle shooting. Each year the high-power phase of these matches traditionally takes place during the first two weeks of August. The **Wimbledon Cup** is awarded for the winner of a 1000-yard shooting match — in which the rules permit use of *"any sight,"* including telescopes. This young Marine corporal made a name for himself in 1965 and his talent was recognized.

TOUR OF DUTY - SHARPSHOOTER

Hathcock was shortly thereafter deployed to Vietnam for the first time in 1966. He was deployed as a military policeman, but immediately volunteered for combat and was soon transferred to the 1st Marine Division Sniper Platoon stationed at Hill 55, South of Da Nang. This is where Hathcock would earn the nickname *"White Feather"* -- because he always wore a white feather on his bush hat, daring the North Vietnamese to spot him.

He had not only the eye to be a long distance target shooter but the other skills to be a feared sniper. Snipers had been critical to military operations since the advent of the long rifle. The term sniper dates back to the 1770s when British marksmen were known to be able to hunt snipes from a distance. Snipes are small fast birds found in marshes. Sniper replaced the German derived term "sharpshooter" in the lexicon. Hathcock had joined a brotherhood of respected and feared shooters.

The U.S. Military had long rifle sharpshooters in the Revolutionary War. Again in World War I, the military employed such marksmen in response to German sharpshooters. After the war to end all wars, the U.S. military stopped training and equipping sharpshooters. When World War II rocked the world the Army and Marines were without such trained long distance shooters. Again the U.S. military had to react and train up and equip these shooters. Unfortunately the lesson was not learned and again the military stopped training and equipping shooters. This on and off affair with sharpshooters was rooted in the belief that such snipers were ungentlemanly pathological killers and not as dignified as regular soldiers and artillery men. Target competitions were acceptable but deploying snipers had an uncomfortable feel to it. Being a sniper was not a career path to achieving higher rank.

Carlos Hathcock (USMC)

Sniper training in the U.S. had been ad hoc and informal. The situation quickly changed as the U.S. military adjusted its attitude and approach towards snipers and sniper training. One of the men behind this new emphasis on sniping was U.S. Marine Corps (USMC) Major Edward James "Jim" Land. He established the first organized sniper training program in 1961 in Hawaii for the USMC. According to him, the school was the springboard for early sniper schools in Vietnam for both the 1st and 3rd Marine Divisions. According to Peter Senich in his book "Long--Range War: Sniping in Vietnam" (1994), the U.S. Army did not begin organized, in--country, division--level sniper training programs until early 1967. By mid--1968, however, the Army had several well--organized in--country sniper schools supported by the U.S. Army Marksmanship Unit (USAMU).

By the time of the Vietnam War the military leadership again embraced the role of sharpshooters in the military strategy. Hatchcock's skills were put to use as were many other snipers. The snipers are part of a 39-man platoon which is assigned to regimental headquarters as a supporting element similar to tanks or artillery. Each regiment in the Marine Corps, under the new table of organization, would have such a platoon. If a battalion or company commander needed one or more sniper teams, he would request them from the regiment in the same manner as he requests other attached supporting elements. The sniper battalion was quartered on Hill 55, about 12 miles south of DaNang.

As his reputation grew, with the body count he left behind, the People's Army of Vietnam (PAVN) placed a bounty of $30,000 USD on Hathcock's life for killing so many of its soldiers. Rewards put on U.S. snipers by the PAVN typically ranged from $8 to $2,000. Hathcock held the record for the highest bounty and killed every known Vietnamese marksman who sought him to try to collect it.

LEGENDARY KILLS

Hathcock is credited with a record-breaking 2,500 yard kill of a guerilla fighter with an M2 .50-caliber machine gun with a single shot. The basis for his legend is not this roughly 1.4 mile shot − while extraordinary, it is based on some of the other kills.

Beyond Belief: True Stories of Marine Corps Heroes

The legend of Carlos Hathcock is centered around his 93 confirmed kills and likely 300 - 400 unconfirmed kills. In Vietnam a *"confirmed kill"* required confirmation by the spotter and an officer, which explains the wide difference.

To understand the extraordinary effort snipers underwent you must think about the terrain, weather, and opposing troops. The terrain could be hilly, mountainous, or swampy. There was almost always dense vegetation that needed to be accounted for to find the right angle for a shot. Vietnam is geographically located in the tropical zone but the weather varies significantly by latitude and longitude. The Central Highlands receive dry and hot winds. The Highlands are susceptible for hurricanes and flooding. The South is generally hot all year round with two seasons – rainy and dry. Such diverse weather results in a diversity of vegetation including forests made up of evergreens, deciduous trees, bamboo, and tall grasses. The Mekong Delta is a wide and swampy region. Such wide ranging landscapes result in unusual and plentiful animals only found in Vietnam. This unique biodiversity includes 12 species of mammals, seven species of birds, 45 species of reptiles, 58 species of amphibian species, 80 species of freshwater fishes and seven species of saltwater fish. The jungles are home to more than 200 species of snakes in Vietnam, and about 25% of them are venomous.

The American snipers, out in the jungles as predators themselves, had to worry about the animal predators that could poison them or give away their location. Additionally, the American snipers were prized targets for the NVA troops and NVA snipers. The enemy always had a say in the battle. Or to say it another way, the prey has a say also, not just the hunter.

The weaponry of the day in the 1960s was not all that sophisticated and leaned on the skill of the marksman. There

Winchester M70 calibre 30/06

were no laser sights or computer assists. Hathcock generally used a

Winchester Model 70 chambered for .30-06 Springfield cartridges, with the standard 8 X Unertl scope. On some occasions, however, he used a different weapon: the M2 Browning machine gun, on which he mounted an 8X Unertl scope, using a bracket made by Seabees metalworkers. Hathcock made a number of kills with this weapon in excess of 1,000 yards, including his record for the longest confirmed kill at 2,500 yards. Hathcock also carried a Colt M1911A1 pistol as a sidearm.

The Unertl scopes were simplistic and rugged. The **Unertl Optical Company, Inc.** was a manufacturer of telescopic sights in the United States from 1934 until 2008. They are known for their 10× fixed-power scopes that were used on the Marine Corps' M40 rifle, and made famous by Marine Corps scout snipers. So armed, the snipers went to work.

THRU THE SCOPE

A NVA sniper was sent to kill Hathcock. Once a sniper has a reputation, he or she was now more at risk. Known as *"Cobra,"* the NVA sniper was picking off Americans around Hill 55. Obviously the **Cobra** was trying to draw *White Feather* out.

When the NVA sniper killed a friend outside Hathcock's hooch, *White Feather* vowed to take *Cobra* out. Command offered to transfer Hathcock away from Hill 55, but this was personal. He felt that he was a little better than the *Cobra,* but that may have been just Marine swagger talking. They stalked each other for days. At one point a mistake was made, Hathcock tripped over a log and the sound gave *Cobra* a target. *Cobra's* shot hit Hathcock's spotter's canteen, causing no injury. Now Hathcock had a direction to focus on by way of the off target shot. Both *Cobra* and Hathcock patiently played cat and mouse. However, *Cobra* was facing the sun and a quick glint off his scope prompted *White Feather* to shoot. It was nothing more than a glint, not an outline of a man or the profile of a shooter. As Hathcock has stated, *"I shot straight through the scope, did not touch the sides. It did a pretty good job on his eyesight, you could say."*

Beyond Belief: True Stories of Marine Corps Heroes

FEMALE VC LEADER

Another legendary shot was his termination of a woman known as *"Apache."* She was platoon leader known for torturing Americans. She was known to skin her captives, thus earning her nickname.

In November of 1966, *Apache* captured a Marine Private and tortured him within earshot of his own unit. *"She tortured him all afternoon; half the next day,"* Hathcock recalled. *"I was by the wire ... He walked out, died right by the wire."* Apache skinned the private, cut off his eyelids, removed his fingernails, and then castrated him before letting him go. She kept him alive and enjoyed the screaming until she turned him loose to run into the razor wire.

This shot also became personal for Hathcock. *"She was a bad woman,"* said Hathcock of the woman known as *Apache*. Normally, enemy kill squads would just kill a Marine and take his shoes or whatever, but the *Apache* was very sadistic. She would do anything to cause pain. *"I was in her backyard, she was in mine. I didn't like that,"* Hathcock said. *"It was personal, very personal. She'd been torturing Marines before I got there."*

Later, Hathcock saw a group of five NVA who were on a trail. At 700 yards out, a woman squatted to pee and *White Feather* knew it was the woman known as *Apache*. *"I saw a group coming, five of them. I saw her squat to pee, that's how I knew it was her. They tried to get her to stop, but she didn't stop. I stopped her. I put one extra in her for good measure."* His single shot kill, plus the extra lead missile, stopped all of her future torturing of Marines.

THE NVA GENERAL

Any good hunter has to understand his prey. Where it feeds, hunts, drinks, sleeps, or prowls are questions asked by every game hunter. A sniper must answer these same questions to understand the person he is seeking. Early morning and early evening were Hathcock's favorite times to strike. *"First light and last light are the best times,"* he said. *"In the morning, they're going out after a good night's rest, smoking, laughing. When they come back in the evenings, they're tired, lollygagging, not paying attention to detail."*

"Carlos became part of the environment," said Edward Land, Hathcock's commanding officer. *"He totally integrated himself into the environment. He had the patience, drive, and courage to do the job. He felt very strongly that he was saving Marine lives."*

A difficult target may take days to zero in on. Hathcock called it *"squirmin' and wormin'."*

Wearing a *"ghillie suit"* he customized, he was more than camouflaged; he was part of the environment. Ghillie suits trace their history back to the Scots. The original ghillie suits were used by servants assisting sportsmen. The first known military use was a Scottish Highland regiment that went on to become the British Army's first sniper unit in about 1916 during the Second Boer War.

A mission to take out a NVA General was assigned to the snipers. Hathcock felt it was the most difficult of missions and took it on rather than send a less experienced snipper. He would have made the Scots proud and was so well hidden the NVA troops cooking and camping outside the General's headquarters, never saw or stumbled upon Hathcock. It took four days of *squirmin' and wormin'* to get close enough to the camp. At no time did the NVA think a single troop would take on such a mission. During that ordeal, Hathcock had a venomous snake slither over him without incident, but not without causing his blood pressure to rise. Finally, on the forth morning when the NVA troops *"were lollygagging,"* he saw his opportunity. At 700 yards, he *"dumped the guy"* with a single shot. The General was dead.

After the kill, a sniper must then escape. Carlos was glad to see the NVA run in the opposite direction where there were more trees. They had no idea how many troops were going to follow up on the single shot. The chaos that was created was the retreating sniper's friend and he made his way back to Hill 55. Shortly thereafter, in 1967, he was sent back to the United States.

Beyond Belief: True Stories of Marine Corps Heroes

THE ACTIONS OF A MARINE HERO

Hathcock returned to Vietnam in 1969, taking command of a sniper platoon. Like many Marines, he missed the action and felt most alive in-country.

On September 16, 1969, Hathcock was riding in an AMTRAC that was struck an anti-tank round. He was injured, but his instinct, drive, and adrenaline kicked in. He went back into the AMTRAC to pull seven Marines out. He ended up with burns over 90% of his body and was sent home. Nearly 30 years later, he received a Silver Star for this action.

The President of the United States of America takes pleasure in presenting the Silver Star to Staff Sergeant Carlos N. Hathcock, II (MCSN: 1873109), United States Marine Corps, for conspicuous gallantry and intrepidity in action while serving as a Sniper, Seventh Marines, FIRST Marine Division, in connection with military operations against the enemy in the Republic of Vietnam on 16 September 1969. Staff Sergeant Hathcock was riding on an Assault Amphibious Vehicle which ran over and detonated an enemy anti-tank mine, disabling the vehicle which was immediately engulfed in flames. He and other Marines who were riding on top of the vehicle were sprayed with flaming gasoline caused by the explosion. Although suffering from severe burns to his face, trunk, and arms and legs, Staff Sergeant Hathcock assisted the injured Marines in exiting the burning vehicle and moving to a place of relative safety. With complete disregard for his own safety and while suffering excruciating pain from his burns, he bravely ran back through the flames and exploding ammunition to ensure that no Marines had been left behind in the burning vehicle. His heroic actions were instrumental in saving the lives of several Marines. By his courage, aggressive leadership, and total devotion to duty in the face of extreme personal danger, Staff Sergeant Hathcock reflected great credit upon himself and the Marine Corps and upheld the highest traditions of the United States Naval Service.

Carlos Hathcock (USMC)

Lieutenant General P. K. Van Riper, Commanding General Marine Corps Combat Development Command, congratulates Gunnery Sgt. Carlos Hathcock (Ret.) after presenting him the Silver Star during a ceremony at the Weapons Training Battalion. Standing next to Gunnery Sgt. Hathcock is his son, Staff Sgt. Carlos Hathcock, Jr. ID: DM-SD-98-02324

POST WAR

At the time, Hathcock did not want any awards or recognition for his efforts. He was doing what any Marine would do to help his mates.

After returning to active duty, Hathcock helped establish the **Marine Corps Scout Sniper School** at the Marine base in Quantico, Virginia. He was in near constant pain due to his injuries, and in 1975, his health began to deteriorate. After being diagnosed with multiple sclerosis, he was medically discharged in 1979.

He received a 100% disability payment for life but the Gunnery Sergeant was separated just 55 days short of 20 years and missed out on retirement pay. Feeling forced out of the Marines, Hathcock fell into a state of depression. With the help of his wife, and his newfound hobby of shark fishing, Hathcock eventually overcame his depression.

Beyond Belief: True Stories of Marine Corps Heroes

In a book written by Peter Senich, The One-Round War: USMC Scout-Snipers in Vietnam (1996 ed.), Hathcock said about his career as a sniper: *"I like shooting, and I love hunting. But I never did enjoy killing anybody. It's my job. If I don't get those bastards, then they're gonna kill a lot of these kids dressed up like Marines. That's the way I look at it."*

Hathcock passed away February 22, 1999, from complications of multiple sclerosis. Sadly, there has not been sufficient study to link Agent Orange exposure, which Hathcock clearly had *squirmin' and wormin'* around, to multiple sclerosis. According to the VA, one study from 2017 did report: *"While this study did not evaluate any specific exposure, they did find that active duty service members that were deployed to a combat zone had a 22.4% higher rate of MS compared to those that were not deployed."*

While Carlos Norman Hathcock II survived Vietnamese snipers and antitank rounds, it may have been Agent Orange that got him in the end, at age 75. He was buried with full military honors at Woodlawn Memorial Gardens in Norfolk, Virginia.

Anthony Wood (USMC)

Evacuation of Saigon
A Story of Marine Might and Will

BY COLIN KIMBALL

The handwriting was certainly on the wall in Vietnam in 1975. Phouc Long, the provincial capital only 75 miles north of Saigon on the border with Cambodia, had fallen to the North Vietnamese Peoples Army of Vietnam (PAVN) in the first week of January 1975, after less than a month of fighting.

President Richard Nixon had promised air support to South Vietnamese President Thieu, to repel any invasion of PAVN forces in South Vietnam. However, Nixon was no longer in office. Furthermore, the U.S. Congress would not authorize any further military action. The absence of the decisive American airpower that has sustained American and Vietnamese forces for ten years emboldened the Communists of North Vietnam in their quest to unify Vietnam. As a result, Saigon, and the thousands of American diplomats, civilians, and third-country nationals who were part of America's Mission in Vietnam, were vulnerable. The end of a divided Vietnam was only a matter of time.

In March, the Communist PAVN forces laid siege to the village of Ban Me Thuot in the Central Highlands of South Vietnam. Though the Army of the Republic of Vietnam (ARVN), the South Vietnam Army, were numerically superior, the highly motivated and well-organized PAVN troops decimated the ARVN forces, which lost 75% of their soldiers in this battle that lasted the better part of two weeks.

Worse yet, thousands of civilians lost their lives as they tried evacuating to Saigon along Route 7, a major north-south transportation route in South Vietnam. Once again, the American air power promised to help defend South Vietnam was completely absent. The Communist conquest of South Vietnam was far ahead of their planned schedule.

The American mission, led by civilians in the State Department, remained unprepared and nonchalant. As a result, thousands of American lives were at risk. The head of the American Mission was Ambassador Graham Martin, a career diplomat who was staunchly anti-communist with an overbearing authoritarian manner known to be subject to unreasonable outbursts of rage. He limited his exposure to the masses of South Vietnam, likely due to injuries he suffered in a vehicle accident, and openly associated with and took his cues from the wealthy elite South Vietnamese in Saigon, to whom he could communicate in French.

Martin's out-of-touch view of South Vietnam from his isolation in Saigon shaped his perceptions. After the PAVN took control of Phuc Long, Martin ignored calls from Washington to draw down the size of the American Mission, especially before May, when the monsoonal season started. William Colby, the Central Intelligence Agency (CIA) head, told Secretary of State Kissinger that he thought Martin was delusional. Colby's observations were remarkably prescient.

Anthony Wood (USMC)

Meanwhile, a young Marine Captain, Anthony *Tony* Wood, was leading a small Recon team in northern South Vietnam, trying to resolve cases of Americans who were missing in action. On March 17, after Ban Me Thuot fell, Wood was recalled to Saigon. Joining Wood on the tarmac after he exited his helicopter was a friend from previous duties in Vietnam, Army Special Forces Captain George Petrie. Wood and Petrie had been recalled from the field and ordered to report to U.S. Army Major General Homer Smith, the Defense Attaché in South

Marine Captain Tony Wood

Vietnam. Smith was the highest ranking military officer in Vietnam at the sprawling Defense Attaché Office (DAO) at Tan San Nhut Air Base. in the northwestern part of Saigon.

Both men were combat veterans. In 1968 Wood served as a Platoon commander and advisor to the Korean Blue Dragon Brigade, earning a Bronze Star. As a Green Beret Sergeant First Class, Petrie had earned a Silver Star for actions as Radio Operator and Platoon Leader of a Special Forces patrol on an extended reconnaissance mission in the Central Highlands on August 7, 1967. Three years later as an Army Infantry first lieutenant, he received a second Silver Star for his heroic actions on November 21, 1970,

Army Captain George W. Petrie, Jr.

during the raid at Son Tay, North Vietnam, to attempt to locate and recover American prisoners of war.

On that date, First Lieutenant Pettrie, *"After crash-landing in the assault helicopter inside the prison compound, Lieutenant Petrie led his element in a search and clear action across the open and exposed portion of the compound courtyard to the main gate and gate tower to engage entrenched enemy personnel. Lieutenant*

Petrie, in the face of automatic weapons fire, personally charged the gate tower, clearing it with rifle fire and grenades. Then, with complete disregard for his life, he maneuvered to an exposed position in order to deliver covering fire for the remainder of the assault group. At this time Lieutenant Petrie was confronted with a counterattack, and, from this critical position, he placed accurate fire on the advancing enemy, repulsed the attack, and caused the enemy to flee." He had also earned two Bronze Stars and two Purple Hearts.

As they entered a bunker at the DAO complex, Wood recalled he had never seen a Major General before, let alone reported to one. Major General Smith came in the room and briefed them in a heavily Virginia-accented voice, in very plain language, telling them their situation. The ARVN had collapsed in the highlands. Moreover, the South Vietnamese were beginning to resent and distrust the Americans as we had failed to provide the promised support, both logistical and air power.

The lack of ammunition, spare parts, and fuel, crippled the ARVN's ability to defend their nation. As a result, there was a need to form a Special Planning Group (SPG) to plan for the evacuation of the thousands of diplomats, civilians, and key vulnerable South Vietnamese allies. The situation was dire and, worse yet, the Diplomatic Mission in Saigon, run by the State Department, was conducting a business-as-usual approach to day-to-day activities, as if Saigon was immune to the chaos in the countryside.

At the end of the general's comments, Wood asked, *"Who is this Special Planning Group, and can we meet them?"* Smith responded that Wood and Captain Petrie were the Special Planning Group.

At the end of the briefing, General Smith advised that Ambassador Graham Martin explicitly forbade any overt plans or discussions of an American evacuation of Saigon. It became abundantly clear that Wood and Petrie were to operate in total secrecy from a bunker underneath the DAO, and only report to Smith or Air Force Brigadier General Edward Baughn, the assistant Defense Attaché. Thankfully, the American Military leadership could read the handwriting on the wall.

Anthony Wood (USMC)

Wood and Petrie had no experience in planning for mass evacuations. To assist them, Smith had an assistant drop off two great stacks of paper composed of three staff studies on plans to evacuate Saigon. In addition, there was a fourth smaller plan consisting of a potential helicopter evacuation, elements of which would lay the basis for *Operation Frequent Wind*, a helicopter evacuation to Navy ships offshore.

General Smith believed that the North Vietnamese would attack Saigon within 90 days. Unfortunately for all concerned, he was off by a couple of months. At the end of the briefing, Smith introduced a third member of the SPG, Marine Major Jim Sabater. Before he left, Smith announced one more thing: the SPG would also need to include the third-country nationals working on behalf of the American interests in Vietnam. There were nine governmental agencies and dozens of non-governmental agencies in Vietnam. Wood and Petrie faced a monumental task with no idea how many civilians needed to be evacuated or where they resided. The consequences of failure could be dire.

The first major obstacle the SPG faced was how many people needed to be evacuated, and where did they live? Their initial estimates suggested that they were dealing with upwards of 20,000 people. The second obstacle was how they would get masses of people to the Tan San Nhut Air Base to evacuate them via aircraft transport? Finally, they needed to know the nature of the chaos they would encounter as Saigon fell, so that they could prepare for the consequences and protect the evacuees. They were given strict orders to complete this planning in absolute secrecy, which further compound their mission. Ambassador Martin's out-of-touch demeanor and irascible behavior would propagate disastrous consequences

Like any American Embassy, the Saigon Embassy was protected by a small detachment of Marine security guards. Many of these Marines were seasoned veterans, but a few were new arrivals to Vietnam. They included Lance Corporal Darwin Judge, who arrived mid-March, and Corporal Charles McMahon who arrived on the last civilian flight into Saigon in April. The Marine Security Guard (MSG) detachment was commanded by senior ranking non-commissioned officers that reported to the civilian State Department officials, overseen by the Ambassador.

After taking two days to review the monumental staff studies Major General Smith had provided, Wood's first order of business was to find out how many people needed to be rounded up and evacuated. Wood and Petrie had confidential access to funds from a classified source. Wood used some of these funds to bribe the managers of the various sports clubs in Saigon, where all the elite foreign nationals socialized. These clubs provided him with their membership lists, which were invaluable in identifying the third-country nationals. Now that that population was identified, Wood needed to determine how many Americans were present in South Vietnam, and where they lived.

During one of his ventures of gathering data, Wood was riding in a DAO Taxi that was provided free of charge, to meet the Americans working in Saigon. He noticed that the driver filled out a chit and then carefully placed it in a box beside his seat. Wood asked the driver, *"what do you do with those chits?"*

The driver responded, *"we file them."* Wood further questioned the driver, who revealed that several years' worth of chits had been carefully filed and stored in a warehouse. Wood acquired the extensive chit files that recorded the identity and destinations of those who used the taxi service and sent them to U-Tapao Air Force Base in Thailand. The Americans had a large computer complex at U-Tapao that was used to assist in the POW operations a few years earlier.

After several days of data entry using the old keypunch cards, Wood was provided with a report that precisely defined the locations of the Americans in Saigon. After receiving the information from U-Tapao, he and Petrie created a pin map that was instrumental in helping define evacuation routes. This map was supplemented with data from various other sources, including Commissary and PX records of people authorized to shop there. The pin map defined the evacuation planning as March came to a close. Wood's fortuitous discovery while riding in a cab became a huge factor in the success of what initially seemed an insurmountable task.

Anthony Wood (USMC)

<u>THE FALL OF DA NANG AND HUE CITY</u>

Meanwhile, while all this detailed analysis was underway, the North Vietnamese Army seized the major provinces of Kontum in the Central Highlands, and began to invade from the north across the DMZ, seizing the province of Quang Tri. In reviewing the plans, the SPG concluded that they would have to build an internment camp to hold the Americans, key allies, and third country nationals, if Saigon fell, in order to protect the American Mission.

This camp would be used to house the American Mission while the United States Government negotiated for their release. This was a monumental task that required dozens of skilled individuals. The major impediment was that they could not communicate with the Ambassador or hostile Embassy staff due to the secrecy requirements Major General Smith imposed. In addition, North Vietnam was seizing South Vietnam, and the US Ambassador, Graham Martin, was putting up a façade of business as usual in Saigon, entirely out of touch with the reality in the countryside and the impending threat to the American Mission.

Wood and Petrie needed to know how the indigenous people, various ethnic groups, and ARVN forces would react as the cities were falling so that they could prepare appropriate safeguards for evacuating the thousands of people from the American Mission in Saigon. They placed small tape recorders in their fatigue jacket pockets and headed for the action. They would talk into their recorders to take notes.

Petrie went to Da Nang and Wood to Hue City. While in their respective cities, with chaos all around, they observed how the citizenry reacted. When the PAVN forces threatened the outskirts of the cities, the ARVN would abandon their uniforms and weaponry, seek to find their fellow family members, and flee or become leaderless armed soldiers looking to exploit opportunities. Looting and rioting followed, with the barricading of streets by lawless people looking to rob and exploit anything, and everything, the people under their gun had in their possession. Finally, snipers started to appear, further adding to the chaos.

The MSG Marines assigned to the Consulate in Da Nang abandoned the Consulate on March 29, followed by the abandonment of the Nha Trang Consulate, a little more than 300 miles to the south, on April 1. The information Wood and Petrie gathered was invaluable in preparing for the safe evacuation of the thousands of civilians in Saigon. However, while all this transpired in the north, people, especially third-country nationals, continued to arrive in Saigon. To complicate matters, Saigon also had an influx of hundreds of thousands of refugees from the chaos occurring elsewhere in the country, which were added to the native population.

PREPARATION

In late March, the SPG projected what awaited in Saigon, based on their observations in Da Nang and Hue. However, building an internment camp on short notice was beyond the three-person SPG's capability. So Wood made a bold decision that almost got him expelled from the country. He met with a lady named Sally Vincent, the director of facilities of the DAO. Wood needed help in getting the logistics, billeting, water, plumbing, and construction to build an internment camp at the DAO. This internment camp would be a haven for the thousands of people associated with the American Mission in Saigon if the City fell to communist hands before they could be evacuated.

To complicate matters, the Ambassador was doing nothing to facilitate any evacuation. In explaining this to Ms. Vincent, Wood explicitly violated the secrecy and direct orders from Major General Smith, who called Wood on the carpet and excoriated him for his disobedience, but then agreed that an internment camp was necessary. Fortunately for Wood, his meeting with Salley Vincent escaped the attention of Ambassador Graham Martin, who forbade any plans to evacuate the American Mission. As Wood would discover later, he could have been expelled from the country under the orders of the Ambassador, who was entirely out of touch with the reality facing Saigon.

The SPG now had a plan that called for a dual ground and air evacuation of Saigon. The ground component identified eight transportation routes named after the trails of the American West, lined with nearly a dozen buildings that could serve as emergency rooftop helicopter evacuation points if the ground convoys got disrupted. All the routes leading from the center of Saigon terminated at the DAO, code-named *"The Alamo."* The busses would be armored from the inside with linings of flack jackets to protect against snipers. Knowing the Vietnamese would likely flee, American bus drivers would be needed to drive these buses.

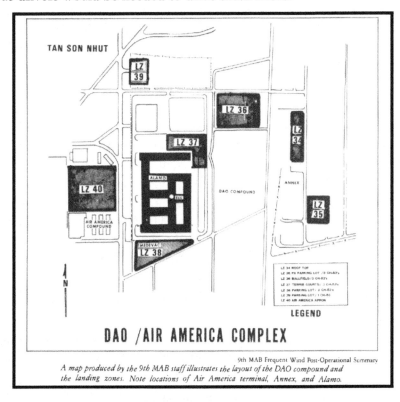

9th MAB Frequent Wind Post-Operational Summary
A map produced by the 9th MAB staff illustrates the layout of the DAO compound and the landing zones. Note locations of Air America terminal, Annex, and Alamo.

Rooftop helicopter landing pads had to be prepared along the route for emergency evacuations. In addition to clearing any obstructing trees and telephone poles, the rooftops had to be protected by hidden stairwell barricades to prevent fleeing South Vietnamese from overwhelming the rooftops during the evacuations. Finally, the bus convoys were to be led by Americans who knew the city. All of these vital functions would be completed by a cadre of more than 100 American civilian volunteers who did the preparation work after hours, in secret, to prevent the Ambassador from finding out — since he was still holding out hope against hope that Saigon would remain in the hands of the South Vietnamese leadership, despite the conquest of South Vietnam by the PAVN and the near total collapse of the ARVN.

Beyond Belief: True Stories of Marine Corps Heroes

Reliable radio communications were needed, and on the advice of some civilian volunteers who used to be in the taxi business, the SPG acquired dozens of the Motorola radios commonly used by cab drivers in the United States. Then, using Marine Corps Communication experts who secretly flew into Saigon on CIA Operated Air American helicopters, they secretly drained a major water tower in Saigon so that they could conceal the antenna needed to facilitate their broadcasts.

As all this work in Saigon was being done in secret, Marine Expeditionary Forces in Japan and the Philippine Islands were preparing for a mass evacuation. Two well-known battalions of Marine Infantry, the First Battalion of the Ninth Marine Regiment (1/9), known as the *"Walking Dead,"* and the Second Battalion of the Fourth Marine Regiment (2/4), known as the *"Magnificent Bastards,"* were assembled offshore along with several squadrons of Marine Helicopter units. In addition, the Third Battalion of the Ninth Marine Regiment (3/9), would augment this force operating as the Ninth Marine Amphibious Brigade (9th MAB), headed by Brigadier General Richard Carey.

Initially, the 9th MAB was formed and mobilized to plan and implement *Operation Talon Vise*, which would subsequently be renamed *Operation Frequent Wind*. Ultimately, they would take up positions off the coast of South Vietnam near Vung Tau on various Navy ships provided by the SEVENTH Fleet.

While the SPG was heavily involved in covert preparations, using more than 100 civilian volunteers working their day jobs and participating in the secret preparations at night, disaster struck on April 4. An American C-5 Transport Aircraft, part of *Operation Baby Lift,* carrying 300 South Vietnamese baby orphans, crashed near Tan San Nhut. The aircraft had previously taken off from Saigon. However, once the aircraft reached an altitude of 20,000 feet, it experienced a major malfunction of a tail ramp door latch that caused the doors to break away and sever the tail elevator controls of the aircraft. Nevertheless, the pilot successfully turned the giant plane around using only engine power, and descended into Saigon. Unfortunately, on his approach to Than San Nhut, the lack of elevator control caused the aircraft to go out of control and crash, killing over 100 passengers, primarily infants, and all 27 female volunteers that the SPG contributed.

It was a devastating blow to the volunteers, who were mostly in their 50s and 60s and were working all day and night without support from the Embassy. Wood called all the volunteers together after this and told them to mourn the loss of their friends and think about

their need to continue, and if they desired, they could withdraw their participation with no negative repercussions. The volunteers acted nearly in unison and returned to their duties working for the SPG

Despite the tragedy of the C-5 crash, *Operation Baby Lift* continued as part of a significant effort by the United States Air Force to evacuate as many people as possible. After the C-5 disaster, the Air Force evacuations kicked into high gear as they flew 375 missions with C-141 and C-130 airlifters out of Tan San Nhut. The C-141s flew in daylight while the C-130s flew at night. The masses of people being evacuated on these flights were processed out of the DAO.

On April 8, Brigadier General Baughn, the Assistant Defense Attaché who was in charge of evacuation planning, sent a message to the Joint Chiefs of Staff requesting a Company of Marines to provide security for the DAO, as things were getting tense due to the masses of South Vietnamese that were converging at this location. When Ambassador Martin discovered this breach of his orders that no overt planning be done for the evacuation, he ordered Baughn arrested and had him immediately flown to Guam.

Even though the chaos in the countryside was causing the local populace to panic – on one occasion they were throwing their children over the walls of the DAO into the arms of Marine Guards,. Ambassador Martin was creating a façade of normalcy inside the Embassy. Martin also suffered from pneumonia and was experiencing severe side effects from the antibiotics. He had a total lack of understanding of the severity of the situation in Vietnam, and the characterization of his *"delusional"* nature by CIA Director William Colby was undoubtedly merited. Considering Wood's violation of Major General Smith's order weeks before when he spoke to Salley Vincent, Wood was lucky not to have been expelled for his work in planning the evacuation.

Many of the Marine Security Guards from the MSG Detachments at Da Nang and Nha Trang were absorbed into the security at the Embassy. No commanding officer will tolerate having the responsibility for individuals under their command who are now reporting to other command authorities. Major Jim Kean, the Company Commander for the MSG Detachments in Vietnam, flew into Saigon on April 17 to wrest control of his Marines that were being absorbed into the SPG at the DAO.

Kean quickly realized that there were two operations taking place. First, the DAO, or *Alamo* as it was now known, was a beehive of activity of people working to secure the evacuation of the American Mission. This necessary work escaped the attention of Ambassador Graham Martin at the Embassy, which in Kean's words, was operating *"complacently"* in a *"controlled façade"* of normalcy. Kean, who took orders from the civilian State Department personnel in the Embassy, eagerly gave up sixteen of his Marines to serve as live-in security at the *Alamo*, as he understood the urgency.

As a handful of Marines were transferred to the DAO to provide security, Wood busied himself with trying to figure out how to protect the convoys. The Ambassador, oblivious to the planning taking place, seriously impeded any reasonable conventional efforts to safeguard the busses as they were en route on the convoy routes. With no options, Wood planned on a giant bluff.

The National Police ruled Saigon with an iron hand and were feared by the local population. Wood created a chop shop in a warehouse, acquired Ford taxis identical to the ones the police used, and had them painted to mimic the National Police vehicles. He placed louvered blinds in the side windows, kept them closed, and put a National Police helmet on the front seat. Since no Vietnamese drivers could be trusted, he had American volunteers drive the fake police cars to escort the buses. It was a daring move, but the only option available.

The civilian volunteers, who Wood says, *"are the true heroes of this story,"* were getting worn out. They were working their day jobs and then most of, if not all night, on preparing concealable escape routes in buildings, cutting vegetation for landing pads, and processing thousands of people out of the *Alamo*. Many had to learn how to drive the large buses in the narrow confines of a parking lot at the DAO by putting the bus in gear, moving forward, then putting it in reverse, and backing up. That was the extent of their bus driving training.

On April 8, a South Vietnamese pilot took off and bombed the Presidential Palace in Saigon. President Nguyn Van Thieu was not injured. By April 9, PAVN forces reached Xuan Loc, just slightly less than 30 miles from downtown Saigon. The ARVN 18th Division made a heroic last stand, but Xuan Loc fell on April 20. PAVN forces were now within artillery and rocket fire range of Saigon. Still, Ambassador Martin remained oblivious to the pending doom of Saigon falling. Martin went so far as to prevent the Marines of the MSG at the Embassy from chopping down trees to make emergency helicopter landing zones within the complex.

Air Force flights continued from Tan San Nhut with thousands of Americans, third-country nationals, and dependents, legal and otherwise, being evacuated on military airlift transports. The Marines hastily acquired from the Embassy were guarding checkpoints outside the DAO that was now taking on the character of its code name *"The Alamo."* One of the significant assets that the SPG created at the DAO was six large helicopter landing zones which could accommodate the large CH-53 helicopters as part of the Ninth MAB that had been assembled offshore.

PAVN forces were now closing to within artillery and rocket range of Saigon. Brigadier General Carey, the Commander of the Ninth MAB, grew very concerned about the Ambassador's inaction regarding evacuating

Marine Brig. Gen. Richard E. Carey

the American Mission and flew out to meet him on April 22. Carey noted his concerns the night before in his log book, stating, *"I pray for a silver tongue and the wisdom of Solomon."*

After meeting with the Ambassador, Carey reported that the Ambassador agreed to move his people to the DAO to prevent evacuation from the Embassy. Further, he stated he might remain behind and seek refuge in the French Embassy as he felt *"duty obligated him to help the Vietnamese friends that had been faithful."* Carey further wrote in his logbook that the Ambassador was an *"honorable, dedicated and highly intelligent human with a great deal of compassion and warmth, but I feel he is too emotionally involved."*

Also, on April 22, the last civilian airliner, a massive **Pan Am** 747, landed in Saigon. Two new Marine Security guards were on that flight, Lance Corporal Bernie Winkleman and Corporal Charles McMahon, Jr. Winkleman observed the array of ships of the U.S. Navy SEVENTH Fleet in the South China Sea before the flight made landfall that contained the Marines of the Ninth MAB. Upon arrival, Winkleman and McMahon, who expected to fulfill their diplomatic Mission as MSG Marines, were immediately issued jungle utilities, helmets, weapons, and ammunition. When Winkleman questioned Major Kean, the MSG Commanding Officer, Kean reminded him in a curt expletive-laden comment that *"every Marine is an Infantryman."*

The day after Winkleman and McMahon arrived, South Vietnamese President Thieu resigned, another ominous sign of the pending takeover of Saigon by the Communist North Vietnamese. Still, Ambassador Martin remained oblivious to the impending danger in Saigon.

Wood and Petrie had planned that the evacuation along the planned routes through Saigon would proceed at night. This would make it easier for the Americans driving the National Police Cars to pull off their bluff, as the chaos in the City generally diminished at night. However, on April 27, PAVN rockets started to fall in Saigon. As a result, the Marine Amphibious Brigade floating offshore upgraded their alert status and began preparations for implementing Operational Plan *Frequent Wind*, the helicopter evacuation of

Saigon. Augmenting the Marine Heavy Helicopter Airlift of CH-53 *Sea Stallions* were 10 Air Force HH-53 *Jolly Green Giants* of the 56th Special Operations Wing (the same airframe with a different service designation), providing a force of 71 heavy airlift capable helicopters supplemented by smaller dual rotor CH-46s and a fleet of 25 Air America UH-1 *Hueys* and Bell *Jet Rangers*. Due to the large size of the *Sea Stallions, Jolly Greens*, and CH-46s, only the smaller UH-1 *Hueys* and *Jet Rangers* could be used to evacuate building rooftops that were strategically located along the evacuation routes in Saigon.

At 4:30 on the afternoon of April 28, two South Vietnamese Air Force A-37 attack aircraft launched airstrikes on the Control Tower and Command Center of Tan San Nhut. The Marines on the ground fired their M-16 rifles in a futile effort to defend themselves. Embassy Marines, now living up to their Infantry heritage, manned various guard outposts around the DAO. In Saigon, Marshal Law had been declared.

At nightfall, Marine Sergeant Ted Murray checked each outpost to assess if there was anything these Marines needed. Outpost 1, at the main entrance of the DAO, was manned by Lance Corporal Darwin Judge and Corporal Charles McMahon. Judge arrived in the country in mid-March, and McMahon had only been in the country a little more than a week. Besides needing sleep that Murray could not supply, they remained alert and on duty. Murray returned to his bunk to get some shut eye when he was violently awakened at 3:30 in the morning from a series of explosions.

The North Vietnamese began launching dozens of 122-mm. rockets against Tan San Nhut and the DAO compound. One 122-mm. rocket landed squarely on Outpost 1. Corporal of Marines Charles McMahon, Jr of Woburn, Massachusetts, and Lance Corporal Darwin Judge, an Eagle Scout from Marshalltown, Iowa, were killed.

They say that Marines are the first to fight, and the Marine Corps lived up to that heritage when they landed in Vietnam in March 1965; these two dedicated Marines were the last Americans to die in Vietnam.

Beyond Belief: True Stories of Marine Corps Heroes

OPERATION FREQUENT WIND

Tan San Nhut Air Base in South Vietnam – April 29, 1975

PAVN 122-mm. rockets rained down on Tan San Nhut and the DAO complex in the early morning of the April 29, 1975. The trailers that housed the SPG members were destroyed. Within 30 minutes after Judge and McMahon were killed, a 122-mm. rocket struck an Air Force C-130 on the taxiway as it was headed to pick up evacuees. The aircraft crew exited the burning plane unscathed and departed on another C-130, preparing to take off in tandem with another C-130. These two C-130s would be the last Air Force flights out of Tan San Nhut.

As dawn broke, South Vietnamese Air Force Pilots began taking off with all sorts of aircraft in a haphazard fashion. A pair of South Vietnamese A-1 attack aircraft and a C-119 gunship was attacking PAVN positions on the base's outskirts. The Marines watched as these planes were shot out of the sky by man-portable surface-to-air missiles.

Army Maj. General Homer D. Smith, Jr.

The Ninth MAB was on alert status and had prepared to launch *Operation Frequent Wind* after dawn broke at 0630. After sunrise, Major General Smith advised Ambassador Martin that the air evacuation from Tan San Nhut was no longer viable and that the helicopter evacuation needed to be activated. True to the delusional or indecisive nature that characterized the Ambassador,

Martin did not believe Smith. As a result, Major General Smith had to waste precious time and escort Martin to the base so he could observe the chaos himself. By 10:48 in the morning, Martin finally agreed to implement *Operation Frequent Wind.* The American radio station immediately began broadcasting Irving Berlin's Christmas song *"White Christmas,"* which alerted all Americans to start their evacuation.

Buses led by fake National Police escorts began to transit six of the eight routes named after the famous trails of the American West, out of Saigon to the *Alamo.* Unfortunately, two of the routes had to be abandoned due to rioting.

Designed as an internment camp, the *Alamo* had been used to process thousands of evacuees from Tan San Nhut during April. It now was the site of six helicopter landing zones. This invaluable asset accommodated the large Marine *Sea Stallions,* Air Force *Jolly Greens,* and the smaller **Air America** *Huey's* and *Jet Rangers.* The smaller **Air America** helicopters brought evacuees from building rooftops in Saigon to the DAO, where they would ultimately board the larger heavy-lift helicopters to be carried offshore to the Navy ships on station off the coast of Vung Tau. It was a remarkably well-choreographed operation controlled by Landing Zone Control Teams flown out from the Ninth MAB.

Wood's plan for a night bus evacuation was thrown out the window by the rapid advance of the PAVN forces and our Ambassador's inept understanding of the situation. The first bus of evacuees arrived at the *Alamo* at noon.

According to the Ninth MAB Command Chronologies, General Carey released the execute message launching *Operation Frequent Wind* at 1246 hours. The delay in implementing this plan was due to Ambassador Martin's intransigence and disbelief that the air evacuation from Tan San Nhut was no longer viable. General Carey landed at the DAO at 1350, followed by several helicopters containing Marine Security Force personnel. The first helicopters to carry evacuees away from the DAO lifted off at 1512 with 149 evacuees on board. The helicopters received small arms and anti-aircraft fire as they entered and exited Saigon airspace.

Wood was now involved in executing the plans he developed by riding with the convoys. In one harrowing incident, Wood was being driven in a U.S. **Jeep** by Marine Sergeant Kevin Maloney, one of the MSG Marines from the Embassy, when they encountered some ARVN soldiers who aggressively bore down on them with their weapons. Maloney reached for his M-16, prompting Wood to grab Maloney's wrist very aggressively, squeezing it to prevent him from raising it. Outnumbered by the ARVN at the roadblock, Wood knew it would have been suicide for them to engage the aggressive ARVN soldiers. Fortunately, the ARVN maintained their discipline, and as Maloney would say, " *we were escaping to live, and they were staying to die.* "

Soon after, Wood and Maloney started taking sniper fire, and their jeep overturned. Maloney grabbed his M-16 and was ordered to get the convoy moving, and Wood dashed off with a .45 pistol and disappeared to mount another bus and get it moving.

Those busses that could not escape the roadblocks directed their passengers to rooftop landing zones that the SPG preprepared along the route. However, these rooftops could only accommodate the smaller *Hueys* and **Bell** *Jet Rangers* operated by **Air**  America as they shuttled evacuees from Saigon to the *Alamo*. One of the most famous photos from the Evacuation of Saigon shows an Air America Huey extracting people from the rooftop of a CIA building that was one of the alternate landing sites built into the plan Wood and Petrie devised. There were roughly a dozen of these buildings that were used to help shuttle evacuees from the rioting in the streets to the *Alamo*, where they could be airlifted to ships of the Navy SEVENTH Fleet assembled offshore.

In a lack of good judgment, the Ambassador, oblivious to the pending takeover of Saigon by the Communists from North

Vietnam, had flown in an estimated 12 Million Dollars for payroll purposes a few days before Saigon fell. With the City falling into communist hands, locals' possession of American currency would have been a dead giveaway and sign of collaboration once the Communist Government took control. Those in possession of American currency would have been at grave risk. The money was ordered destroyed, adding mightily to the burdens of a small group led by George Petrie as they were destroying classified documents in the DAO.

The flak vests inside the buses saved lives. Many of the busses were peppered with small arms fire, and the flak vests safely absorbed the bullets. Not a single bus passenger was harmed by sniper fire. In the late afternoon, three buses were attacked by mutinying members of the ARVN and caught fire outside the entrance to the DAO. General Carey authorized a flight of *Cobra* gunship helicopters to disperse the ARVN Troops by force if necessary. When the *Cobras* showed up, their presence was sufficient to stop further attacks, and no shots were fired by the ARVN soldiers. The wear and tear on the buses were extreme due to the constant braking and overloading of passengers. Several had to be abandoned due to the loss of brakes outside the walls of the *Alamo.*

Meanwhile, the Embassy, which the Ambassador had previously promised would be emptied of Americans, became overwhelmed with evacuees and rioting South Vietnamese. Finally, on the April 29, the Marines made landing zones within the Embassy complex by cutting down vegetation and light poles that the Ambassador had previously forbidden. As a result, the Embassy could now be integrated into *Operation Frequent Wind*, and helicopter airlifts from the Embassy were eventually initiated late in the day.

The fake National Police Car bluff also worked. Again, no American was captured or harmed as they bluffed their way through the chaos and riots on the streets of Saigon.

By midnight of April 29, the Marines from 2/4, sent in as ground security, had evacuated the DAO that was being destroyed by thermite grenades to demolish the complex. Wood and Petrie would fly out on one of the last helicopters. The Ninth MAB Command

Beyond Belief: True Stories of Marine Corps Heroes

Chronologies record that by 2300 an estimated 6,393 people had been evacuated from Saigon, mainly from the DAO, and an estimated 900 more evacuees remained at the Embassy. The DAO was finally evacuated at midnight as the compound was on fire from the demolition charges deployed by the Marines who came in with the security forces.

Helicopter airlifts continued from the Embassy with ten flights of single *Sea Stallions* and CH-46s flying in at 10-minute intervals. At 0345 on April 30, the President ordered that only 19 more helicopter lifts were authorized and that the Ambassador was to depart on the last lift. He had also ordered the aircrew of the CH-46 sent to retrieve Ambassador Martin to arrest him, if necessary, to affect his removal from Saigon. By 0420, Command Chronology reports indicate 737 evacuees had been lifted from the Embassy in 18 lifts. In addition, more Vietnamese nationals were arriving at the Embassy.

After the Ambassador was airlifted at 0458, an estimated 200 Americans remained at the Embassy. Small arms fire was reported in the Embassy from adjacent buildings. After the first light at 0605, an estimated 80 - 90 Marines remained at the Embassy. Command Chronologies said that 782 had been evacuated from the Embassy after the DAO missions were completed and that 35 Marines remained behind on the roof, prepared to make their last stand. They were finally evacuated after sunrise at 7:53 on the morning of the April 30. They were the last American combat troops to leave Vietnam.

Unfortunately, two Marines were left behind — Lance Corporal Darwin Judge and Corporal Charles McMahon, Jr. Immediately after their deaths, their remains were transported per Embassy protocol to the Hospital Morgue run by the 7th Day Adventists in Saigon. Unfortunately, confusing reports on their proper recovery, coupled with the chaos of the events on April 29, caused them to be overlooked and left behind. It took the efforts of Senator Edward Kennedy to negotiate their return almost a year later, in February 1976.

Anthony Wood (USMC)

Marine Lance Corporal Darwin Lee Judge of Garwin, IA, and Marine Corporal Charles McMahon, Jr. of Woburn, MA, were killed in action during the evacuation of Saigon on April 29, 1975. They were the last American casualties of the Vietnam War.

U.S. Air Force Historic Division sources report that as many as 45,000 civilians, and 5,600 Americans, were processed out of the DAO between April 20 - 29 on daily C-141 and C-130 flights – more than double the original 20,000 that the SPG estimated in mid-March. The Marine helicopter airlift, supplemented by Air Force and CIA helicopters during *Operation Frequent Wind*, was the largest helicopter airlift in history. While the number of sorties flown by Air American pilots is unknown, their small fleet of helicopters had dwindled to thirteen due to operational issues and ground losses to enemy fire. The Ninth Marine Amphibious Brigade reports that 682 sorties were flown on April 29 and 30, evacuating 6,968 people. One pilot was credited with 22.5 hours of continuous flight time.

All the civilians involved in the evacuation returned home as unknown heroes. They built infrastructure and provided the human resources to escort and process tens of thousands of people fleeing for their lives. They drove buses and fake police cars through barricaded streets under fire from snipers. Sadly, they were given no parades and no medals. Yet, their efforts contributed directly to sparing tens of thousands of lives.

Unfortunately, many fleeing Vietnamese were left behind as refugees and continued to flee South Vietnam via boats and aircraft after the last American boots left the ground on April 30.

In the last days of the Vietnam War, a secret operation by a small **Special Planning Group** consisting of two Marines and one Army Special Forces Captain was completed covertly against unbelievable odds in defiance of the out-of-touch civilian leadership. It prevented the potential catastrophic loss of lives of Americans, key Vietnamese allies, and third-country nationals of the American Mission.

George Petrie retired from the Army as a major. He passed away in 2011 and rests in Honored Peace at the Dallas National Cemetery in Texas. Jim Sabater and Tony Wood retired from the Marine Corps as colonels. Richard Carey retired from the Marine Corps as a lieutenant general and, along with Tony Wood, resides in the Dallas Fort Worth Area. Countless people live today because of their efforts.

The success of *Operation Frequent Wind* was made possible by the SPG's planning, preparation, and execution, and the dedication of the civilians who made the preparations and risked their lives evacuating those who got out. The DAO was never used as an internment camp as conceived initially. Still, it functioned brilliantly as a secure collection and transfer point to receive those coming in from busses and small helicopters, transferring them to larger heavy-lift helicopters that flew them to freedom on Navy ships waiting offshore.

In contrast to the Iranian Hostage debacle that occurred just four short years later, the evacuation of Saigon remains a remarkable achievement that was completed against seemingly insurmountable odds from a few mission-oriented Marines willing to risk their own lives and careers for the sake of others.

Anthony Wood (USMC)

ACKNOWLEDGMENTS AND ATTRIBUTIONS

The author would like to acknowledge and extend my appreciation and gratitude to Colonel *Tony* Wood, USMC (Ret.), and Lieutenant General Richard Carey, USMC, (Ret.) for their interviews and comments on their first-hand involvement in this final American episode of the Vietnam War. In addition, many references and quotes from the Marines involved were obtained from sources provided by the Fall of Saigon Marine Association published on FallofSaigon.org.

Figures on the number of people evacuated during the fall of Saigon vary widely due to the chaos of the period, and the many different modes of transportation used. Statistics cited on dates, times, and volumes of people evacuated came from the U.S. Air Force Historical Division report *"1975 - Operation Baby Lift and Frequent Wind,"* and Official USMC Command Chronology Reports from the Ninth Marine Amphibious Brigade for the period of March 26 to April 30, 1975. Brigadier General Carey's logbook was also very illuminating, providing insight into the challenges of the Marine mission. These references are preserved and housed in the **Sam Johnson Vietnam Archive** at Texas Tech University.

May those many Marines, Servicemen, and civilians who participated in this unbelievable operation know that their exceptionalism, duty, and courage have rarely been matched and that our country owes a great debt of gratitude to them.

For those who have passed on, may they forever Rest in Honored Peace.

Beyond Belief: True Stories of Marine Corps Heroes

Jason Dunham (USMC) & William Kyle Carpenter (USMC)

Lessons from Marines That Jumped on Grenades

By Jim Fausone

This is the story of two incredible Marines that performed similar acts of heroism that resulted in being awarded the Medal of Honor. Each man has his own story but the lessons to learn are similar. What compels a young Marine to risk his life by jumping on a grenade to save his buddies? Is it their upbringing before the Corps or is it the training received while in the Corps? After reading about these men you will ask yourself, could I have done what they did? Was the reaction simply training, instinct, or a higher calling?

For action in Iraq in 2004, Jason Dunham was the first Marine to receive the Medal of Honor since the Vietnam War. For action in 2010 in Afghanistan, Kyle Carpenter was the youngest Marine in the War on Terrorism to receive the Medal of Honor. Both made a decision to protect their fellow Marines by jumping on a grenade.

CORPORAL JASON LEE DUNHAM

Jason Lee Dunham (November 10, 1981 – April 22, 2004) was a corporal in the United States Marine Corps. He was posthumously awarded the Medal of Honor in 2007 for his actions while serving with Third Battalion Seventh Marines during the Iraq War in 2004.

While on a patrol in Husaybah, his unit was attacked and he deliberately covered an

Beyond Belief: True Stories of Marine Corps Heroes

enemy grenade to save nearby Marines. When it exploded, Dunham was gravely injured and died eight days later. His life and story are short. The lessons he provides and his all-too brief life were more than a short story. He was the kind of young man that the Marine Corps seeks, and that our Country needs — those who want to be the best and to be tested.

Jason was from a family of service, military and public. His father, Dan, was an Air Force veteran. His mother, Deb, was a public schoolteacher in Scio, New York. This small hometown of 1,800 people in upstate New York is surrounded by hills and creeks. Jason played high school basketball and like a lot of young men growing up, would describe himself as an athlete. That is where he learned to test himself, the value of teamwork, the disappointment of losing, and the joy of sharing wins. Jason was a typical young man, full of life and sometimes mischief. He had a smile that would light up a room and make his high school friends, and later his Marines, feel good. Jason was a big guy with a big heart. High school graduation led him to joining the Marine Corps in 2000.

During the next four years he absorbed all that the Corps had to teach about teamwork, sacrifice and pushing oneself beyond expected limits. By 2004, Dunham was a squad leader in Iraq. In the United States Marine Corps, a rifle squad is usually composed of three fireteams of four Marines each and has a squad leader who is typically a sergeant or corporal. This is the building block of leadership in the Corps.

On April 14, 2004, the battalion commander's convoy came under attack near Husaybah, Iraq, and Fourth Platoon was dispatched on patrol to investigate. Dunham and his squad intercepted a number of cars that had been spotted near the scene of the attack, which the patrol detained to search for weapons. When the squad approached a

Jason Dunham & Kyle Carpenter (USMC)

white Toyota Land Cruiser and saw AK-47s in the back, the driver exited, trying to skirt away. Dunham was closest and engaged the insurgent. During hand-to-hand combat to subdue the insurgent he yelled, *"watch his hands"* and then the insurgent dropped a Mills 36M hand grenade. Dunham turned his attention to the grenade while another Marine shot the insurgent dead as he tried to escape.

In a flash, Jason Dunham had to react to protect others. He instantly covered the grenade with his Kevlar helmet, seeking to contain the blast. He was severely wounded and two Marines of his squad (William Hampton and Kelly Miller) were also struck by grenade fragments. The helmet was shredded, as was Jason.

Why does someone do that? For decades, young Marines have asked themselves, *"What would you do in such a situation?"* It is idle talk during downtime of war. **Wall Street Journal** staff reporter Michael M. Phillips wrote in 2004 that such a conversation of *"What would you do?"* had indeed involved Dunham: *"Early this spring (2004) , Corporal Jason Dunham and two other Marines sat in an outpost in Iraq and traded theories on surviving a hand-grenade attack,"* he wrote. *"Second Lieutenant Brian 'Bull' Robinson suggested that if a Marine lay face down on the grenade and held it between his forearms, the ceramic bulletproof plate in his flak vest might be strong enough to protect his vital organs. His arms would shatter, but he might live."*

Corporal Dunham had another idea: A Marine's Kevlar helmet, held over the grenade might contain the blast. *"I'll bet a Kevlar would stop it,"* he said, according to Second Lieutenant Robinson.

"No, it'll still mess you up," Staff Sergeant John Ferguson recalled saying. It was a conversation the men would remember vividly a few weeks later when they saw the shredded remains of Corporal Dunham's helmet, apparently blown apart from the inside by a grenade.

In 2005, Phillips published **The Gift of Valor: A War Story** which told Dunham's life story. The men who Dunham saved would refer to his act as *"the Gift"* and speak of the need to live their lives in a manner that paid honor to the gift they had been given by Jason's sacrifice.

Beyond Belief: True Stories of Marine Corps Heroes

Corporal Jason Dunham was posthumously awarded the Medal of Honor by President George W. Bush in January 2007, the first Marine to receive the nation's highest honor for valor in combat since the Vietnam War.

The President of the United States of America, in the name of Congress, takes pride in presenting the Medal of Honor (Posthumously) to Corporal Jason L. Dunham, United States Marine Corps, for conspicuous gallantry and intrepidity at the risk of his life above and beyond the call of duty while serving as a Rifle Squad Leader, 4th Platoon, Company K, Third Battalion, Seventh Marines (Reinforced), Regimental Combat Team 7, FIRST Marine Division (Reinforced), on 14 April 2004. Corporal Dunham's squad was conducting a reconnaissance mission in the town of Karabilah, Iraq, when they heard rocket-propelled grenade and small arms fire erupt approximately two kilometers to the west. Corporal Dunham led his Combined Anti-Armor Team towards the engagement to provide fire support to their Battalion Commander's convoy, which had been ambushed as it was traveling to Camp Husaybah. As Corporal Dunham and his Marines advanced, they quickly began to receive enemy fire. Corporal Dunham ordered his squad to dismount their vehicles and led one of his fire teams on foot several blocks south of the ambushed convoy. Discovering seven Iraqi vehicles in a column attempting to depart, Corporal Dunham and his team stopped the vehicles to search them for weapons. As they approached the vehicles, an insurgent leaped out and attacked Corporal Dunham. Corporal Dunham wrestled the insurgent to the ground and in the ensuing struggle saw the insurgent release a grenade. Corporal Dunham immediately alerted his fellow Marines to the threat. Aware of the imminent danger and without hesitation, Corporal Dunham covered the grenade with his helmet and body, bearing the brunt of the explosion and shielding his Marines from the blast. In an ultimate and selfless act of bravery in which he was mortally wounded, he saved the lives of at least two fellow Marines. By his undaunted courage, intrepid fighting spirit, and unwavering devotion to duty, Corporal Dunham gallantly gave his life for his country, thereby reflecting great credit upon himself and upholding the highest traditions of the Marine Corps and the United States Naval Service.

His parents, Dan and Deb Dunham, accepted the medal from President Bush in the East Room of the White House. They grew this young man who would sacrifice his life for his buddies. Dan and Deb may have found comfort in the Christian Bible verse: *"Greater love hath no man than this, that a man lay down his life for his friends."* (John 15:13)

President George W. Bush presents the Medal of Honor to the family of Corporal Jason Dunham of the Marine Corps during a ceremony on January 11, 2007.

Their faith would also strengthen them in 2004 when the family made the decision to pull the plug on the ventilator that was keeping Jason alive. He had discussed with his father that if something happened, he did not want to be kept alive by machines. Jason wrote his living will to indicate that his father should make the decision and pull the plug.

Jason's story has continued to inspire because he didn't hesitate to cover that grenade and shield his fellow Marines from the brunt of the blast.

His mother, Deb, wrote of her son and her loss in 2007:

MY SON'S GONE – BUT HEROES FIGHT ON

"I'll leave it to others to debate the politics of the war in Iraq. I'm a mother, not a politician. For me, discussing my son is personal, not political.

I want to remember Jason and to offer some thoughts to other parents whose sons and daughters are in combat serving this country.

There were so many facets to Jason's personality, you can't lock into any one thing.

He had a mischievous sparkle in his eye. You could play a joke on him and he would roll with it, but you could be pretty sure that he would come back with something when you weren't expecting it.

He was competitive and sports were often the way that he channeled that spirit. Jay played soccer, basketball and baseball – he still holds his high school's record in baseball.

Jason's teams often won. When he won, he wouldn't make the other team feel bad. He would congratulate his teammates and then go shake hands with the other team.

But it was his quiet sense of kindness that I remember most. He would always want to help out the little guy, the underdog, even when he was young.

Jason received the Medal of Honor for sacrificing himself to save others. What he did is great. But my son would have said, "Oo-rah! Let's go have a beer."

There was always one more challenge for him to find and meet in his life.

Like many families across America, my husband Dan and I would not have been able to afford college for our four children. Jason knew that and in the summer of his junior year in high school, we would sit in the living room and talk about what he wanted to do.

My husband was in the Air Force and he believes that everyone should serve a few years in the military, because it polishes you.

So Jay went into the Marine Corps – because it's the toughest training and something he could hold over his father's head. He'd say, "I work in the men's department of the military."

Jason joined the Corps before 9/11, but he believed in what he was doing in Iraq. His sense of right and wrong was keen. He thought that when someone has a lot of power and a lot of strength, you have a responsibility to help the little brother.

I just miss him.

For those parents who still have children in Iraq, I say, support your child.

Jason Dunham & Kyle Carpenter (USMC)

> *This is a volunteer military that we have – these men and women have more courage, more dignity and more patriotism than I have seen in years.*
>
> *Take the phone calls, send the letters and the care packages. They know you are scared, but they don't need to go through two types of war.*
>
> *It's not a political issue when it's your child. They are doing what they believe is right.*
>
> *Jason may be gone, but we've gained thousands of new sons."*

The Dunhams raised a son of strong timber - an American son. He was up to the challenge. He was an example for his siblings and his squad. He cut his life short to give others a gift.

LANCE CORPORAL WILLIAM KYLE CARPENTER

William Kyle Carpenter, born October 17, 1989, is a medically retired United States Marine who received the United States' highest military honor, the Medal of Honor, for his actions in Marjah, Helmand Province, Afghanistan in 2010. Kyle Carpenter was the youngest living Medal of Honor recipient at the time.

Kyle grew up in a loving household where sports, hard work, and dedication were supported. While this is a Marine that, as he says, *"cuddled a grenade"* and lived to tell about it, he is another example of how good men answer the call. His is also a story of overcoming the devastation of war with family love and hard work.

He was born in Mississippi and spent some time in Alabama, Georgia, and Tennessee. His family ended up in South Carolina, which he calls home. He had the typical young kid in the south upbringing. Football was his passion, younger twin brothers looked up to him and he felt like he had solid, loving parents and upbringing.

Like many kids at the end of high school, the options are college or military service. In March of 2009 Kyle went off to Marine boot camp at Parris Island. He explained to VeteransRadio.net in an interview in 2019 why he chose the Marines:

"I wanted to do something bigger than myself. Regret and unfilled potential is, besides hand grenades now, my only two fears in life. I just wanted to do something that was bigger than any one individual and I wanted to do it and not have the fear of waking up one day when I had missed my opportunity and have regret about not joining and not committing myself, and now my body and my life, to something greater than myself or any one person or individual."

On November 21, 2010, Carpenter's life changed forever. He went on to describe the actions that day for VeteransRadio.

"Roughly, a day and a half to two days before, on November 19, myself and the rest of my squad moved to a village in a rotation south of the small patrol base that we had been living and operating out of for the first four months so far in our deployment. Looking ahead, we were over the halfway point and for anyone not completely familiar with how things work, combat zones are when other units are coming to relieve you. Before those next units come in and you go home, what you want to do is expand your presence from how you found it and took it over from the unit that you relieved. We went into Marjah. We wanted to push out and expand our presence. That helps not only to continue to push the enemy further out, but also with making things safer, more comfortable for the locals. Then, once the threats are gone, people start coming out more; they want to take advantage and, hopefully, one day be able to send their children to school and have paved roads and

Jason Dunham & Kyle Carpenter (USMC)

running water. Just pushing that out to create more and more stability.

"We had pushed out to a village south of our position, and within the hour, very soon after we took over that compound, the first grenade attack came. For the next 24 to 36 hours, we were attacked constantly by AK47s, small arm fire, snipers and multiple attacks with hand grenades. When all was said and done, it was time a few days later for my squad after myself and many of my fellow Marines were injured to go back to the base where we had initially started out at. We were almost at 50% casualties and we had barely left our 4 walls of safety of the base that we were currently occupying.

"The day I was injured, November 21, 2010, myself and a fellow Marine, one of the most amazing and greatest Marines that I had ever had the pleasure of serving with and someone I am thankful to call a best friend, Nick Eufrazio, we were on top of a roof together on post. Post is essentially, for those not familiar with military terminology, it's a look out position. We were on this roof looking for more hand grenade attacks. Any attacks that might injure the Marines who are not vigilant and on watch and either cleaning their weapons, eating or resting inside the compound. We were at the end of our 4 hour shift, which was the afternoon of November 21.

"Unfortunately, I don't remember anything in the moments leading up to that daylight grenade attack. The only thing I remember from the day before is that morning, rolling out of my sleeping bag around 7:45 or 8:00 a.m. – we were getting attacked. It was a day break attack with AK47s. That had kind of become our alarm clock over there. I remember unzipping my sleeping bag and rolling out and kind of thinking, here we go, another day in Afghanistan.

"Fast forward to that afternoon, and really the only thing I remember from that day and the attack is, after the grenade exploded, I remember physically how I felt. At first, I was extremely disoriented and I was reeling from the blast. I just felt that I had got hit really hard in the face and I was trying to put the pieces together. I was thinking, okay, I was in Afghanistan, the last

307

thing I remember was on a roof, but what could possibly injure me this bad from a roof? Maybe I got off and went on patrol and I stepped on an IED? Maybe this is just the last thing I can remember. Those thoughts and me trying to put those pieces together was interrupted by the feeling of what I was thinking at the time to be, warm water.

"It just shows you how much Marines love each other and how much we pick on each other because I was thinking, man, in this banged up and terrible shape and state that I am in, my buddies are still messing with me. The pieces quickly and unfortunately, fell into place and gave me the surreal realization that what I was feeling was not warm water, it was blood, and I was bleeding out very quickly."

As reported by his mates, there was a grenade thrown up on the roof and instinctively Carpenter covered the grenade to protect his squad mate, and his body and Kevlar took the brunt of this grenade explosion, which blew through the roof. There was an amazing effort by his squad and the medics and everybody else to save his life, as he was bleeding out. The resulting medevac, and multiple hospital stops in Germany and Walter Reed was reported in his 2019 book, **You Are Worth It: Building a Life Worth Fighting For.**

The President of the United States of America, in the name of Congress, takes pleasure in presenting the Medal of Honor to Lance Corporal William Kyle Carpenter, United States Marine Corps, for conspicuous gallantry and intrepidity at the risk of his life above and beyond the call of duty while serving as an Automatic Rifleman with Company F, Second Battalion, Ninth Marines, Regimental Combat Team 1, FIRST Marine Division (Forward), I Marine Expeditionary Force (Forward), in Helmand Province, Afghanistan, in support of Operation ENDURING FREEDOM on 21 November 2010. Lance Corporal Carpenter was a member of a platoon-sized coalition force, comprised of two reinforced Marine rifle squads partnered with an Afghan National Army squad. The platoon had established Patrol Base DAKOTA two days earlier in a small village in the Marjah District in order to disrupt enemy activity and provide security for the local Afghan population. Lance Corporal Carpenter and a fellow Marine were manning a rooftop security position on the perimeter of Patrol Base DAKOTA when the enemy initiated a daylight attack with hand grenades, one of which landed inside their sandbagged position. Without hesitation and with complete disregard for his own safety, Lance Corporal Carpenter moved toward the grenade in an attempt to shield his fellow Marine from the deadly blast. When the grenade detonated, his body absorbed the brunt of the blast, severely wounding him, but saving the life of his fellow Marine. By his undaunted courage, bold fighting spirit, and unwavering devotion to duty in the face of almost certain death, Lance Corporal Carpenter reflected great credit upon himself and upheld the highest traditions of the Marine Corps and of the United States Naval Service.

Kyle Carpenter's story is of recovery, struggle, redemption and perseverance. Today, Carpenter may be one of the most grateful and well-adjusted Medal of Honor recipients in recent history. This again highlights a strong supportive family structure he had

Kyle Carpenter receiving the Medal of Honor from President Barack Obama

before joining the Marines, and its impact on his recovery. He explained to VeteransRadio.net in 2019:

"Wow, where to start. .... On a foundational level, just to have someone beside you that says, 'hey, I support you, I love you, and I'm here for you.' Veteran or not, military or not, injured or not, just as a person and as a human being, to have people and my family, and yes, the amazing staff at Walter Reed. Just from the moment I woke up to have the love and support I did. It was hard for me almost to not stay positive. I woke up and I was alive.

Beyond Belief: True Stories of Marine Corps Heroes

Incredible, amazing Step #1. I just could not believe it because I truly thought when I felt myself bleeding out, that that was it.

"Then I wake up to this bonus round. Yes, I've been fighting for my life. It was so hard and terrible to breathe through a tube for months. It took me a long road to recovery to get back on my feet. At the foundation of it all, to just be loved and supported and have a helping hand around my shoulder was enough to help me be able to continue to knock out the baby steps and strive to reach that potential in whatever recovery I was in."

"Here is this bad ass Lance Corporal Marine, the guy jumps on a grenade and one of the things that really helps him get through the down times is this fluffy white 9½ pound dog named Sadie.

"Thankfully, there are a lot of dog lovers out there so if I'm being judged ... Sadie was like any great dog. After I spent my initial lifesaving three months at Walter Reed, the casualty rate coming in was astronomical. At one point, there were hospital beds in the hallways at Walter Reed so when it came time for me to still need to be taken care of medically, but also I didn't have to stay in-patient every second of every day, I was allowed by the military and the staff at Walter Reed to go home and recover until that following September. I got done at Walter Reed at the end of January, but I got to home for seven months and recover. All I could do was lay on the couch and I had the tough job of eating mom's amazing homemade southern cooked food all the time. I just laid on the couch. Sadie likes her personal space and doesn't like to be bothered all the time if she is in that mode. I think she knew. She sat there with me every second of every day for those seven months and helped me get better and she's the best."

Naturally, Carpenter felt he was *damaged goods* and that nobody was going to love him. You have to work through the recovery both physically and mentally after you cuddle a grenade.

"That is a great question and I'm glad you brought that up because out of everything that I talk about in the book, this one extremely low moment was not only a defining moment in my recovery but my life.

310

Jason Dunham & Kyle Carpenter (USMC)

"It was very shortly after I had left the hospital at the end of February, so this was spring 2011. I think, up until that point, through all of the pain, the time at Walter Reed, just the surgeries, I think that I was strong and as good as I was, I pushed as hard as I did because aside from all of my physical stuff and my injuries, it was equally as much, if not more, an emotional and mental burden on me knowing that my family and my parents, I knew how heart wrenching it had to be for them. So I tried not to show anything but positivity. My dad said he never believed me but I always would say I'm not in any pain because I didn't want to hurt them anymore.

"But I was at home, in the spring of 2011, it was about 10 o'clock at night, and it was a very movie-like setting, the lights were kind of dim, mom was the only one still up, and I was in the kitchen by myself and I hadn't had any of my nerve surgeries on my arm, I could barely operate enough to make a bowl of cereal. I finally get this bowl of cereal made and I try to start eating it. I can barely hold the spoon and that's a challenge. Up until a couple of weeks before this point, my mom was still brushing my teeth, putting on my underwear, tying my shoes. My doctors, I can't even express how amazingly they rebuilt and put my face and my jaw back together, but the grenade blew most of my teeth out on the bottom and some on the top, and really just completely destroyed my entire lower jaw and part of my upper jaw, pretty much everything from my eye socket down.

"I'm sitting here trying to eat my cereal with no teeth. I can't feel my chin because my nerves are severed. I noticed milk is all over my face, dribbling down my chin, and something inside me completely broke.

"I started crying harder and harder until I was borderline hysterically crying. My mom rushes in and her first thought is, of course, I'm in pain and what is wrong? I just looked at her and said, 'who is ever going to love me again?'

"Yes, it was a low moment and so hard. At the time, I regretted saying it because I could see that it absolutely tore her in two. My book is essentially lessons that over time, and reflection,

and personal growth, I realized a life lesson that I wanted to convey to people.

"Now looking back, I'm so thankful for that moment, that low, terrible moment at the kitchen counter because I realized that as upset and down as I was, that I could either get up, take one small step and put one foot in front of the other, and continue to push through not only my recovery, but the rest of my life and make the best with the cards that I have been dealt. Or the only other option that I had, and that we have in life, is when we are knocked down... I could have sat at that kitchen counter for the rest of my life.

"I'm thankful I made the choice that I did and I didn't know exactly what I was doing at the time, all I knew was that I could have got up and made the best of it and pushed forward. Or, I would have stayed right there, down and out, crying and trying to eat that bowl of cereal for the rest of my life. The turning point in my recovery, and really where I have decided that I was always going to move forward and never look back, and what happened, happened, is right there sitting at that kitchen counter."

Amazingly, Kyle lived after his selfless act of covering a grenade. How you are going to live after a tragedy is a choice. He had to decide how to live and if he was going to hide his scars.

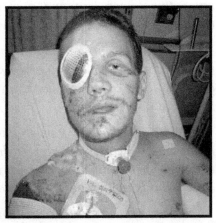

"At one point in my recovery, I tried scar revision therapy. After I got out of surgery, the doctors kind of said, 'hey, we have this laser treatment and we can smooth a lot of these scars out on your face.' I was there for three years. It was there and available, so I said, 'why not, I'll try it.' I came out of that and my face was swollen. It really looked like I stuck my head in beehive. I got back to my room and I was looking at myself in the mirror and I had a 'what am I doing' type moment.

Jason Dunham & Kyle Carpenter (USMC)

"I asked that to myself for two reasons. One, trying to smooth out the scars on my face, would that be possible? Yes, with a certain number of treatments, it would probably make me a little bit prettier. It would be hard, but it might make me look a little bit prettier. Then you go down and you get to a massive scar on my neck that goes from my ear all the way to the other side of my neck. My trach scar . . . then we don't have enough time the rest of the day to talk about the scars from the neck down.

"I tell people to own their scars, who am I if I sit here trying to get scar revision therapy and trying to get rid of the things that I am telling people to be proud of and to own?

"Through that thought process, I kind of solidified in my thought process that as far as scars, they are really beautiful. And people may see them as physically different or physically ugly, but scars show our physical representation that you have not only lived but you've been knocked down, or you've been injured, or you bled, or you had these hard times.

"Scars can be absolutely just as much mental and emotional, as physical. Those are much tougher, obviously, because people can't see them for a lot of time, and people might not want to talk about them. But as far as my physical scars, and people's physical scars, be proud of those. They show that you have lived life and you pushed through whatever gave you those scars. Now, you might have a scar but you have knowledge, and experience, and more reliance, and perseverance, when the next challenge or the next life obstacle comes your way. Above that, not only for yourself, but you can connect with other people who have struggled.

"Struggle was kind of my lightbulb term. When I realized that the angle that I could take is struggle because everyone on this planet, that is that common thread through us all. Mental, physical and emotional. Scars – own them. Be thankful for them because you are still living and you are still breathing. You are better and stronger than you were before."

Sacrifice often leads to struggle. Dunham's sacrifice has led to struggle for his squad members who are learning to live with the gift

313

of life that he gave them and of which they may not feel worthy. Dunham's family has had to struggle with his loss and its meaning.

Carpenter's sacrifice led to immense pain, surgeries and scars. He and his family had to work out these struggles. But they had the joy that he lived and was now again living. He embraced his scars.

These men, who cuddled a grenade, acted in a way that is beyond belief. Such acts of valor often come with the cost of loss of life. On occasion the men survive and to live with the resulting scars and struggles. They remind us of the importance of family and foundational values. We can learn from them both in their acts of heroism but also in putting the pieces of life back together.

Gomer Pyle U.S.M.C.

America's Most-Famous "Marine"

By C. Douglas Sterner

War is not a laughing matter – or is it?

During World War II dramatic depictions of Soldiers, Sailors, Airmen and Marines served important roles from inspiring the American public in support of the war effort to the important task of promoting war bond sales and rationing at home. Perhaps one of the greatest impacts of these dramatic depictions of combat and heroism, presented with patriotic fervor, was that they inspired young men and women to visualize themselves as these members of the military service, and inspiring them to enlist for military service.

Beyond Belief: True Stories of Marine Corps Heroes

Well known actors like John Wayne, who had never served in the military, portrayed characters from all branches of military service in combat roles, even including the new Navy Seabees. Within months of the heroic but tragic defense of Wake Island in December 1941, Brian Donlevy, Robert Preston, Macdonald Carey and William Bendix brought their story to the big screen in *"Wake Island."* That same year, John Wayne appeared in the film *"Flying Tigers"* about American pilots fighting in China. One of Wayne's last of several such movies released during the war, "They Were Expendable" was released in 1945. John Wayne played the role PT Boat Commander John Duncan Bulkeley (called Brickley in the movie), a Medal of Honor recipient, during the earliest days of the war in the Philippine Islands.

The positive impact of these dramatic depictions of Americans at war is evident by the unprecedented support the military gave to the production of the movies. In fact, in an effort to increase recruiting in the U.S. Army Air Forces, Hollywood icon Clark Gable was enlisted and sent to England in 1943 to fly and film air missions as an aerial gunner in the EIGHTH Air Force for "Combat America," a planned movie about the air war, specifically targeted at recruitment.

When the war ended, the American public continued to want additional movies of the war's greatest heroes. In 1955 Audy Murphy, who emerged from World War II as one of the two most-highly decorated Infantrymen, played himself in the biopic *"To Hell and Back."* Other lesser known veterans of that war went on to become actors staring in Hollywood productions from war movies to non-military related features, including Lee Marvin, Charles Durning, Art Carney, Mell Brooks, Eddie Albert, James Arness, and others.

During the war, and in the ten years after the war's end, most of these movies were dramatic representations of men at war. The drama was in the combat itself, and there was little hint of interpersonal conflict . . . after all, these movies were meant to inspire and to promote patriotism. But all that changed in 1954 with the release of *"The Caine Mutiny."*

Set in World War II, it was based on a 1951 Pulitzer Prize winning novel by Herman Wouk, who had served aboard two destroyer-minesweepers during the war. This time the drama was not between the U.S. Navy and the Japanese, but rather between the ship's commander Captain Queeg (Humphry Bogart), a tyrannical and mentally unstable officer, and his crew. Queeg's ship, the focus of the movie, is the *U.S.S. Caine,* named for the Bible Story of Cain who killed his brother Abel, which in itself, give a hint as to the premise of the drama that unfolds. It established a new formula for military movies and subsequent television shows, pitting those in authority (the new enemy) against the everyday Soldiers, Sailors, Airmen and Marines who served under them.

In 1955, *"Mister Roberts,"* with a star-studded cast that included Henry Fonda, James Cagney, William Powell, Jack Lemon, and Ward Bond, was released to wide acclaim. Amid the dramatic conflicts between Mr. Roberts, a low-level Navy Officer pitted against a harsh and unpopular captain, the movie also had more than a few events that drew laughter, yet another twist in the evolution of military entertainment.

The authority vs. everyday soldier came to life that same year on television, this time as a flat out, peace-time comedy at a laid-back Army post in the fictional town of Roseville, Kansas. *The Phil Silvers Show* (1955 – 1959) was about Sergeant Bilko (played by Silvers, and the show actually was often called *"Sergeant Bilko"* by the audience), who with authority clashes now becoming a staple of military entertainment, pitted against his commanding officer, Colonel John T. Hall (Paul Ford). This time, however, the conflict was not as personal.

The lead character this time was Master Sergeant Bilko, a career soldier with a variety of money-making side-hustles. In fact, the original title, subsequently dropped, was *"You'll Never Get Rich."* In charge of the Motor Pool, Sergeant Bilko was always trying to scam someone and make a quick buck. Sometimes his rank-and-file soldiers were in on the scheme, but at other times Bilko was not immune to taking advantage of them, despite always being careful to protect them. There was a comradery among them all, but Bilko's approach to his get-rich-quick schemes have been described as: *"They were his men and if anyone was going to take them, it was going to be him and only him."* Like the soldiers, the authoritarian Colonel Hall, was also likeable. The comedy was often slap-stick, with the hustle being performed right behind Colonel Hall's back.

Unlike the military comedies that would follow, *"The Phil Silver Show"* was filmed before a live audience in New York City. It featured several secondary characters and cameos, including Ed Sullivan's first cameo appearance on television, becoming too expensive to continue beyond the fourth season. From his jail cell, where Bilko and some of his men were being held after a recent scam, he signaled the end of the show with the words, "Th-th-that's all folks!"

In 1958, a young and rising actor named Andy Griffith starred in *"No Time For Sergeants,"* a truly comedic military movie. Griffith played William Stockdale a bumbling country-boy thrown into the structure of Air Force life. Together with his friend and equally bumbling recruit Ben Whitledge (Nick Adams), they become a *thorn in the flesh* of their all-military Master Sergeant Orville C. King (Myron McCormick).

Promoted as *"The Picture that is Winning Every Medal for Mirth,"* it was in many regards a trend setter for a series of military comedies that would become popular in the next two decades. Like

The Phil Silver show it too, depicted everyday military life. *"No Time for Sergeants"* would in fact, return to CBS Television for one season (1964 – 1965).

In 1960, Griffith would reach new heights in the entertainment world with the debut of a non-military comedy, *"The Andy Griffith Show"* starring in 249 episodes through 1968. During the show's first two seasons Aaron Ruben, who was creator of *"The Andy Griffith Show,"* suggested that the shows namesake visit The Horn show club in Santa Monica, California, where a funny-looking fellow with a country-bumpkin persona was belting out tunes in a strong baritone voice that belied his appearance. Thus it was that Andy Griffith first became aware of the multi-talented Jim Nabors.

James Thurston Nabors was born June 12, 1930, in Sylacauga, Alabama, the only son of police officer Fred Nabors and Mavis Pearl (Newman). He grew up with two sisters and loved to sing, often singing for both his high school and his church. While attending the University of Alabama he began acting in skits. After graduation he moved to New York City, where he worked as a typist for the United Nations for a year. After moving to Chattanooga, Tennessee, he got his first job in television as a film cutter at WRGP-TV and also substituted as co-host of the *"Holiday for Housewives"* show.

Suffering from asthma, he moved to Los Angeles to continue his career as a film cutter at NBC, while also performing at The Horn. There, where he was managed by Dick Link, he sang in his powerful voice, and occasionally slipped into his more high-pitched, comedic voice. He became close friends with a stand-up comic, also managed by Link, named Ronnie Schell. Nabors was once invited to appear on *"The Steve Allen Show,"* but it was cancelled before he was able to make the appearance. His television debut was as Jimmy Nabors on the *"Today in Dixie"* show in Augusta, Georgia.

Beyond Belief: True Stories of Marine Corps Heroes

Nabors and Schell became close friends, touring together and performing small gigs in Las Vegas and around the country, before that fateful night when Andy Griffith came to **The Horn** to hear him sing. Duly impressed by both Nabors' comedic persona as well as his incredible singing voice, Nabors was invited to join the cast of his show, playing the party of Gomer Pyle, the kind-hearted and soft-spoken rube who worked at the Mayberry, North Carolina, service station.

Gomer's Mayberry character was created by two writers of the show, Everett Greenbaum and Jim Fritzell. He was named after Gomer Cool, a writer, and Denver Pyle who played in several episodes, and later went on to play Jesse Duke in *"The Dukes of Hazard"* (1979 – 1985). Nabors was originally scheduled to play that part in only one episode.

Mayberry's Gomer Pyle role, however changed Nabor's life. Gomer Pyle gained a quick following and he appeared in 23 episodes of *"The Andy Griffith Show"* from 1962 to 1964. Nabors was a good man, with a kind heart and a strong sense of loyalty, and as his star began to rise, he would not forget his friend Ronnie Schell, who had been with him through the early days.

As Gomer Pyle was making his first appearances in Mayberry as a civilian, on October 11, 1962, the first military-related comedy came to television. Ernest Borgnine, a World War II Navy veteran and Academy Award winning dramatic actor, assumed the role of Lieutenant Commander Quinton McHale, commander of a World War II PT boat in *"McHale's Navy"* (1962 – 1966).

Joseph Flynn, who had entertained troops with the Army Special Services Branch in World War II, played the part of by-the-book Captain Wallace *Wally* Binghamton, better known by his men as *Old Leadbottom*. In many regards it followed the format of the earlier *"Caine Mutiny"* and *"Mister Roberts,"* but without any effort at drama, and piles of laughs. Binghamton, although *the* enemy in a World War II military show, was not as evil or borderline unstable. He was more of an authoritarian and incompetent narcissist. These traits made him more comical than hate-able. The bumbling rube, almost now requisite for such shows, was Ensign Parker, launching the comedic career of Tim Conway. It was, perhaps, entertainment's first true military comedy in a pattern that would be followed by many more highly successful such television comedies over the next two decades.

Back in Mayberry, North Carolina, or at least the show's Desilu Studies in California, Producer/Writer Ruben had an idea for another creation. Building upon the popularity of Mayberry's service station attendant, he decided to throw the country-bumpkin with a heart of gold into the structured world of Marine Corps service. Thus was born the idea for *"Gomer Pyle, U.S.M.C.,"* that for five years would become one of the most popular shows on television.

To play opposite Jim Nabors, the loveable but clumsy Private Gomer Pyle, Ruben began looking for the right person to play the part of Sergeant Vincent Carter, Pyle's boot camp drill instructor and the authority figure to be the enemy. He found his man in the strong visage of veteran actor Frank Sutton, who literally looked like a Marine Drill Instructor, and had the booming command voice to match.

Born in Clarksville Tennessee, on October 23, 1923, Frank Spencer Sutton developed an interest in acting at age nine which he pursued further in the drama club at East Nashville High School, where he graduated in 1941. After a brief stint as a radio announcer in Clarksville, he attempted to enlist in the Marine Corps but was rejected on medical grounds – he was color blind. So Sutton, eager to do his patriotic duty, joined the U.S. Army. From 1943 to 1946 he served with the 293rd Joint Assault Signal Company in the Pacific Campaign, achieving the rank of sergeant and earning a Bronze Star for Valor and the Purple Heart for wounds received in action, as well as 5 battle stars on his campaign ribbon. Throughout his combat service in the Pacific he participated in 14 landings including Luzon, Bataan, and Corregidor.

Beyond Belief: True Stories of Marine Corps Heroes

After his honorable discharge he attended the Columbia University of General Studies, graduating cum laude with a degree in drama in 1952. Multiple small roles followed throughout the 1950s, and in 1955 he had a role in the Academy Award winning movie *"Marty."* Most of his work was as a dramatic actor, quite in contrast to the role he would play in *"Gomer Pyle, U.S.M.C."*

To prepare for his role as Gunnery Sergeant Vincent Carter, despite his prior military service, Sutton was sent to Camp Pendleton in California for a month to observe real Marine sergeants in action. While Gomer Pyle's character had been well-scripted throughout his episodes on *"The Andy Griffith Show,"* Sergeant Carter's profile was developed from scratch. *"The writers were making a brutal s.o.b. out of him,"* he noted in one interview. Indeed, that was the formula of the past: the viciously cruel and narcissistic Captain in *"Mister Roberts,"* played by Jim Cagney; the by-the-book and heartless Master Sergeant King in *"No Time For Sergeants"* and the pompous and condescending *Old Leadbottom* in *"McHale's Navy."*

"I am an actor," Sutton once noted. *"I like doing characters that are real people. I want (Sergeant) Carter to have a whole real life instead of just getting into embarrassing coming situations. I started writing his biography on the last page of the scripts. I made him a high school dropout; the whole thing bored him, not enough action. The war's on in Korea; bam! – he volunteers. Carter has a mother; an allotment goes out. He lost his father. I'm inventing that now."*

Sutton often spoke of what he witnessed among the hard-charging, rule enforcing, and forceful education of Marine recruits by real Marine Drill Instructors (DI). He saw in them not only strong, dedicated professionals, but human beings with softer sides – leaders of men who underneath it all cared about the men that were their responsibility. He built that into his character. It was the kind of character just about every military veteran can identify with. During training the DI was seen as mean, heartless, and demanding. In retrospect, most veterans came to revere their DIs as dedicated leaders, men whose challenge was to train and prepare everyday young men and women for military service, fulling realizing that they may one day need these skills to survive at war.

Gomer Pyle, U.S.M.C.

Ask any veteran, and especially any Marine, and decades later they can still recall the name of their Boot Camp DI. As an Army veteran myself, fifty years after attending the Army's NCO School, I can literally sometimes hear the distinctive lisp of Tac Sergeant Shultz yelling at me, *"Cooopl Sterner, what in the hell do you think you are doing?"* And then, I smile with the memory.

"Gomer and Carter will become more closely related, but will never be buddies" Sutton said in one interview during the early days of the series. *"It wouldn't be realistic for a gunnery sergeant and a private to be buddies. Besides, it would ruin the show,"* he added, noting that the secret of the show's success was the interplay between Gomer and Carter. There was indeed a chemistry there that caused the viewer to like both characters, and enjoy the interplay between them, sometimes even sympathizing with Sergeant Carter.

On May 18, 1964, the pilot for *"Gomer Pyle, U.S.M.C."* aired as the final episode of *"The Andy Griffith Show's"* fourth season. In it Gomer joins the Marines, and Andy Griffith drives him out to the base and stays briefly to see how Gomer assimilates. The less kind Sergeant Carter had not yet begun to materialize, and Sergeant Carter immediately rejects the eager but

clumsy would-be private, and starts working on a plan to send him home. Learning this, Andy works hard to finally get Sergeant Carter to cut Gomer some slack, and let him pursue his dream of being a United States Marine.

As the series itself went into production, the two key figures were both outliers – Gomer Pyle was certainly not your typical person, much less typical Marine recruit; and Sergeant Carter was himself atypical, save for his counterparts in the real Marine Corps. Reuben was looking for a third key figure, someone more average that the general public to relate to. Nabors, remembering his long time friend and fellow performer, turned to Ronnie Schell to fill that important need.

Beyond Belief: True Stories of Marine Corps Heroes

Ronald Ralph Schell was born in Richmond, California, on December 23, 1931. Upon graduating from high school, Ronnie enlisted in the United States Air Force. *"I'm very pro-military,"* he noted in a recent interview, *"I had uncles and cousins who served in the military, and one of my high school classmates was killed in the early days of the Korean War."*

He admits he was a bit of a *"cut up"* during his service days, though not to the level of Private First Class Gilbert *Duke* Slater that he portrayed in four of the show's five seasons. His was a personality suited to comedy, and in his last year-and-a-half of service he toured with the U.S. Air Force Dance Band performing stand-up comedy during breaks in their show.

He appeared on the TV quiz show *"You Bet Your Life,"* hosted by Groucho Marx on May 28, 1959, demonstrating a comic barrage of beatnik jive talk. He went on to develop his stand-up routine at the **hungry i** nightclub in San Francisco, and partnered with Jim Nabors at **The Horn** and in subsequent performances in Las Vegas and other venues around the country. Schell, happy-go-luck and always with a side-hustle only slightly more innocent than Sergeant Bilko, completed the triumvirate that made *"Gomer Pyle, U.S.M.C."* an entertainment hit, and a boon for Marine Corps publicity and recruiting. He was Gomer's (and Nabors') best friend.

Gomer Pyle, U.S.M.C.

"Gomer Pyle, U.S.M.C." debuted CBS on September 25, 1965, and gained an immediate audience, including thousands of real U.S. Marines. The Marine Corps had given the show *limited cooperation* according to Sutton who noted, *"For a blanket seal of approval you'd have to give script approval, and that just can't be done on a comedy show."* Indeed, the opening scene with Sergeant Carter yelling at Private Pyle was filmed on-site at Camp Pendleton with real Marines and real Marine sergeants in formation.

Sergeant Carter's uniform reflects an interesting resume as well. Carter is a Marine veteran of combat in Korea, but Sutton was allowed to wear some of his World War II awards, including the Bronze Star and Purple Heart that would be appropriate for a Marine in any war. He also wears his World War II Victory Medal, along with the appropriate campaign ribbons the fictional Carter would have received for his Marine Corps service in Korea.

There were also Marine advisors who worked with the script writers and actors on the set at Desilu Studios. Sutton, who was left-handed, once requested a side-arm holster he could wear on the left side. He explained that in an episode of *"Gunsmoke"* that he had once appeared in, while called upon to do a quick draw from a holster on the right, he had clumsily cleared the holster but not his leg, burning it. Also, during filming of an episode of *"Naked City,"* his ineptness with his right hand wound up with him shooting himself in the arm. *"They may be blanks but they can give you a rough burn. That's why I'm adamant about using a left-handed holster, even if they do have to be specially made. At best, I'm clumsy as hell."*

"The Marine Corps advisors pointed out there's no such thing in their branch of the service as a left-handed holster," he recalled. *"So I promptly called to their attention an incident that happened to me while serving overseas in the Army (during World War II). It was in 1943, a date I acquired my first left-handed holster in a swap deal with a Marine. How come, I wanted to know, did he have one if they're not issued?"*

The Marine advisors commented that it must have been specially made, but the bottom line is that Sergeant Carter won that

Beyond Belief: True Stories of Marine Corps Heroes

round, and can be seen throughout the series wearing his side arm on the left hip.

The role of those Marine Corps advisors, as well as the fact that two of the three main characters were themselves veterans of real military service, is quickly recognizable by real veterans, which no doubt led to the loyal military and veteran audience the show quickly gained. Uniforms are immaculate and starched, the barracks orderly and frequently inspected, and there is no shortage of those silly things of military life any veteran recalls such as the endless raking of rock gardens, or digging a hole for no reason and then filling it back in. After a visit to the Marine Corps base in San Diego, Sutton remarked, *"The fellows there all love the show. Especially the sergeants."*

The real appeal of the show, however, far beyond its wide audience of current and former members of military service, was the nature of the three key characters, and the chemistry they seemed to have. Of course Nabors and Schell were long time friends, and very close so the chemistry was already there. Sutton, a good man with a kind heart and uncommon work ethic quickly was embraced. They would be close friends long after the show's five seasons.

Gomer Pyle was the star, but Sutton developed his own following as well. He explained their chemistry and appeal when he said, *"He (Gomer Pyle) trusts everybody in his own, innocent, untarnished way. I trust nobody. Except Gomer, of course. Who wouldn't trust Gomer?"*

"When I scream at Gomer – 'I can't hear you?' and that kind of stuff – Gomer just gazes back with those beagle eyes of his and grins. Then he said, 'I don't love you, but I like you' with that hillbilly accent. Why, ever viewer at home knows this Carter really isn't such a bad guy after all."

The audience came to know Gomer, Carter, and *Duke* as real, and as believable people with their own idiosyncrasies, problems, and challenges. Pyle himself was believable because everyone knew about Mayberry, North Carolina, and the young *"Marine's"* roots. During the five years of the show, *"Andy Griffith Show"* regulars including Andy, Aunt Bea, Opie, and Goober made guest appearances. There was a realistic appeal of the soldier and his hometown ties.

Gomer Pyle, U.S.M.C.

Despite the oddity of Gomer's personality, he represents the Marine Corps well. As an infantryman, he is dedicated to the Corps and always goes the extra mile to be a good Marine, often to the extreme. As a person, he comes across as a very caring and loyal person, always quick to come to the aid of a homeless stranger while on leave, honest to a fault, and loyal to his sergeant. Gomer is the Boy Scout who is always ready to help the little old lady across the street, sometimes innocently enough, when she didn't even want to cross the street.

In one episode where Gomer is hurting the platoon by his ineptness on the obstacle course, Sergeant Carter becomes exasperated by his sleeping late, only to learn that at nightfall, Gomer had been secretly visiting the obstacle course, running it throughout the night to finally master it. In yet another, when Gomer mis-reads Sergeant Carter's frequent anger and frustration with him, he requests a transfer – something Sergeant Carter had often dreamed of. In his absence, Corporal Chuck Boyle (Roy Stuart), helps Sergeant Carter realize how much he will miss Private Pyle. In his own gruff way, he comes to realize how symbiotic is his relationship to Gomer Pyle.

Stewart was only main cast member besides Nabors without prior military service, but he portrayed his role well through four seasons, looking every bit like a Marine Corporal. As Sergeant Carter's right-hand man, the interaction in the privacy of the platoon office and the two NCO's billet, Corporal Boyle provides the venue for the audience to see the more likeable side of Sergeant Carter.

Lieutenant Colonel Edward Gray (Forrest Compton) appeared in 58 episodes as the Commanding Officer, looking every bit the immaculate part of a Marine Corps officer. His uniform sports a Silver Star and Navy and Marine Corps Medal. The latter is one of the rarest of all military awards, presented for life-saving heroism in a noncombat situation. (In fact, in history only 17 Marines have been awarded both.). He also wears a Purple Heart and, almost overlooked, the Marine Corps Good Conduct Medal, which marks him as a *Mustang*, an officer who came up through the ranks.

Compton was, in fact, an Army combat veteran who served with the 103d Infantry Division in Europe during World War II. As Colonel Gray, he epitomizes a high ranking officer with a strong sense of demand, but an understanding attitude towards his men. More than once Gomer's faux paus come back to place Carter on the hot seat with the colonel, but he always responds with measured authority and structure.

Although it was indeed a comedy, and a very good one at that, the cast took their roles seriously and always tried to present a realistic appearance in keeping with Marine Corps standards. *"I've seen military shows where characters had long hair, were unshaven, or even had beards,"* said Schell recently. Not so on the set of "Gomer Pyle, U.S.M.C."

"Because of the military backgrounds of so many of the cast, when you see us in formation, or in a parade, we liked to look like Marines you would see at Camp Pendleton, or any other Marine base around the world."

In Season 1, viewers are introduced to Bunny (Barbara Stuart), Sergeant Carter's girlfriend who appeared in 21 episodes through all five seasons. His romance with Bunny gave further insights into Carters quirky, but loveable character, and the fact that Bunny really liked Gomer as a person, was fodder for more than one funny conflict between the sergeant and his private. In Season 3 actress Elizabeth MacRae appeared as Lou Ann Poovie, a sweet but naïve girl who grew up not far from Mayberry and who came to California to build a musical career, despite being tone deaf.

She and Gomer become instant friends, and as the series progresses, even boyfriend/girlfriend. In one episode, Sergeant Carter and Bunny even double date with by now Private First Class Pyle and Lou Ann. It is an incomprehensible scenario, the sergeant and his private on a double date. The cleverly crafted script, however, makes it more than believable with Carter being coerced into it by Bunny and, of course, Pyle is more than eager for the date. The most unbelievable scenarios became believable in "Gomer Pyle."

Gomer Pyle, U.S.M.C.

When the show premiered in 1964, the United States was at peace, save for a few military advisors serving in Vietnam. In fact, most Americans at that time had never heard of Vietnam, and could not find it on a map. All that changed in 1965, when the Vietnam conflict morphed into our nation's longest war up to that time.

That war was never written into the scripts, or even referenced, in episodes of *"Gomer Pyle."* It was not a matter of willful ignorance, or a conscious effort to weight in politically on what would quickly become an unpopular war with American populace. Rather, the TV sit-com was focused more on the everyday life of Marines at home. Throughout the remaining four seasons, the only acknowledgement that America was at war began in Season 3 (1966 – 1967), when the Marines were seen wearing the National Defense Service Medal on their dress uniforms. That award is presented to every member of military service, regardless of where they are stationed, during a time of war.

In the spring of 1966, with the filming of Season 2 complete, the cast went on a brief vacation. Frank Sutton used this respite to purchase a ticket to Vietnam. There, in Marine Corps uniform as Gunnery Sergeant Vince Carter, he performed a 22-minute comedy show 56 times in eight days for the Marines who were fighting that new war. In character as Sergeant Carter, he would chew out his audience: *"Dirty! Dirty! Dirty,"* he would scream. *"Marine, do you know that button is dirty?"*

Travelling by jeep and helicopter, he visited Marines in the field, usually opening with the words, *"Fellows, I'm very upset. All I hear about these days is the Green Beret. What's so great about the Green Beret? I've known guys in Hollywood who wore green berets. . . green purses . . and green dresses,"* and the laugher began. He also noted that, *"In every unit someone would say, 'You've got to see our Gomer Pyle,' and then call out 'Go get so-and so'."*

Beyond Belief: True Stories of Marine Corps Heroes

Indeed, the characters of the show, no matter how far-fetched it might seem on the surface, always reminded real Marines of someone they knew in their unit: Sergeant Carter, Private Pyle, Private First Class *Duke* Slater, Lieutenant Colonel Gray, or any of the other myriad of funny characters.

On his last day in Vietnam, Marine Lieutenant General Lewis Walt invited Sutton to lunch. *"That's quite a gesture for a Parris Island DI – or even for a Hollywood performer,"* Jim Lucas, a staff writer for Scripps-Howard wrote.

Of his motivation, Carter recalled his own experience during World War II when comedian Joe E. Brown came to entertain the troops. *"What he accomplished was a miracle and I swore right then and there that if the opportunity ever presented itself, I'd follow Joe's example of entertaining where the need was greatest.*

"My identification was with the young, healthy guys fighting," Sutton continued. *"I wanted to be a part of it,"* he said. *"I know what it means to die in a rice paddy with the stink and filth. I saw boys all shot up. I saw a quadruple amputee and blind.*

"They (Vietnam Marines) are far superior both physically and emotionally speaking, to troops in World War II. They are much more aware of what is going on in the world."

He also expressed his appreciation for the lack of racial prejudice he witnessed among the Marines, having served in World War II where racial prejudice was common, and military service often segregated.

"When I got back," he noted, *"everybody put me down. You'd think I was practically a Nazi. I am surrounded by dovish people in my business."*

If the anti-war crowd didn't appreciate Carter's trip, the Marine Corps did, in a twice special way. Sutton returned home on June 2 to prepare for filming of Season 3 of *"Gomer Pyle."* Before he could get started, however, he received an invitation with a special surprise – the opportunity to meet his inspiration. *"Now, after 20 years, I'll be meeting (Joe E. Brown) at last,"* Sutton noted with excitement adding, *"I just hope I don't bust out crying."*

The event was the SECOND Marine Division Association's convention in Los Angeles. There, on July 16, 1966, California Senator George Murphy, President of the Screen Actors Guild from 1944 to 1946, and recipient of an honorary Oscar in 1951, presented special citations to Brown, Sutton, Nabors, and Betty Hutton for *"their untiring and outstanding contribution to the Marines."* Frank Sutton received the rare distinction of being named an Honorary Sergeant of Marines.

"BUY U.S. SAVINGS BONDS"
Says Sarg and Gomer

Sergeant Carter and Private First Class Pyle, throughout the five-year run of their hit comedy show, repeatedly found ways in real life to support the Marine Corps and their nation. They promoted Savings Bonds, and other good causes, and were always active in their communities, often forging friendships with real Marines.

In 1967, **Hobo Kelly** (Sally Baker), the top-rated children's personality with a weekday show, conceived a Christmas project to benefit the thousands of homeless children in the Los Angeles area. With the Marine Corps Reserve's Toys for Tots program, she launched a three-hour telethon on December 2 to insure that these children

would have a happy Christmas. Among the celebrities that joined her in the effort that made it possible to collect more than 50,000 toys for underprivileged children through one of the Marine Corps' longest lasting social programs, were Sergeant Vince Carter and Private First Class Gomer Pyle.

Keeping the top-rated show always in the top ten was long hours and hard work. Sutton was the consummate professional, returning home after a day of work to review his script and memorize his lines often late into the evening. *"He was a totally Type-A*

Beyond Belief: True Stories of Marine Corps Heroes

person," Schell recalled. *"He would show up early the next morning totally prepared for work. Nabors, on the other hand was, well, Gomer Pyle. He'd show up and say, 'Okay, what am I doing today."*

During the show's five-season run, several additional characters were introduced, many of them also veterans of prior military service. Their presence kept the show always new, and always different. For some, the show became a springboard to bigger things.

Sergeant Carter's drinking buddy and fellow NCO Staff Sergeant Charley Hacker (Allan Melvin), appeared in 16 Episodes, including one in which he tried to steal Gomer for his kitchen when he learned that Gomer was a very good cook. Hacker was often Carter's nemesis, but the two had much in common and were friends, much like the friendship NCOs develop among themselves in the real military. Melvin was himself a veteran of military servicer in the Navy during World War II. He also had guest appearance in *"The Andy Griffith Show,"* and later went on to appear in several episodes of *"All in the Family,"* among others.

Larry Hovis was another comedian discovered by Andy Griffith, and hired to play Private Larry Gotschalk in 11 episodes of *"Gomer Pyle,"* (1964 – 1965) and also in two episodes of *"The Andy Griffith Show."* Hovis was also a writer, and wrote most of the comedy sketch for Sergeant Carter's visit to Marines in Vietnam.

Hovis would go on to become a regular in the World War II comedy about prisoners of war, *"Hogan's Heroes"* where he appeared in 168 episodes.

Another rising star was William Christopher who appeared in 15 episodes of Gomer Pyle as Private and later Corporal Lester Hummel, as well as two episodes of

Gomer Pyle, U.S.M.C.

"The Andy Griffith Show." Christopher would go on to play Father Francis Mulcahy, the chaplain in the hit comedy "M*A*S*H.

While Hovis and Christopher were both too young to have served in World War II, and were not called to service during the Korean War, other veterans appeared from time to time. Peter Hansen, who was a Marine Corps F4U fighter pilot in the Pacific during World War II appeared in four episodes in Season 1 as Lieutenant Colonel George Van Pelt. John *Buck* Young, who had served in the Army Air Forces during War II, appeared in 10 episodes at Staff Sergeant Whipple.

In a series of four episodes to play off the common inter-service rivalries when Sergeant Carter's men go to sea for exercises from a Navy Ship, Tige Andrews played the role of the overbearing and condescending Navy Senior Chief Petty Officer Wayne Simpson. Tige was a veteran actor who had appeared in *"Mister Roberts"* and *"The Phil Silvers Show:"* Andrews served with the Army's 45th Infantry Division in World War II, and was medically discharged as a Second Lieutenant in 1944 after he was injured when his ship sank in the Mediterranean.

Private First Class *Duke* Slater disappeared at the end of Season 3, when Ronnie Schell departed to star as a disc jockey in his own short-lived sit-com *"Good Morning World"* He returned for season five, newly promoted to corporal, creating new opportunities for comedic conflict with the best friend, still a Private First Class, and as Sergeant Carter's right-hand man.

No doubt due to its popularity, the skill of its writers, and the versatility of its cast, *"Gomer Pyle, U.S.M.C."* might well have gone on for many more seasons. But Nabors, now type-cast as Gomer Pyle, wanted to break and return to his first love, singing. The show ended on April 16, 1965 after 150 episodes, 12 of them in color from Seasons 2 through 5. Its successful run had entertained the public, humanized military service, and became the springboard for many military comedies to follow including: *"Hogan's Heroes"* (1965 –

Beyond Belief: True Stories of Marine Corps Heroes

1971, *"F-Troop"* (1965, *"M*A*S*H"* (1972 – 1983), *"Operation Petticoat"* (1977 – 1978), *"Private Benjamin"* (1981 – 1983), and many others.

Jim Nabors went on to star in his own variety show *"The Jim Nabors Hour"* from 1969 to 1971. When he made his departure from the set at Desilu Studios, he took with him his two closest friends, Frank Sutton and Ronnie Schell. For Schell this was an easy transition, having performed with Nabors for years before *"Gomer Pyle, U.S.M.C."* changed their lives. For Frank Sutton, the transition was not so easy.

"When Jim made the decision to go into variety and asked me to come along, I had misgivings, sure," he said. *"The first time my 15-year-old son Joey saw me in this outfit (bellbottom rehearsal slacks and dancing shoes), it broke him up."*

But being the inveterate professional, he spent his free hours for a year in dancing classes, and also took singing lessons. Still, the look on his face screams, *"Oh my God, Gomer, what have you got me into this time?"*

In 1970, I was myself in the military, serving as a young Army sergeant in Vietnam. As Christmas approached, our Commanding Officer asked which us of wanted to be on the list to travel to Da Nang to see the **Bob Hope Christmas Show**. My small base was north of Hue and far north of Da Nang, at the edge of the A Shau Valley. Going meant I would have to arise at 3 a.m. and make the multiple-hour and often dangerous convoy south to Da Nang. In the end, I opted out.

One year later I was still in Vietnam, albeit now at Camp Eagle, closer to Da Nang. I said to myself, "Self, you simply cannot spend two Christmas in a war zone and not see Bob Hope." Then, as I started seeing publicity for that years show, I quickly noted that among the beautiful starlets Hope was bringing, there was also someone I really wanted to see – Jim Nabors. It sealed the deal and I quickly put my name on the list.

That day I was one of tens of thousands of Soldiers, Sailors, Airmen and Marines crowed into the small amphitheater to see the show, but it was enough – I was not disappointed. Not only had I seen Bob Hope, but like Sergeant Carter five years earlier, Gomer Pyle had finally come to Vietnam.

Of that visit, Nabors said, *"When I went to Vietnam in 1971 with Bob Hope, we went to Da Nang, which was a Marine base. I just have to say it was one of the biggest thrills I've ever had."*

He returned home to the United States to a busy and versatile career. He continued his work with his own variety shows, as well as Christmas Specials. He recorded several widely popular record albums and took full advantage of his new opportunities to showcase his love of music and his amazing singing voice.

Beyond Belief: True Stories of Marine Corps Heroes

Tragically Frank Sutton died unexpectedly of a heart attack in his dressing room on June 28, 1974. He was 50 years of age, and he was deeply mourned by all who knew and had worked with him.

Nabors continued his entertaining in his own variety shows and others, even appearing on an episode of "The Muppets." He lived in a very close world of dear friends who had risen together in show business: Ronnie Schell, Andy Griffith, and the entire cast of both shows.

He appeared in every season premier of the popular Carol Burnett show, and the two were also close friends. Burnett herself had appeared in two episodes of "Gomer Pyle, U.S.M.C." as Marine Lance Corporal and later Sergeant Carol Barnes.

In the 1980s, Nabors appeared in three feature-length films including *"The Best Little Whorehouse in Texas"* (1982) with his friend Burt Reynolds. He and Reynolds also played in *"Stroker Ace"* (1983), and *"Cannonball Run II"* (1984). In 1986, he reprised his role as Gomer Pyle in a reunion of the Mayberry family in the made-for-television movie *"Return to Mayberry."* From 1972 to 2014, Nabors also joined the Purdue All-American Marching Band to sin *"Back Home Again in Indiana"* before each **Indianapolis 500** race.

In 1994, after a visit to India, he contracted hepatitis B which damaged his liver and nearly took his life. Nabors underwent and survived a life-saving liver transplant, thanks in part to Carol Burnett's intervention on his behalf with the head of the liver transplant division of the University of California, Los Angeles. After recovery, Nabors moved to Hawaii where he had often visited and had a villa, and entered semi-retirement. Before his annual rendition before the **Indianapolis 500**, Nabors announced that it would be his last public performance.

In 2001, the U.S. Marine Corps promoted Private First Class Gomer Pyle, aka Jim Nabors, to Corporal. Six years later in Hawaii, on the Marine Corps' 238th birthday, he was promoted to an Honorary Sergeant of Marines.

Retired Marine Corps Lieutenant General Hank Stackpole, a resident of Honolulu, noted that Nabors was *"devoted to the Marine Corps as vice versa. He spent a lot of time giving his time and his voice to the Marines. He had the entire Marine Corps Ban drum and Bugle Corps at his house and he shook hands and took pictures with one after the other with all of them. It really touched my hear to see him do that."*

Jim Nabors died in his home in Honolulu on November 30, 2017 at the age of 87. Ronnie Schell said, *"There are only two people in my entire life who have never had a negative word said about them, my wife of 52 years, and Jim Nabors. Everyone loved Jim."*

As a Vietnam Veteran myself, in retrospect, I believe what Gomer Pyle, Sergeant Carter, and Duke Slater did for veterans went far beyond just making people laugh, or promoting the Marine Corps. During our nation's most divisive war, when men and women in uniform were often only seen in combat footing on the evening news, and when many suffer indignities and disrespect from those who opposed the war, those three would-be Marines, and their comrades, reminded us that all that those who serve are people – human beings with fault, frailties, families, hopes, and dreams. They are indeed, simply dedicated public servants and patriotic soldiers.

Today, Ronnie Schell is the last regular member of the cast of *"Gomer Pyle, U.S.M.C."* still living. When I interviewed him for this story, he had just returned from a reunion of the Mayberry cast, where he was one of the few still living.

Following the last season of *"Gomer Pyle, U.S.M.C."* and his work with Nabors on the "Jim Nabors Hour, " he continued to have a successful career as an actor and comedian. His resume of TV appearances are too numerous to list. In 2007 he was part of a touring cabaret show "5 Star Review," and in 2009 starred in the off-Broadway production of *"Don't leave it All to Your Children,"* a comedic and musical revue dedicated to aging baby boomers. In 2009 he was comedy advisor to Richard Dreyfuss in the 2019 Netflix film *"The Last Virgin."*

Today, at age 88, Schell hasn't slowed down much. He is a busy guy, still entertaining audiences, autographing posters and books, and reminding us of the many wonderful characters from Mayberry, North Carolina, and a Marine Corps base, which made us laugh and who stole our hearts.

My sincere thanks to Ronnie Schell for taking time out of his busy schedule for a lengthy interview, and to his Talent Manager Leonard C. Carter, III, for helping make this story possible.

Sincerely,
Doug Sterner

MEET THE AUTHORS

ADAM BALLARD

Adam Ballard is an active duty sergeant in the United States Marine Corps and currently serves as a Combat Instructor with the Advanced Infantry Training Battalion, School of Infantry West, Aboard Camp Pendleton, California. Adam is also the son of Navy Corpsman, and Medal of Honor Recipient Donald Ballard. Outside of training Marines, Adam spends most of his time volunteering with the Medal of Honor Character Development Program and supporting many different charity events including Skyball and Snowball Express.

SCOTT BARON

Scott Baron is the author of eighteen books on American military history including *They Also Served, Forged in Fire*, and *Forgotten No More*, and wrote a column for "Stars and Stripes" on celebrities who served in the military. He is a Vietnam-era veteran and former law enforcement officer who has spent the last twenty-one years as a U.S. history teacher. He has a master's degree in teaching and lives in California with Marisela, his wife of forty-three years.

MARIO BIRLOCHO

My name is Mario but I sign my work Birlocho, I am an Ecuadorian artist, born in a small city named Portoviejo. I love to draw sexy girls, adding a bit of humor in the process, and it has turned out into a full-time job. When I was a kid, I dreamed of drawing using nothing but computers. Grandma used to say I was "wasting my life." I like to see life through what I like to call "my vision." The main victims of that so-called vision are my characters "Mabú & Lorenzo," the topic of my stories are parodies of world class pop culture through the eyes of a girl from a small city in a coast province in a Sudamerican country . . . and her cat.

JIM FAUSONE

Jim Fausone has been a lawyer for four decades and a veteran advocate since going to law school on the GI Bill. He founded Legal Help for Veterans, PLLC; is a podcast host for VeteransRadio.net; and maintains HomeofHeroes.com a website dedicated to Medal of Honor recipients. He is a board member of Michigan Military and Veterans Hall of Honor. A former Lt.(j.g.) in NOAA Corps, he graduated from the University of Michigan College of Engineering and Gonzaga University School of Law. He has co-authored the books *How to Get into a Military Academy*; *Answers to Common Veteran Disability Questions*, and *Vietnam Stories - Best of Veterans Radio*. He has hosted the largest and longest Veterans Summit in SE Michigan for a dozen years getting information out to veterans about benefits and health care. He is married to his college sweetheart, a nurse and fellow veteran advocate, Brigadier General Carol Ann Fausone (ret.) USAF/Michigan ANG.

JIM FURLONG

James "Jim" Furlong was a combat infantryman in Vietnam. Serving with Company B, 2d Battalion, 14th Infantry Regiment, 25th Infantry Division. Jim was wounded and earned a Purple Heart and Distinguished Service Cross for extraordinary heroism. After the war, Jim returned home and continued his education receiving his master 's degree in Economics from the University of Denver. He started working in the private sector for large computer manufacturers selling integrated services to highly classified government installations. Now retired, Jim is frequently asked to speak about the war, focusing not on his personal experiences but giving voice "to those who will always be twenty-one" in our hearts.

COLIN KIMBALL

Colin Kimball of McKinney, Texas, served in the U.S. Air Force as a weather radar technician in the post-Vietnam era and used the GI Bill to attain a bachelor's and master's degree in Geology. Growing up as an Air Force brat, he became the "man of the house" when his father served in Vietnam in 1969 and 1970. He was haunted by the loss of the fathers of neighboring friends as well as his childhood best friend and older brother figure, PFC Franklin D. Lacey, USMC, who was killed in at Khe Sanh in 1968. Our nation's rush to forget the war and those who served in it disturbed him for decades. This experience, as well as the negative feelings from the public towards our military after Vietnam that he experienced when he served, inspired him to begin painting portraits of our nation's heroes so that their legacies would not be forgotten. Beginning with Frankie, whose portrait hangs in his mother's home and who has a local ballpark named after him, Colin founded the North Texas Fallen Warrior Portrait in 2013. To date it has placed seventy-nine portraits of local fallen warriors and law enforcement officers on permanent display in the Russell A. Steindam Courts Building in his home county of Collin County, Texas, north of Dallas. Kimball was also influential in persuading the local county commissioners to name their courthouse after 1st Lt Russell A. Steindam, a local hero who received a posthumous Medal of Honor in Vietnam. An avid historian, he uses his portraits as a vehicle to tell the stories of our military and law enforcement heroes. Colin has completed hundreds of portraits and his work is displayed in homes nationwide and at military and public institutions from Vicenza, Italy, Quantico, Virginia, to the University of Texas. He is currently working on a compendium of portraits of posthumous Medal of Honor recipients to preserve their legacies, and that their family names can be honored and remembered.

KEVIN MANSFIELD

Kevin Mansfield is a veteran of thirty years military service in both the Marine Corps and the Army National Guard with two deployments during Operation Iraqi Freedom. He holds master's degrees in both Operations Management and Business Administration. Prior to the Beyond Belief series, he has contributed research information for numerous other Hero Books Publishing titles. Kevin lives with his wife, Rebecca, in Jacksonville, Arkansas.

C. DOUGLAS STERNER

Doug Sterner is a decorated, two-tour veteran of the Vietnam War. For the last thirty years he has compiled the largest and most complete database of U.S. Military Award citations, curates the *Military Times* HALL OF VALOR, and has become recognized as one of Americas foremost authorities of military awards and American military heroes. A life member of the Veterans of Foreign Wars, he is one of only two Americans in history to be granted Honorary, Lifetime Membership in the Legion of Valor. He has written scores of articles on U.S. military heroes for periodicals, contributed to *Chicken Soup for the Veteran's Soul*, and authored more than seventy-five reference books of award citations. His books can be found at www.herobooks.store. Doug makes

his home in Pueblo, Colorado, a city he and his wife were instrumental in being officially designated as "America's Home of Heroes."

PAMLA M. STERNER

Pamla Sterner is an accomplished author, speaker, and public performer. As a ventriloquist, and stand-up comic, she has authored numerous books related to these arts. She started her own comedy company, Pueblo Pfunny, which she promotes on Facebook. With her husband she has written such non-fiction works as the couple's 500+ page treatise on Baby Boomers titled *The Defining Generation*. In 2004, as a political science student at Colorado State University-Pueblo, she wrote a paper for a class assignment that became the basis for the landmark Stolen Valor Act, passed by Congress in 2006, struck down by SCOTUS in 2012, and subsequently revised and nearly unanimously passed by Congress the following year. In her hometown of Pueblo, Colorado, she is best known for her efforts to honor and recognize Medal of Honor recipients, and as the driving force behind her city being named "America's Home of Heroes."

DWIGHT JON ZIMMERMAN

Dwight Jon Zimmerman is an award-winning, #1 *New York Times* bestselling author. In a career spanning more than forty years he has written everything from comic books (for Marvel Comics and DC Comics) to hundreds of military history articles and more than two dozen books. His book *First Command*, about the first commands of famous generals, was an award-winning documentary aired on the Military Channel. He co-authored *Uncommon Valor: The Medal of Honor and the Warriors Who Earned It in Afghanistan and Iraq* which won the Military Writer Society of America's Founder's Award, the organization's highest honor, and was the first book to contain the complete history of the Medal of Honor. He lives in Brooklyn, New York.

Visit My Website

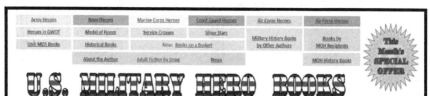

Army Heroes | Navy Heroes | Marine Corps Heroes | Coast Guard Heroes | Air Corps Heroes | Air Force Heroes
Heroes in GWOT | Medal of Honor | Service Crosses | Silver Stars | Military History Books by Other Authors | Books by MOH Recipients
Unit-MOS Books | Historical Books | New: Books on a Budget | |
About the Author | Adult Fiction by Doug | News | | MOH History Books

U.S. MILITARY HERO BOOKS

81 HERO BOOKS
23 Million Words
37,500+ Pages

If someone had told me that these numbers would define my life-work, I'd have never believed it possible. It was certainly nothing I planned.

More than two decades ago I began building a website (www.homeofheroes.com®) and developing a database containing the citations for the highest valor awards to American Soldiers, Sailors, Airmen and Marines. Fortunately I had the *shoulders* of great historians like Harry Stringer (WWI), Jane Blakeney (Marine Corps) and above all, the late Colonel Albert Gleim, to stand on.

I understand the passion of these great historians because I felt the same drive and passion to insure that the accounts of men and women who have received our highest combat decoration should never be "lost to history".

The military services neither track awards or compile award citations for any award other than the Medal of Honor. Two decades ago I began the seemingly impossible mission of fixing that problem. Unfortunately, my efforts including testimony before Congress, have failed to get a positive official response to the need for a comprehensive database of highly decorated American heroes.

I have estimated that somewhere near 350,000 awards above the Bronze Star have been awarded in history. My two decades of research has identified 200,000 of these, including 95% of all who received awards of the Silver Star or higher. I have compiled and digitized more than 80,000 of these awards including the citatons for every Medal of Honor, Marine Corps Brevet Medal, Navy Cross, Air Force Cross, and 85% of the Distinguished Service Crosses.

When I began this project in the early 1990s there were very few books available, even related to the Medal of Honor. In recent years much has been published about the Medal of Honor and recipients of that award, but other highly decorated Americans are vastly overlooked. I am determined to change that. In addition to continued research and digitizing of citations, over the last few years I have begun to these citation compendiums available in print form. It is my way of insuring that my decades of research and work "outlive me."

Feel free to click through the various pages of this, my new website. You are sure to find books that will interest you. In fact, not infrequently have individuals found a friend or relative listed in the database I curate for "Military Times" (https://valor.militarytimes.com/) that did not even know that person had received such high awards. In a couple of instances, I have heard from combat veterans who found themselves listed for awards as high as the Distinguished Service Cross and Silver Star, who themselves, never knew they had received that high accolade.

These cases, and the fact that I know that these heroes will live on in history, is what motivates me. If all these books become my legacy, I will be satisfied to know I did my best and accomplished something important.

www.herobooks.org

BEYOND BELIEF

True Stories of
American Heroes
That Defy
Comprehension

True Stories of "
Navy Heroes
That Defy
Comprehension

True Stories of
Military Chaplains
That Defy
Comprehension

True Stories of
Civilian Heroes
That Defy
Comprehension

Medal of Honor Books

Army (Civil War-WW I)

Army (WWII-GWOT)

Navy

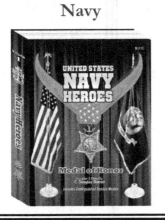

Marine Corps

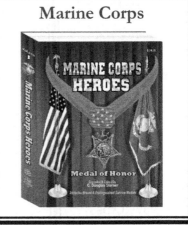

Air Force

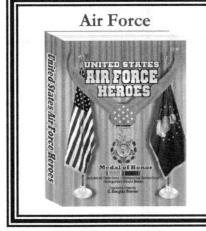

Coast Guard

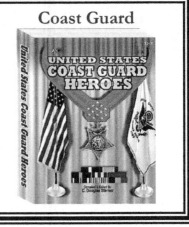

The following 24 volumes of **U.S. Military Heroes by Branch of Service** comprise the largest collection of award recipients ever published. Each 8 ½" x 11" book contains the names, citations, and often a photo and brief biography of the listed recipients. Often the last volume in any set (MOH, DSC, Navy Cross, Silver Star) and when broken down by war, includes informational appendixes analyzing awards by the rank of recipients, military occupational specialty, and unit, as well a list of recipients by how state and town. These represent more than 20,000 pages of detailed information on our most highly decorated heroes.

United States Navy Heroes

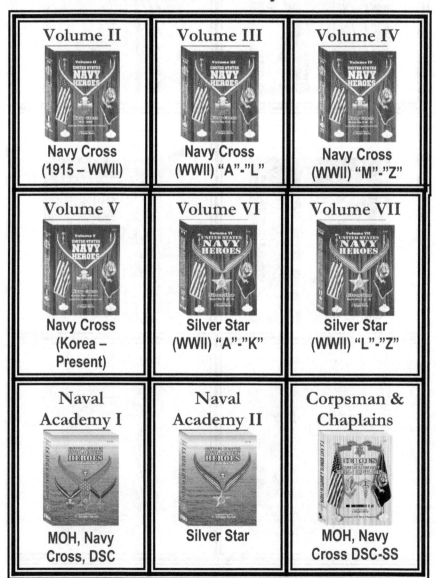

Volume II	Volume III	Volume IV
Navy Cross (1915 – WWII)	Navy Cross (WWII) "A"-"L"	Navy Cross (WWII) "M"-"Z"
Volume V	**Volume VI**	**Volume VII**
Navy Cross (Korea – Present)	Silver Star (WWII) "A"-"K"	Silver Star (WWII) "L"-"Z"
Naval Academy I	Naval Academy II	Corpsman & Chaplains
MOH, Navy Cross, DSC	Silver Star	MOH, Navy Cross DSC-SS

United States Army Heroes

Volume II

DSC (1873 – WWI) "A"-"G"

Volume III

DSC (WWI) "H"-"R"

Volume IV

DSC (WWI) "S"-"T" & Siberia

Volume V

DSC (WWII) "A"-"G"

Volume VI

DSC (WWII) "H"-"R"

Volume VII

DSC (WWII) "S"-"Z"

Volume VIII

DSC (WWII) USAAF

Volume IX

DSC (Korea)

Volume X

DSC (RVN – GWOT)

Volume XI

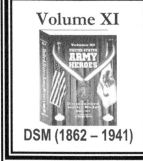

DSM (1862 – 1941)

Volume XII

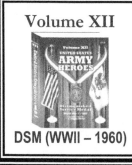

DSM (WWII – 1960)

Volume XIII

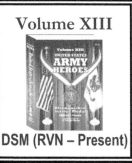

DSM (RVN – Present)

West Point Heroes

MOH, DSC, Navy Cross

West Point Heroes

**Silver Star
1875 – WWII (A-J)**

West Point Heroes

**Silver Star
WWI (K -Z)**

West Point Heroes

**Silver Star
Korea, Congo**

West Point Heroes

**Silver Star
RVN (A-L)**

West Point Heroes

**Silver Star
RVN (M-Z) to GWOT**

United States Marine Corps Heroes

	Volume II Navy Cross (1915 – WWII)	**Volume III** Navy Cross (Korea - Present
Volume IV Silver Star (1900 – 1941)	**Volume V** Silver Star (WWII) "A"-"K"	**Volume VI** Silver Star (WWII) "L"-"Z"
Volume VII Silver Star (1947 – Korea)	**Volume VIII** Silver Star (RVN) "A"-""L"	**Volume IX** Silver Star (RVN "M"-"Z" & GWOT

United States Air Force Heroes

Volume II	Volume III	Volume IV
MOH, DSC, SS USAAS (WWI)	DSC USAAF (WWII)	Silver Star (WWII) "A"-"C"

Volume V	Volume VI	Volume VII
Silver Star (WWII) "D"-"H"	Silver Star (WWII) "I"-"N"	Silver Star (WWII) "O"-"S"

Volume VIII	Volume IX	Volume X
Silver Star (WWII) "T"-"Z"	MOH, DSC, SS (Korea)	DSM (1918-1965)

Coming in 2022

Volume X	Volume XI	Volume XII
Distinguished Service Medals	Soldier's Medals (WWII)	Soldier's Medals (Korea)

SPECIAL COLLECTIONS

Vietnam War POWs		MOH at Arlington	CHAPLAINS

AIR FORCE	USA, USN, USMC, CIV	Citations, Photos, & More	MOH, DSC, NX, SS

WAR ON TERRORISM HEROES

Navy Heroes in the War on Terrorism

Citations for all awards of the Medal of Honor, Navy Cross, and the majority of Silver Star to members of the U.S. Navy in the wars in Iraq and Afghanistan. Appendixes provide analysis of recipients by unit, by specialty, by rank/rating, as well as a chronological analysis of these awards.

Marine Corps Heroes in the War on Terrorism

Citations for all awards of the Medal of Honor, Navy Cross, and Silver Star to U.S. Marines **and attached Navy Corpsmen** in the wars in Iraq and Afghanistan. Appendixes provide analysis of recipients by unit, by specialty, by rank/rating, as well as a chronological analysis of these awards.

Air Force Heroes in the War on Terrorism

Citations for all awards of the Air Force Cross and Silver Stars to members of the U.S. Air Force during the wars in Iraq and Afghanistan. Appendixes provide analysis of recipients by unit, by specialty, by rank, as well as a chronological analysis of these awards.

Army Heroes in the War on Terrorism (OIF)

Citations for all awards of the Medal of Honor, Distinguished Service Cross and Silver Stars to members of the U.S. Army during Operation ENDURING FREEDOM in Afghanistan. Appendixes provide analysis of recipients by unit, by specialty, by rank, as well as a chronological analysis of these awards.

Army Heroes in the War on Terrorism (OEF)

Citations for all awards of the Medal of Honor, Distinguished Service Cross and Silver Stars to members of the U.S. Army during Operation IRAQI FREEDOM in IRAQ. Appendixes provide analysis of recipients by unit, by specialty, by rank, as well as a chronological analysis of these awards.

U.S. Army Heroes by Division

This is the most comprehensive compilation of citations ever published. Each volume the names of the recipients of our highest military awards, and in many cases brief biographical information, a photo of the recipient, and personal data such as Date and Place of Birth, Home Town, Date of Death, and Burial Location. Appendixes break down the awards by rank, military specialty, unit, and more.

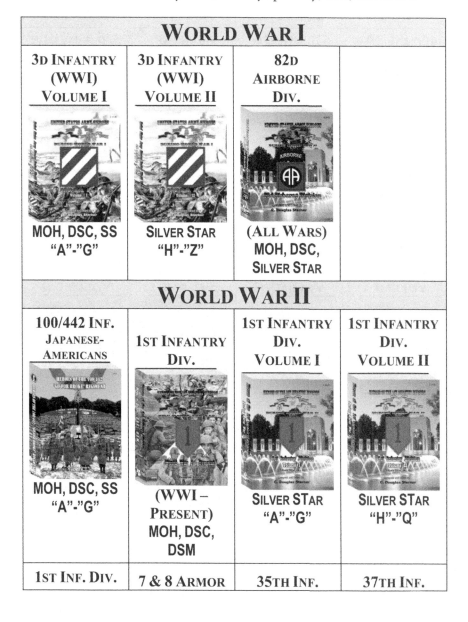

WORLD WAR I			
3D INFANTRY (WWI) VOLUME I MOH, DSC, SS "A"-"G"	**3D INFANTRY (WWI) VOLUME II** SILVER STAR "H"-"Z"	**82D AIRBORNE DIV.** (ALL WARS) MOH, DSC, SILVER STAR	
WORLD WAR II			
100/442 INF. JAPANESE-AMERICANS MOH, DSC, SS "A"-"G"	**1ST INFANTRY DIV.** (WWI – PRESENT) MOH, DSC, DSM	**1ST INFANTRY DIV. VOLUME I** SILVER STAR "A"-"G"	**1ST INFANTRY DIV. VOLUME II** SILVER STAR "H"-"Q"
1ST INF. DIV.	**7 & 8 ARMOR**	**35TH INF.**	**37TH INF.**

VOLUME II	DIV.	DIV.	DIV.

SILVER STAR "R"-"Z"	MOH, DSC, SILVER STAR	MOH, DSC, SILVER STAR	MOH, DSC, SILVER STAR
42D INF. DIV.	63D INF. DIV.	80TH INF. DIV.	82D ABN. DIV.

MOH, DSC, SILVER STAR	MOH, DSC, SILVER STAR	MOH, DSC, SILVER STAR	(WWI – PRESENT) MOH, DSC, SS

KOREAN WAR

2D INF. DIV. VOLUME I	2D INF. DIV. VOLUME II	3D INF. DIV. VOLUME I	3D INF. DIV. VOLUME II

MOH, DSC, SS "A"-"K"	SILVER STAR "L"-"Z"	MOH, DSC, SS "A"-"K"	MOH, DSC, SS "A"-"K"

24TH INF. DIV. MOH, DSC, SILVER STAR	**24TH INF. DIV.** MOH, DSC, SILVER STAR		
VIETNAM WAR			
11TH ARMORED CAV. MOH, DSC, SS, LOM, DFC, SM	**82D AIRBORNE DIV.** (WWI – PRESENT) MOH, DSC, SS		

WINGS OF VALOR

*A Projected 6-Volume History of
Army & Air Force Heroism in the Sky*

Volume I—The Birth of Military Aviation

Read the evolution of early combat aviation in World War II through the lives and actions of the 4 WWI Air Service Medal of Honor recipients. Follow the continuing efforts to establish a military air arm in the interim from 1918—1941.

Volume II—At War in the Pacific

From the attack on Pearl Harbor on December 7, 1941 until the close of 1943, the tide of war turned quickly in the Pacific. Through the lives, heroism, and in too many cased their death, the eight Pacific War Medal of Honor recipients from 1941 to 1943 reveal inspiring tales of the continuing evolution of combat aviation.

Volume III—Bombs Over Europe

The stories of 18 Medal of Honor recipients demonstrate how the United States Army Air Forces went head-to-head with the vaunted German Luftwaffe, and gained the aerial superiority necessary to enable the subsequent D-Day ground invasion.

THE DEFINING GENERATION

True Stories of a generation that challenged the traditions of the past, and in its search for meaning and purpose, redefined the world we live in today.

Fifteen years in development, "The Defining Generation" is a 600+ page tribute to the children of "The Greatest Generation." Baby boomers themselves, authors Doug and Pam Sterner weave personal vignettes, history, and the inspiring true stories of heroes and leaders of their generation. It is a positive portrayal of a generation in rebellion that rose up against traditions of the past, rejecting "the establishment" and its narrow views of life, equality, poverty and world need. The genesis of their thesis: "The Greatest Generation indeed saved our world (in World War II), but their children redefined it, making it better."

GO FOR BROKE:

The Nisei Warriors of World War II Who Conquered Germany, Japan, and American Bigotry

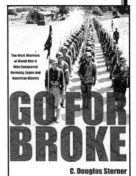

During World War II, Japanese-Americans were forcefully removed from their homes and businesses, and placed in "relocation" camps throughout the West. With countless instances of "Gestapo-like" tactics used against them, no one would have faulted them for being bitter or angry at the country that held them captive. Instead, the remarkable story of these Nisei (first generation Japanese born outside of Japan) warriors explains why they were eager to defend their American homeland, and how they became the most decorated fighting unit ever assembled in U.S. military history. Go For Broke is the incredible story of how these soldiers, known as the purple Heart Battalion," helped liberate Europe, the Pacific, and America from its pervasive and systemic bigotry.

A Splendid Little War

"A Splendid Little War" recounts the chronology of events leading up to and during the fighting of the Spanish-American War. Perhaps no war in our history has been more popular at home or among those who fought it. American media played a significant role in instigating war, and fanning the patriotic fervor that made it so. In these pages you will meet the heroes of both sides and follow the chronology of battle through the actions of the aging Civil War heroes that commanded the American forces, and the young Soldiers, Sailors, Marines and Army Nurses who were conspicuous by their gallantry and devotion to duty and to each other.

Day of Infamy

A Tribute to the Heroes of Pearl Harbor

The Japanese surprise attack on Pearl Harbor, Hawaii, on December 7, 1941 was perhaps the most cataclysmic event of the 20th Century. Within two hours the U.S. Navy 's Pacific Fleet was almost completely destroyed and Americas air forces at Hawaii and in the Far East were nearly annihilated. "Day of Infamy" takes the reader through the chronology of that fateful day through the actions of the 15 Sailors whose heroic actions in earned them the Medal of Honor. The little known stories of other heroes, and interesting snippets of human interest, enhance the narrative. Liberally illustrated with photos, maps, and pictures of individual heroes, this book is more than a history book—it is a look inside the human character of those who faced unbelievable odds in the most trying of times.

SHINMIYANGYO—THE OTHER KOREAN WAR

This book details the first American incursion in Korea in 1871, with narratives that are woven through the actions of the 14 Marines and Navy Bluejackets who received Medals of Honor for this first foreign war.

BOOKS BY AND ABOUT US

HOW PUEBLO BECAME THE HOME OF HEROES

Don't Fight City Hall - Entice them to Join You

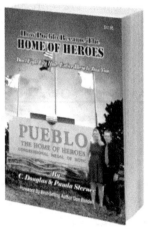

How Pueblo Became the Home of Heroes is much more than a fun read which is hard to put down. It is a memoir about the unique couple who spearheaded the drive to make Pueblo the Home of Heroes: Doug and Pamla Sterner. Doug and Pam are both magicians, singers, ventriloquists, but more important, patriots.

Pueblo, Colorado, the town they live in, at one time, was the only city in America which was the home of four living recipients of the Medal of Honor of Honor. It prompted a President of the nation to ask, "Is there something in the water out there?"

The stories of the celebrity-filled visits to Pueblo by celebrities, such as Wayne Newton and Adrian Cronauer (Good Morning, Vietnam!) and too many Medal of Honor recipients to share are neat and interesting.Few have done more to honor Medal of Honor recipients and other recipients of valorous military awards for all branches than the Sterners. It is great to read the story behind the stories.

Don Bendell (Best-Selling Author)

RESTORING VALOR

One Couple's Mission to Expose Fraudulent War Heroes and Protect Americas Military Awards System

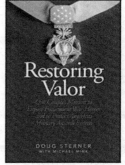

Stolen valor occurs when a person lies about receiving military decorations that he or she has in fact never earned. It has become a major societal problem that has been discussed numerous times in the news and, most recently, by the US Supreme Court. In Restoring Valor, Doug Sterner provides riveting case studies of the stolen valor imposters he has investigated and exposed, and the serious crimes—including murder—they have committed. He chronicles the evolution of stolen valor from the inception of the republic to today. Sterner demonstrates why the federal law he and his wife Pam helped to enact, called the Stolen Valor Act, is necessary.

JAMIE 's STORY: GOD IS GOOD

A True Story of Friendship and Faith

Jaime Pacheco, one of the last Army Rangers killed in the Vietnam War, was the close friend of this author. In this small booklet, Doug Sterner details his own missions as a combat correspondent with Jamie 's Ranger Team, the impact on his life of Jamie 's death after Doug returned home, and the unexpected reunion with Jaime 's family decades later. Originally written as a personal memoir, this touching story set the stage for Doug 's subsequent work in his Home Of Heroes website, and much more.

Made in the USA
Middletown, DE
20 July 2023

35235600R00205